THE
ELITE
OF OUR
PEOPLE

Edited by Julie Winch

THE
ELITE
OF OUR
PEOPLE

Joseph Willson's
Sketches of Black Upper-Class Life
in
Antebellum Philadelphia

The Pennsylvania State University Press
University Park, Pennsylvania

Library of Congress Cataloging-in-Publication Data

Willson, Joseph.
   [Sketches of the higher classes of colored society in Philadelphia]
   The elite of our people : Joseph Willson's sketches of Black upper-class life in antebellum Philadelphia/Joseph Willson ; edited by Julie Winch.
      p. cm.
   Originally published: Sketches of the higher classes of colored society in Philadelphia. Philadelphia : Merrihew and Thompson, printers, 1841. With new introduction and extensive annotations.
   Includes bibliographical references (p.   ) and index.
   ISBN 0-271-02020-2 (cloth : acid-free paper)
   ISBN 0-271-02021-0 (pbk. : acid-free paper)
   1. Afro-Americans—Pennsylvania—Philadelphia—History—19th century.
2. Upper class—Pennsylvania—Philadelphia—History—19th century.
3. Philadelphia (Pa.)—Social conditions—19th century. I. Winch, Julie, 1953–
II. Title.

F158.9.N4 W54 2000
974.8'1100496073—dc21
                                                                         99-055383

Copyright © 2000 The Pennsylvania State University
All rights reserved
Printed in the United States of America
Published by The Pennsylvania State University Press,
University Park, PA 16802-1003

It is the policy of The Pennsylvania State University Press to use acid-free paper for the first printing of all clothbound books. Publications on uncoated stock satisfy the minimum requirements of American National Standard for Information Sciences—Permanence of Paper for Printed Library Materials, ANSI Z39.48–1992.

For Lou

Should a stranger desire to see the elite of our people, he must visit Philadelphia.
 —"Travelling Scraps" in *Freedom's Journal,* July 11, 1828

Our white countrymen do not know us . . . they are strangers to our characters, ignorant of our capacity, oblivious to our history. . . . What American artist has not caricatured us? What wit has not laughed at us in our wretchedness? What songster has not made merry over our depressed spirits? What press has not ridiculed and condemned us?
 —James McCune Smith, "The Suffrage Question, 1860"

Contents

Prefaces xi
Acknowledgments xiii
Abbreviations xv

Introduction:
   Joseph Willson's Philadelphia 1
   Joseph Willson, "Our Talented Young Friend" 50

*Sketches of the Higher Classes of Colored Society in
   Philadelphia by "A Southerner"* 79

Notes 121
Bibliography 175
Index 187

Preface

This book is an edition of a little-known work entitled *Sketches of the Higher Classes of Colored Society in Philadelphia by "A Southerner."* Originally published in Philadelphia in 1841 by the firm of Merrihew & Thompson, this elegantly written and eminently readable book has been largely ignored, and that is a great pity. As a result of his parentage and upbringing, author Joseph Willson, who used the pen name "A Southerner," was painfully aware of the complexities of race and class in antebellum America. A wealthy and well-educated man of color, he wrote not for fame or for profit, but to help in some small way to bridge the racial divide he saw growing wider by the day in the city that had become his home.

I first came across a copy of *Sketches of the Higher Classes of Colored Society* at the Library Company of Philadelphia some twenty years ago. I was intrigued both by the book and by its author. I eventually discovered that Joseph Willson was a Georgia native who spent the better part of two decades in "the city of brotherly love." Tracking Joseph Willson and the Willson family across two continents and over more than two centuries has proven a fascinating—and occasionally frustrating—task, but it is one that has revealed much about the contours of race, family, and community in America. As for Joseph Willson's book—the only one he wrote—it remains as relevant at the dawn of the twenty-first century as it was in 1841. I hope it will resonate with readers today as Joseph Willson intended it to do when he first put pen to paper more than a century and a half ago.

Acknowledgments

I would like to begin my acknowledgments by expressing my gratitude to the staff of the various archives I visited while doing the research for this book. Every single library seemed to be in the process of moving or undergoing massive renovations. Research takes on a unique flavor when one is trying to avoid ladders, using back stairs one never knew existed, and finding a solid wall where there had been a door only the week before.

Ward Childs and the staff at the Philadelphia City Archives, especially Jefferson Moak and Natalie Caldwell, deserve a special mention. They kept their sense of humor and their dedication to patrons as their archives literally moved across the city to a new location. They kept boxes of papers out of the hands of the movers to allow me just a few more minutes before items I needed were labeled "temporarily inaccessible" for weeks. Thank you again. Researching at the Philadelphia City Archives is *never* dull.

The Historical Society of Pennsylvania was undergoing much the same process during the time I was there. In that case it was not a move across town but a series of much-needed renovations. I would like to say a special word of thanks to HSP staffers Daniel Rolf and Ronald Medford.

The staff at the Pennsylvania State Archives in Harrisburg were dealing with what seemed to be a rebuilding of the entire area around the complex. They still took time to make my week there a pleasant and productive one. Thanks to the renovations there, the National Archives regional facility in Philadelphia is now a much more user-friendly place to work in. Throughout their upheavals the staff have always been "user friendly." I can say the same of the New England Historic Genealogical Society in Boston. The renovated building was worth the wait, and the staff in the Microtext Department proved immensely helpful, even when their section was temporarily reduced to two superannuated reader-printers in a back room. The Microtext Department at the Boston Public Library remains desperately in need of a major structural overhaul. The staff, however, do a wonderful job under trying circumstances.

As for the reference librarians and interlibrary loan staff at the Healey Library at the University of Massachusetts at Boston, their assistance has been invaluable. Despite staff shortages and the vagaries of a new computer system, they worked to track down sources and to process innumerable interlibrary loan requests. Special thanks go to Joel Fowler and Stephen Haas.

I also want to thank Phillip Lapsansky at the Library Company of Philadelphia. Without Phil there are so many sources and illustrations I would never have found. As for Emma Lapsansky, what can I say? In terms of scholarship, I owe her a tremendous debt of gratitude. Her own work on nineteenth-century Philadelphia has suggested to me and to many others new ways of looking at this remarkable city and its people. Emma generously read my manuscript for Penn State, and I have benefited greatly from her suggestions, as well as from those of James Brewer Stewart of Macalaster College. I would also like to thank my editor at Penn State, Peter J. Potter, for seeing my manuscript through all its various stages to publication.

A stipend from the Faculty Development Committee at the University of Massachusetts at Boston made it possible for me to do much of the basic research for this book, and a course-load reduction for one semester gave me the time to complete it.

Thanks go also to my brothers, both of whom gave me house-room at various times as I worked on this book during visits to my native England. The renovation motif persisted across the Atlantic. Peter Winch and Anne Harrison have now replaced their ceiling after the flood. As for Roy Winch, the presence of a small cement mixer next to the desk in his half-finished living room was an unusual but effective aid to contemplation.

To my companion, Louis Cohen, I owe a great deal. His sense of humor has helped me throughout this project. As for his technical assistance, without him to fix my computer, retrieve lost files, and so on, this book really would not have been written. Lou, this one's for you.

Abbreviations

Newspapers

AAM	*Anglo-African Magazine* (New York)
AR	*African Repository* (Washington, D.C.)
ASA	*Anti-Slavery Advocate* (London)
ASB	*Anti-Slavery Bugle* (Salem, Ohio; New Lisbon, Ohio)
ASR	*Anti-Slavery Record* (New York)
CA	*Colored American* (New York)
CR	*Christian Recorder* (Philadelphia)
Eman	*Emancipator* (Boston; New York)
FDP	*Frederick Douglass' Paper* (Rochester, New York)
GUE	*Genius of Universal Emancipation* (Mount Pleasant, Ohio; Greenville, Tennessee; Baltimore, Maryland; Washington, D.C.; Hennepin, Ohio)
HR	*Hazard's Register* (Philadelphia)
JM	*The Juvenile Magazine* (Philadelphia)
Lib	*Liberator* (Boston)
NASS	*National Anti-Slavery Standard* (New York)
NECAUL	*National Enquirer and Constitutional Advocate of Universal Liberty* (Philadelphia)
NEW	*National Era* (Washington, D.C.)
NR	*National Reformer* (Philadelphia)
NS	*North Star* (Rochester, New York)
NYT	*New York Times* (New York)
PA	*Pacific Appeal* (San Francisco)
PF	*Pennsylvania Freeman* (Philadelphia)
Poulson	*Poulson's American Daily Advertiser* (Philadelphia)
PL	*Public Ledger* (Philadelphia)
ProvF	*Provincial Freeman* (Windsor, Ontario; Toronto, Ontario; Chatham, Ontario)
RA	*Rights of All* (New York)
Trib	*Philadelphia Tribune* (Philadelphia)
VF	*Voice of the Fugitive* (Sandwich, Ontario; Windsor, Ontario)
WAA	*Weekly Anglo-African* (New York)

Archives and Journals

AANYLH	*Afro-Americans in New York Life and History*
ACS	American Colonization Society
AH	*American Heritage*
AQ	*American Quarterly*
BAP	Black Abolitionist Papers
BPL	Boston Public Library
EIHC	*Essex Institute Historical Collections*
HSP	Historical Society of Pennsylvania
JAH	*Journal of American History*
JER	*Journal of the Early Republic*
LC	Library Company of Philadelphia
LibC	Library of Congress
NA	National Archives
NCHR	*North Carolina Historical Review*
NGSQ	*National Genealogical Society Quarterly*
PA Hist	*Pennsylvania History*
PCA	Philadelphia City Archives
PMHB	*Pennsylvania Magazine of History and Biography*
PSA	Pennsylvania State Archives
RCH	*Richmond County History*
UPA	University of Pennsylvania Archives
WMQ	*William and Mary Quarterly*

INTRODUCTION

Joseph Willson's Philadelphia

If the plight of the entire free community of color in antebellum America was an unenviable one, what was it like to be a member of the nation's "higher classes of colored society"? To have money and want the opportunity to make more? To aspire to enjoy the privileges that came with wealth? To have education and seek to use it? To want a role in the political process? To exert influence within the black community and expect to have that influence recognized by the white community? In short, to be acknowledged for what one had achieved instead of what one was in a society where to be of discernible African ancestry was to be forever excluded from the inner circles of power and prestige?[1]

Obviously such concerns were far removed from the day-to-day existence of the vast majority of free people of color, whose lives were consumed, as were those of most whites, by the struggle to keep a roof over their heads, food on the table, clothes on their backs, and put a little aside to tide them over the crises that were sure to befall them—illness, unemployment, old age, the death of a breadwinner. And yet, in a very real sense, the fate of the men and women in the "higher classes of colored society" was inextricably bound up with that of the rest of their community. In some cities, among them Joseph Willson's Philadelphia, housing was not as rigidly segregated by race as it would be after the Civil War, but the relatively small size of these cities meant elite African Americans, even when they could buy a house on one of the more desirable streets,

---

1. Willard B. Gatewood's focus in *Aristocrats of Color: The Black Elite, 1880–1920* (Bloomington and Indianapolis: University of Indiana Press, 1993) is on the post–Civil War era, but he does address the earlier period in the first chapter of his book. Leon Litwack includes a brief analysis of class (179–86) in *North of Slavery: The Negro in the Free States, 1790–1860* (Chicago: University of Chicago Press, 1961). On the wealth of elite free people of color in the South in the period 1800–1861, see Loren Schweninger, *Black Property Owners in the South, 1790–1915* (Urbana and Chicago: University of Illinois Press, 1990), chap. 4. On their social status and their view of themselves, see Ira Berlin, *Slaves Without Masters: The Free Negro in the Antebellum South* (New York: Vintage Books, 1976), 273–83. For a brief but illuminating discussion of class in the antebellum black community, see Richard L. Bushman, *The Refinement of America: Persons, Houses, Cities* (New York: Vintage Books, 1992), 434–40.

2   The Elite of Our People

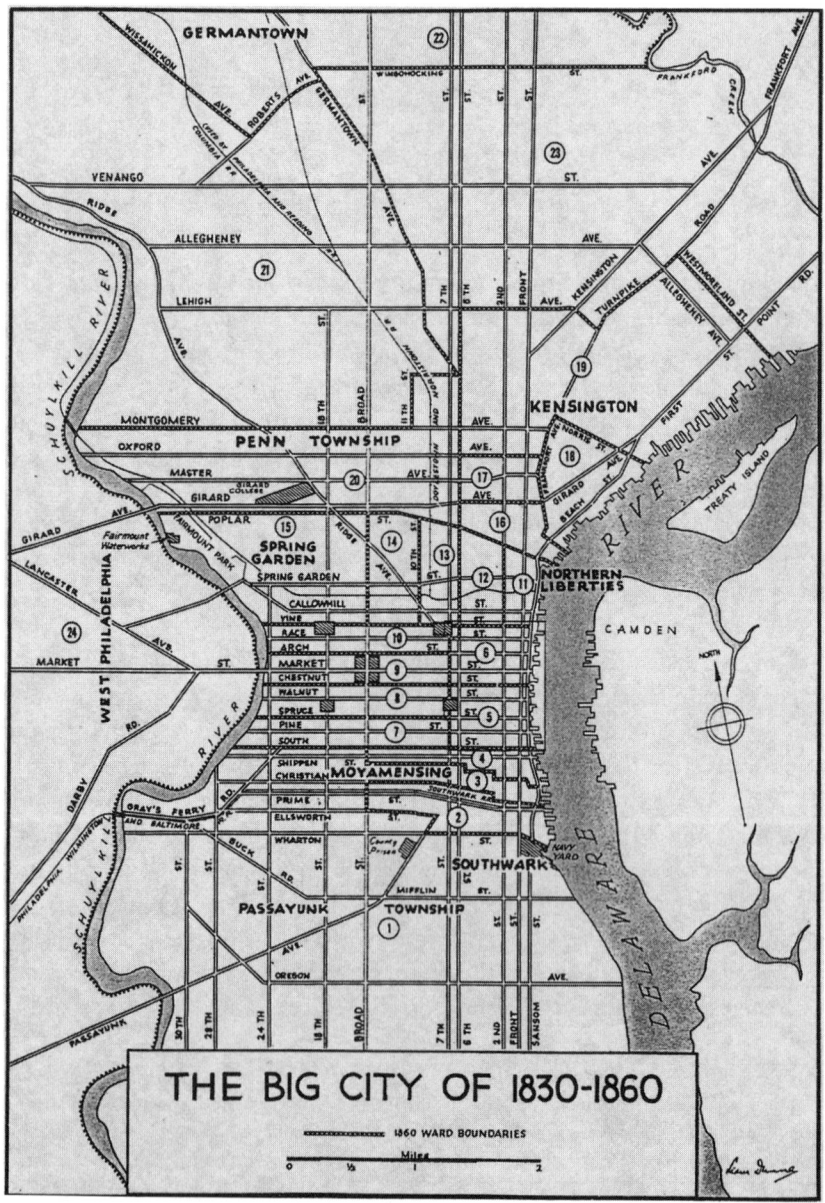

The Big City of 1830–1860. The numbers are those of the various wards after Consolidation in 1854. From *The Private City: Philadelphia in Three Periods of Its Growth*, by Sam Bass Warner. Copyright 1968 by the Trustees of the University of Pennsylvania. Reprinted by permission of the University of Pennsylvania Press.

still lived in close proximity to poorer blacks. The well-to-do owned comfortable homes on the main thoroughfares, and the poor rented hovels in the sunless, squalid alleys and courts that were only a matter of yards away. The "better sort" could not remain unaware of the plight of the less fortunate.[2] The "higher classes" might congregate at certain churches, but no black church was without its humbler and less fortunate members. As for racial violence, it was as likely—and sometimes more likely—to be directed against the homes and persons of the "better sort" as frustrated whites vented their rage against those of their neighbors who had the audacity to be both black and prosperous. As for seeking redress in court or making one's sense of outrage felt at the ballot box, that was next to impossible. By the early 1840s few free people of color lived in states where they could vote, and still fewer lived in states where they could vote on exactly the same basis as whites.[3]

Occasionally a well-intentioned legislator tried to get a law passed which, in relation to this or that aspect of daily life, would secure for the "respectable" members of the African-American community some better treatment than that accorded the mass of black people.[4] Such efforts were seldom successful. By and large, the laws of the various states made no distinctions because the majority of whites saw none. Joseph Willson knew this all too well. He had traveled extensively in the South and the North. He had wealth and education. In 1839 or 1840, when he began collecting data for his *Sketches of the Higher Classes of Colored Society in Philadelphia,* he realized he would be addressing white readers who had "long been accustomed to regard the people of color as one consolidated mass, all huddled together, without any particular or general distinctions, social or otherwise." It was that notion—that black people were all alike because they were black, that ancestry and phenotype somehow outweighed all other considerations—that Joseph Willson set out to challenge. Before the nation was engulfed in a bloody and protracted civil war, before all black men and women became "free" in law, if not in reality, Willson endeavored to convince white Americans that race was not an absolute, that the African-American community was not a monolith—in

---

2. For a discussion of residential patterns in antebellum Philadelphia, see Emma Jones Lapsansky, *Neighborhoods in Transition: William Penn's Dream and Urban Reality* (New York: Garland, 1994), especially chap. 3.
3. Litwack, *North of Slavery,* 91.
4. That was the case in Pennsylvania when the Reform Convention disfranchised all men of color. Several delegates tried to preserve the privileges of the black "better sort."

short, that "the sight of one colored man . . . whatever may be his apparent condition, (provided it is any thing but genteel!)" was not "the sight of a community."

Joseph Willson was exceptionally well qualified to comment on the lives, the achievements, and the frustrations of those in the "higher classes of colored society." In an America where the distinctions between "black" and "white" seemed to be more sharply drawn with each passing day, he was painfully aware that most whites would look at him and see not the self-assured young gentleman that he was, the son of a white Georgia banker, but a pushy, ambitious man of color who needed to be reminded that one could not be a "gentleman" if "the discerning eye of prejudice" could detect any sign of African ancestry. It mattered very little to most white observers that Willson and his siblings were well educated, well-to-do, and eminently respectable, or that their father and their great-grandfather were white men. They themselves were not quite "white" enough.[5]

Legislation intended to keep the Willsons and people like them firmly "in their place" had driven them out of Georgia in the early 1830s. They had come to Philadelphia hoping for better things, for opportunities they knew they could not find back home. What they experienced in "the city of brotherly love," while less oppressive than the situation they had fled from, was a level of racism that pervaded virtually every aspect of their lives. However, even while he condemned prejudice, Joseph Willson took pride in the achievements of free people of color in Philadelphia and elsewhere in the North. He was critical of them in some respects, but he was still impressed by the complex and culturally rich community they had established—a community of churches and schools, mutual benefit societies, charities, and self-help organizations. If whites would only look at their black neighbors, especially those who constituted the "higher classes of colored society," they would see, Willson insisted, men and women in every way qualified for the rights and privileges of citizenship. His plea was not for universal equality, since he did not believe all people were

---

5. On the debate over definitions of "whiteness" as an ideological construct in antebellum America, see David R. Roediger, *The Wages of Whiteness: Race and the Making of the American Working Class*, 2nd ed. (New York : Verso, 1999); Eric Lott, *Love and Theft: Blackface Minstrelsy and the American Working Class* (New York: Oxford University Press, 1993), especially chaps. 1–6; and James Brewer Stewart, "The Emergence of Racial Modernity and the Rise of the White North, 1790–1840," *JER* 18 (Summer 1998), 181–236.

equally deserving, but for a level of respect that cut across the racial divide. A person's moral worth, he contended, was not related to ancestry, to the texture of the hair or the shade of the skin, but to their capacity for intellectual improvement, their industry, their integrity, and their willingness to work for the betterment of society as a whole. And yet in no sense was Willson calling for a diminished sense of pride in oneself, one's heritage, and one's community. To be a member of the "higher classes of colored society" did not mean "becoming white." What Willson envisaged was arguably more far-reaching than that, and it assumed the cooperation of white people. He advocated the creation of a society in which sterling moral worth and nothing else determined the degree of respect to which an individual was entitled.

Joseph Willson's *Sketches of the Higher Classes* is firmly rooted in Philadelphia. Its message of unanimity within the black community and respect for that community on the part of the larger white community might apply to other cities as well, but the focus of *Sketches of the Higher Classes* is essentially a local one. To appreciate Willson's analysis of the intersection of race and class in antebellum Philadelphia, it is necessary to see the city as he saw it, with all its complexities and contradictions.

Joseph Willson was sixteen in 1833, when he and his family moved to Philadelphia. Thanks to a generous legacy from her white lover, Joseph's mother was able to buy a three-story house on Morgan Street in Spring Garden, one of the city's unincorporated "liberties." It was an area of relatively recent development, and not until the Consolidation Act of 1854 would it become part of the city proper, but it was growing rapidly. The Willsons would have seen few black or brown faces in Spring Garden. Most of their neighbors were whites of German, English, or Irish extraction. If the family experienced any racial animosity, Joseph Willson did not mention it. The Willsons lived on Morgan Street—apparently peacefully—for almost fifteen years.

While the Willsons did not encounter many people of color in Spring Garden, they would have seen and interacted with many more as they began to familiarize themselves with Philadelphia. It was home to one of the largest concentrations of African Americans anywhere in the United States. In 1830 there were more than 14,500 in Philadelphia County, an area that included the city itself and the adjoining districts of Southwark, Moyamensing, the Northern Liberties, Kensington, and Spring Garden.

Black people lived in every ward of the city and each one of the districts, making up just under 10 percent of the total population of Philadelphia County in 1830.[6]

There was no ghetto in the modern sense, although, as the Willsons would soon have realized, the relative numbers of blacks and whites varied greatly from neighborhood to neighborhood. In Spring Garden in 1830, African Americans accounted for less than 4 percent of the population. By contrast, in Moyamensing one in five residents was black. In the city itself there were sharp differences when it came to the relative numbers of black and white residents. In 1830 African Americans made up 24 percent of the population of Locust Ward, 25 percent in New Market Ward, 19 percent in Cedar Ward, and almost the same percentage in Pine Ward. The figures for other wards were strikingly different—4.3 percent for High Street Ward, 5.6 percent for Chestnut Ward, and 4.87 percent for Upper Delaware Ward.[7]

The center of African-American community life was the South Street corridor, the area bounded by Pine Street on the north, Shippen Street on the south, and running from the Delaware west to Eleventh Street. Until Consolidation in 1854, this neighborhood straddled the boundaries of the city proper. South Street was in Philadelphia, while Shippen was in Moyamensing. That was a jurisdictional nightmare (or bonus) for the officers of the law. During times of riot and disorder—and there were many during the antebellum era—city constables would chase law-breakers to the city boundaries and then leave them to be pursued by the authorities in Philadelphia County.

White mobs in search of black victims knew where to find them, and

---

6. The size of Philadelphia's antebellum black population varies according to whether one looks at the city proper or the whole of Philadelphia County. In *The Free Black in Urban America, 1800–1850: The Shadow of the Dream* (Chicago: University of Chicago Press, 1981), Leonard P. Curry notes that the federal census put the number of African Americans in the city at 9,806 in 1830, at 10,507 in 1840, and at 10,736 in 1850 (244–46). For Philadelphia County the totals were 14,554 for 1830, and 19,833 for 1840. Based on statistics for the city alone, African Americans made up 12.19 percent of the total population in 1830. The percentage for the whole of Philadelphia County in 1830 was 9.8 percent. Emma J. Lapsansky, "'Since They Got Those Separate Churches': Afro-Americans and Racism in Jacksonian Philadelphia," *AQ* 32 (Spring 1980), 57; Gary B. Nash, *Forging Freedom: The Formation of Philadelphia's Black Community, 1720–1840* (Cambridge, Mass.: Harvard University Press, 1988), 143; Elizabeth M. Geffen, "Industrial Development and Social Crisis, 1841–1854," in Russell F. Weigley et al., eds., *Philadelphia: A 300-Year History* (New York: W. W. Norton, 1982), 309.

7. For the breakdown of the 1830 census by wards, see *HR*, March 1831, 172–73.

the South Street corridor was plagued with racial violence for the better part of three decades. However, it remained an attractive area for black Philadelphians. It was there that the majority of black churches were located, including the one that Joseph Willson and his family attended. The neighborhood was home to schools, to the black Masonic lodge, to black-owned businesses and places of entertainment. It had more than its share of slums, but it also had its well-to-do black residents who had no thought of leaving homes they had occupied for a generation or more.[8]

Philadelphia's African-American community was larger than that of most other cities. The only comparable communities were in Baltimore, New Orleans, and New York City.[9] It was also a community with deep roots. Black people had been living in Philadelphia since its founding. One of those in the "higher classes," affluent sailmaker James Forten, a man the Willsons would have met at church every Sunday, could boast of being the great-grandson of a slave who had been brought to the fledgling colony within a year or two of William Penn's own arrival.[10] Other black Philadelphians could come close to matching that.

Joseph Willson had grown up surrounded by slaves. He had seen slaves in the streets of his native Augusta. His father had owned and traded in slaves. He had received his early education in Alabama in the home of a slave-owner. His mother had had slaves to work in her household. But she had been born a slave, and a slave she remained until her lover manumitted her. Joseph Willson was very familiar with slavery. But for his father's intervention, he would himself have been a slave.

In Philadelphia, things were different. Slavery had been an integral part of the social and economic fabric of the colonial city, but, as a result of the working of Pennsylvania's Gradual Abolition Act of 1780, there were only eleven slaves in Philadelphia when the 1830 census was taken.[11] How-

8. On the significance of the South Street corridor, see Lapsansky, " 'Since They Got Those Separate Churches,' " 54–78.
9. For population statistics for fifteen major cities, see Curry, *The Free Black in Urban America*, 244–45, 250.
10. Samuel J. May, *Recollections of Our Antislavery Conflict* (Boston: Fields, Osgood, 1869; reprint, New York: Arno Press, 1968), 287. On the early history of Africans and African Americans in Philadelphia, see Nash, *Forging Freedom*, chap. 1.
11. On the significance of slavery in the colonial city, see Gary B. Nash, "Slaves and Slaveowners in Colonial Philadelphia," in Nash, ed., *Race, Class, and Politics: Essays on American Colonial and Revolutionary Society* (Urbana and Chicago: University of Illinois Press, 1986), 91–118. For statistics on the dwindling slave population, see Curry, *The Free Black in Urban America*, 247.

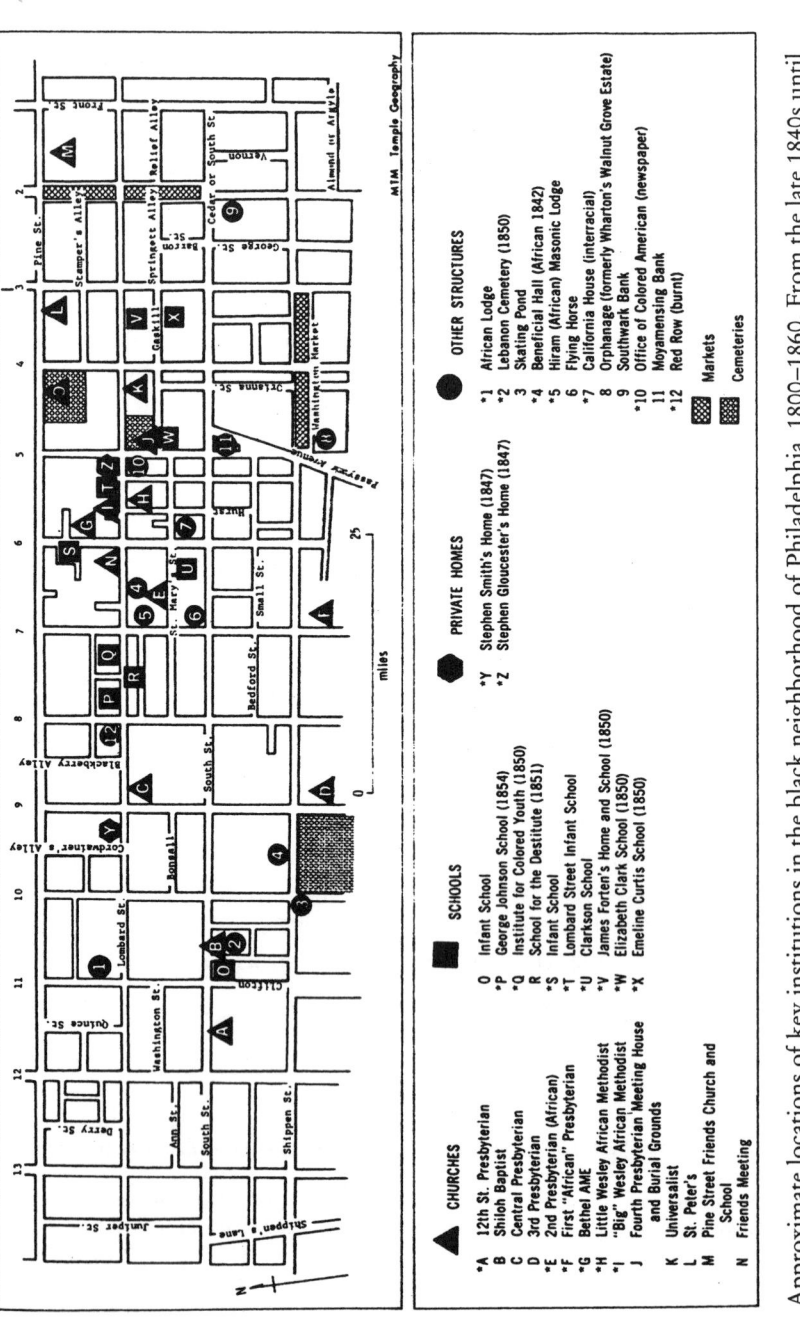

Approximate locations of key institutions in the black neighborhood of Philadelphia, 1800–1860. From the late 1840s until their move to Cleveland in 1854, the Willsons lived in a home at Ninth and Shippen. From Emma J. Lapsansky, "'Since They Got Those Separate Churches': Afroamericans and Racism in Jacksonian Philadelphia," *American Quarterly* 32 (Spring 1980), 54–78 (fig. 1, p. 59). © 1980. The American Studies Association. Reprinted by permission of the Johns Hopkins University ever, there were many black migrants to Philadelphia, including some of the people in the "higher classes," who had been born into slavery. Some had been emancipated by their owners, and others had purchased their freedom. A significant minority had fled to freedom and lived in constant fear of recapture. They were not eager to have the census-taker record *their* presence. Plenty of Philadelphians who were legally free had family members still in bondage in the South.

Exploring Philadelphia, coming to know its African-American community, Joseph Willson would soon have realized how diverse a community it was in terms of people's origins. There were men and women whose families had lived in and around the city for two, three, or even four generations. There were those whose parents had arrived in the 1790s or early 1800s from the Upper South as manumission had become easier for a time in Delaware, Maryland, Virginia, and even North Carolina. There were those who were themselves migrants. One contingent was from South Carolina. The wave of repression that occurred in that state in the wake of the Denmark Vesey conspiracy of 1822 had prompted some to relocate, while others had come simply because Philadelphia seemed to offer more opportunities for gainful employment. Shortly before the Willsons' own arrival, a number of free families of color had fled Virginia as whites, driven into a frenzy of fear and rage after Nat Turner's rebellion, had turned upon them. The first safe haven they found north of the Mason-Dixon line was Philadelphia.

There were migrants from Georgia, although few were as rich or as well educated as the Willsons. Among the recent arrivals from North Carolina were Junius C. Morel, the son of a white slaveholder and "his chattel personal" (Morel's own description), who emerged as a powerful and controversial spokesman for the black community, and Frederick Augustus Hinton, a talented and resourceful man from Raleigh, who eventually married into the Willson clan. Some migrants, like Amos Webber, came from Pennsylvania's rural counties. Webber may have learned to read and write before he left Bucks County, but it was in Philadelphia, with its network of African-American schools and literary societies, that he had the chance to further his education, and it was during his lengthy sojourn in the city that he began to compile his "memory books."[12] People of color arrived from neighboring New Jersey, unsure of their future in a

---

12. On Webber's adjustment to life in Philadelphia, see Nick Salvatore's *We All Got History: The Memory Books of Amos Webber* (New York: Random House, 1996), chaps. 1–3.

state where slavery was taking a very long time indeed to die. Individuals came to Philadelphia from other parts of the North because they had married Philadelphians. That was the case with Amy Matilda Williams, a friend of Joseph Willson's sister, Emily. She was the daughter of a prominent New York City minister. In her teens she met and married Philadelphia barber Joseph Cassey. Still others arrived because their work brought them to the city. John Bowers, for instance, was a sailor from Boston. Around 1807 or 1808, his ship sailed up the Delaware to Philadelphia. He liked what he saw and stayed.

Then there were the immigrants. Willson would have met people from the Caribbean. Some, like well-to-do barber Robert Douglass Sr. and Sarah Ann Gordon, matriarch of the affluent Gordon family, were from the British colonies—Douglass from St. Kitts and Gordon from Barbados. A sprinkling of French names—Montier, Duterte, Appo, and Dupuy—resulted from the influx of *gens de couleur* and slaves from Saint Domingue in the 1790s. Whether they spoke French or English, most of the West Indians quickly put down roots in the city, marrying into "local" families.[13]

Few Philadelphians were African-born by the 1830s, but there were some. Willson might have heard the last name "Ganges" applied to a number of people in the community and wondered about it. If he inquired, he would have been told about dozens of Africans set free several decades before from an illegal slaver and named for the vessel that had rescued them.

Some of the migrants kept alive ties with friends and family back home. Sarah Gordon's son lived for a time with her brother on Barbados. Frederick A. Hinton announced his marriage in the Raleigh papers as well as the Philadelphia ones. Amy M. Cassey provided friends in Philadelphia with contacts in New York City. When they attended a women's antislavery convention in New York in 1837, a group of young women of color from Philadelphia stayed with her parents. Friends visited friends. People wrote letters of introduction for one another, easing the transition into a strange city or making a visit safer and more pleasant. Joseph Willson was able to

---

13. Some Caribbean immigrants still valued their distinctive identity enough to organize their own mutual benefit society. The Friendly West Indian Society was incorporated in 1816. Most of its thirty-three charter members had decidedly "English" names (John Brown, Richard Bennett, and so on), but the names of a few members, such as David Bastien and John Jematrice, suggest French West Indian origins. Charters of Incorporation, Book 2, 234; PSA.

tap into that kind of network of friends when he went to New England to train as a printer.

News was passed back and forth, sometimes over remarkable distances. Junius C. Morel and James Forten had correspondents in the West Indies. Forten's son-in-law looked after the business affairs of a friend in Liberia. Surprisingly large numbers of black Philadelphians traveled overseas. Most did so as sailors. The world they saw was generally that of the great "sailortowns" like Liverpool and Rio de Janeiro, New York and Marseille. A few saw a very different world. When the independently wealthy Robert Purvis went to Britain to advance the antislavery cause, he ran into Irish patriot Daniel O'Connell in the lobby of the House of Commons! Others went abroad to raise funds for churches and schools. A few went for higher education or the kind of professional training they could not get in the United States. Whether they went as sailors or students, what they found outside the United States often gave them a very different perspective on their identity as Americans and people of color.

In no sense was the Philadelphia community an isolated and insular one. Although many people lived their whole lives within a few blocks of the place where they had been born, others traveled across town, across the state, or across the ocean. Philadelphia became home to thousands of African-American migrants, but black migrants from Philadelphia also headed out for other communities. Joseph Willson was a case in point. Born in Augusta, Georgia, he lived briefly in Huntsville, Alabama. Then he came to Philadelphia. From there he went to Boston for a year or two. He returned to Philadelphia, made his home there for some years, left for Cleveland, and then relocated to Indianapolis.

Whatever factors had drawn individual black migrants to Philadelphia, they shared one major concern with the long-established residents. How could they make a living? What job opportunities could the city offer men and women of color? For many the only work to be had was of the most menial and arduous kind.

Very few African-American women in Philadelphia knew what it was like to supervise servants, or to enjoy the rather more modest luxury of keeping house for their families while their husbands fulfilled single-handedly the role of breadwinner. Generally, black women worked in the homes of whites. Some "lived in," while others lived with their families and trudged to work every day to clean and cook for upper- and middle-class white women. Still others took in laundry. Being a laundress or a washerwoman was low-paid and certainly without prestige, but it was work they could do at home while they cared for their children.

Most of the female wage-earners in the black community were in domestic service of one kind or another. There were some, though, who were streetvendors, selling a wide range of delicacies, from pepper-pot soup to ginger-cakes and candies. Others were seamstresses and milliners. The work was often poorly paid, and it took a toll on one's eyesight, but again it could be done at home. Some women, especially widows, kept boardinghouses. At least bustling about and tending to the needs of their boarders meant boardinghouse keepers were working for themselves, and caring for their children could be combined with their paid work.

A few black women became teachers, opening their own schools or working in schools run by the Abolition Society or other charitable groups. However, the standing an African-American teacher enjoyed in her own community was seldom translated into respect from whites. Sarah Mapps Douglass, a genteel young woman whom Willson had no hesitation in including in his "higher classes," recalled a traumatic encounter in New York, where she taught for a time. She had been raised a Quaker by her mother and had accompanied her to Friends' Meeting in Philadelphia since childhood. In New York she located a meeting and began attending. Most of the white Friends completely ignored her. "I had been attending one month, when a Friend accosted me thus—'Does thee go out a house cleaning?'—I looked at her with astonishment—my eyes filled with tears, & I answered 'no.' 'What does thee do then?' 'I teach a school'—'oh, then thee's better off'—Judge what were my feelings! a stranger, in a strange land! . . . I wept during the whole of that meeting, & for many succeeding sabbaths."[14]

The range of jobs available to black men was appreciably greater than that available to black women, but it was narrowing rapidly by the time the Willsons came to Philadelphia. The vast majority worked as unskilled laborers, who cleaned the city's streets, dug ditches, hauled away trash, and in short did whatever they could to eke out a living. Low-paid and physically very demanding, laboring also gave a man little job security. He was hired by the day or by the week. In addition, black laborers found themselves competing with each new wave of white immigrants. One

---

14. Testimony of Sarah Mapps Douglass, quoted in Sarah M. Grimké, "Letter on the Subject of Prejudice against Colour amongst the Society of Friends in the United States," 1839; BPL.

Introduction 13

"Pepper Pot, Smoking Hot." From *The Cries of Philadelphia: Ornamented with Elegant Woodcuts* (Philadelphia: Johnson & Warner, 1810). (Courtesy of the Historical Society of Pennsylvania). African-American street vendors, male and female, were a common sight in Philadelphia. Pepper pot was made "chiefly of tripe, ox-feet, and other cheap animal substances, with a great portion of spice. . . . [E]xcepting to weak stomachs, it is a very pleasant feast." Note that this vendor's customers are drawn from various segments of the city's population.

black commentator, himself in comfortable circumstances, was appalled at the unwillingness to give African-American men a chance to earn a few cents by performing even the humblest tasks. "During the late snow storm, thousands of persons were employed in cleaning the gutters, levelling [sic] the drifts, &c. Among the whole number, there was not a man of

Vase of flowers, by Sarah M. Douglass (1843). From the Album of Martina Dickerson. (Courtesy of the Library Company of Philadelphia)

The smaller of these two paintings is signed S.M.D. and is by African-American schoolteacher Sarah M. Douglass. The larger painting is probably also her work. A poet as well as an artist, she was often asked to contribute to the handsome leather-bound albums that members of the "higher classes of colored society" kept to entertain themselves and their friends. The Library Company has three such albums.

Flowers in a vase, watercolor, from the Album of Amy Matilda Cassey. (Courtesy of the Library Company of Philadelphia)

color to be seen, while hundreds of them were going about the streets with shovels in their hands, looking for work and finding none."[15]

Slightly higher up the occupational ladder than the unskilled laborers were the porters. Porters moved anything that needed moving, from furniture and household goods to merchandise for store-owners and luggage for the hundreds of travelers who arrived in the city each day by coach or by river.[16] A refinement on that, toiling on the docks as a stevedore or longshoreman, moved one into the semiskilled category. Loading a vessel to maximize space and to ensure that cargoes did not shift in transit required more than a strong back. Draymen and coachmen enjoyed a certain measure of independence. The coachman might work for a white family, but occasionally he owned his own vehicle.[17] Draymen with their horses and carts provided an essential service, moving goods of all kinds about the city. Sweep-masters were also independent entrepreneurs, going from house to house with their gangs of young chimney-sweeps.[18] Crossing-sweeps and whitewashers, male and female, also did better for themselves than unskilled laborers.

As a port city, Philadelphia had a long history of offering employment to black mariners. Going to sea was tough and dangerous, but it had its positive aspects. Sailors were paid not on the basis of their race but according to the level of their skill.[19] And there were the intangible benefits that offset the hardships and risks of life at sea. One saw something of the wider world. John Bowers sailed to China in 1809. In Canton, as close as foreigners were allowed to get to the mainland, he made an interesting discovery. All non-Chinese, white and black, were regarded as "barbar-

---

15. *Lib*, February 12, 1831. "A Colored Philadelphian," was in fact sailmaker James Forten. This was a pen name he often used.

16. In 1830 nineteen African-American porters banded together to form their own mutual benefit society, the African Porters' Benevolent Society. Charters of Incorporation, Book 4, 419; PSA.

17. Like porters, coachmen had their own mutual benefit organization, the Coachmen's Benevolent Society. It is perhaps an indication of their dominance of the occupation—at least as late as 1828, when the society was formed—that they did not feel it necessary to identify themselves as "African Coachmen" or "Colored Coachmen." All thirty of the founding members were men of color. Charters of Incorporation, Book 4, 263; PSA.

18. On the sweep-masters of another urban center, New York City, and their role as entrepreneurs, see Paul A. Gilje and Howard B. Rock, "'Sweep O! Sweep O!': African-American Chimney-Sweeps and Citizenship in the New Nation," *WMQ* 51 (July 1994), 507–38.

19. W. Jeffrey Bolster, *Black Jacks: African American Seamen in the Age of Sail* (Cambridge, Mass.: Harvard University Press, 1997), 76, 161, 213. However, as Bolster notes, few African-American sailors became mates, and fewer still masters.

"A meeting of the Free & Independent Wood Sawyers, Boot Cleaners, Chimney Sweepers, Porters, &c &c of Philadelphia." Lithograph by David Claypool Johnston, 1819. (Courtesy of the American Antiquarian Society). This is a white artist's satirical rendering of the communal life of Philadelphia's aspiring black entrepreneurs. Several of the men in Willson's "higher classes" were sweeps and porters.

ians" by a culture that had a profoundly different understanding of "race." With travel came a degree of pride. Junius C. Morel, an ex-sailor, boasted: "In the course of a not uneventful life, it has been my case to have visited the four corners of the Globe, and . . . to have been brought into contact . . . with Christians, Mahomedans and Pagans."[20]

If black seafaring had declined from its heyday long before Willson arrived in Philadelphia—in 1810, 22.4 percent of mariners shipping out of

---

20. *CA*, May 3, 1838.

" 'Worldlyfolk' questioning chimneysweeps and their master before Christ Church, Philadelphia." Watercolor by John Lewis Krimmel. The Metropolitan Museum of Art, Rogers Fund, 1942 (42.95.12). John Lewis Krimmel (1786–1821), a German who emigrated to the United States in 1810, captured in a far less satirical manner than other white artists the nuances of socioeconomic status among African Americans in Philadelphia. The sweep-master, a small-scale businessman, is clearly in a very different class from the wretched young sweeps who work for him.

the port on overseas voyages were men of color—it was still significant. The figure was 17 percent in 1830 and, despite downturns as the economy fluctuated, it was still 17 percent in 1853, when Willson began preparing to leave Philadelphia for a new life in the Midwest.[21]

Many black Philadelphians went to sea at some point in their working lives, and many found work in one or another of the maritime trades. Unquestionably the most spectacular success story was that of James Forten, who rose from apprentice to proprietor of one of the largest sail-lofts in the city. At the height of his prosperity, he presided over an integrated (and harmonious) workforce of forty men. Others labored in shipyards, rigging lofts, and mast shops. Still others did the vital work of caulking, making sure seams were watertight before a vessel sailed.

The basic problem with this kind of work, and many of the other better-paying jobs, was that they were skilled. The necessary level of skill was acquired by serving a lengthy apprenticeship. As Joseph Willson discovered when he tried to train as a printer, a young black man seeking to apprentice himself to a white craftsman would have to look long and hard before he found one willing to share the "mysteries" of his craft with him. James Forten, who fully appreciated the advantages he enjoyed and spoke in glowing terms of the white man who had given him his start in business, made a personal commitment to take on apprentices regardless of race. He called on other black men in the skilled trades to make the same commitment. It was essential that they do so because no one else would. "If a man of color has children, it is almost impossible for him to get a trade for them, as the journeymen and apprentices generally refuse to work with them, even if the master is willing, which is seldom the case."[22]

Some black Philadelphians were fortunate in that they had skills, either mastered in slavery or handed down by their parents. Dressmakers like Hetty Burr, wife of community leader John P. Burr and very much a presence in her own right, shared their skills with their daughters. Fathers trained their sons. When he left the sea, John Bowers became a clothes-dealer. His sons, John C. and Thomas, became tailors. Several men who featured in *Sketches of the Higher Classes* were boot- and shoemakers. Charles Brister was a skilled worker in a sugar refinery. The multitalented Paris Salter was a successful builder, combining the skills of a bricklayer, plasterer, slater, and stonemason. Ex-slave James Gibbons built homes and

21. Bolster, *Black Jacks*, 236.
22. *Lib*, February 12, 1831.

James Forten. Watercolor by unknown artist. Leon Gardiner Collection, Historical Society of Pennsylvania. Sailmaker and real-estate speculator James Forten (1766–1842) was one of the richest free people of color in antebellum America. Born free in Philadelphia, he fought for the Patriots during the Revolution and often cited his wartime service to justify his claims to full civil rights. For more than four decades he was an outspoken opponent of slavery and a champion of racial equality.

the furniture to fill them. His son, George Washington Gibbons, graduated from making furniture to coffins, and from coffin-making to undertaking. Of course, whether one could find employment even with a good trade was another matter. Surveys conducted by the Pennsylvania Abolition Society and the Society of Friends revealed that hundreds of black citizens possessed skills they had no opportunity to use.[23]

One sector of employment that African-American men had dominated for decades in Philadelphia was barbering. Many in Willson's "higher classes" were barbers. The designation "barber" embraced everyone from the prosperous hairdresser, wig-maker, and perfumer Joseph Cassey, to John P. Burr, who never earned enough to become a homeowner, to Alexander Hutchinson, a young journeyman who worked in someone else's shop, but Willson included all three in his "higher classes" not because of their wealth or their lack of it, but because of their devotion to the welfare of their community.

On one level, barbering was servile. White customers felt comfortable being shaved by a black barber. The proprieties were preserved. The black man was in deferential attendance on the white man. African-American men who were careful to show they "knew their place" could do well as barbers. Servile though barbering might be in some respects, it could be very lucrative. Joseph Cassey combined shaving customers with "note shaving." As a result of his money-lending activities, which were financed by the capital he derived from his barbershop, he grew very wealthy and eventually retired to live the life of a gentleman. Frederick A. Hinton prospered, becoming the proprietor of the elegant "Gentleman's Dressing Room." Other affluent barbers in Willson's "higher classes" included Robert Douglass Sr. and his son James, Thomas Butler, and James McCrummill. Some, like McCrummill, Jacob C. White, and young Peter Cassey, doubled as dentists and bleeders. For every well-to-do African-American barber, though, there were dozens making barely enough money to live on. Competition was also becoming tougher. By the time Joseph Willson arrived in Philadelphia, the near monopoly black barbers had once enjoyed was being eroded.

There were opportunities for African-American men and women who wanted to become retailers. Not much capital was needed, although still

23. See, for instance, the Pennsylvania Abolition Society's *Register of the Trades of the Colored People in the City of Philadelphia and Districts* (Philadelphia: Merrihew and Gunn, 1838).

far more was needed than most black Philadelphians could hope to amass. There were black grocers, cake-bakers, and confectioners. Some of the individuals Willson included in his "higher classes" were secondhand clothing dealers. Philadelphia had a thriving market in used clothing. The personal servants of the well-to-do expected to be given their employers' castoffs. Having little opportunity to wear such finery themselves, they sold the garments to dealers and pocketed the proceeds (often an important supplement to their wages). The dealers then sold the various items to people eager to buy last season's fashions if the price was right. Of course, one had to take care not to handle stolen goods unwittingly.[24] However, men like Harrison R. Sylva and John Bowers prospered in the clothing trade. In every respect—wealth, status, aspirations—they were in a very different class from the wretchedly poor rag-pickers, who roamed the alleys looking for scraps of cloth to sell to paper-makers.

One sector of the economy that African-American men in Philadelphia succeeded in keeping peculiarly their own throughout the antebellum era was catering. Most of those who prepared and sold food ran fairly modest operations—an oyster-cellar or a small eatery of some sort—but a handful of people, such as Peter Augustine, Robert Bogle, James Prosser, Thomas J. Dorsey, and the Mintons, had establishments that could offer lavish entertainments to affluent white customers able to pay for their services. Bogle's catering skills were legendary. They were the subject of a lengthy poem by Nicholas Biddle, who had probably attended some of Bogle's dinners, and of a shorter satirical piece by another white Philadelphian. Both dwelt on the same theme. No entertainment was complete unless Robert Bogle had had the overseeing of it.[25]

In terms of an African-American professional class, Philadelphia had no black lawyers before the Civil War. As for physicians, there were none who were university-trained, but there were black women and men who practiced medicine in one form or another. Ex-slave James J. G. Bias was a highly regarded bleeder and practitioner of the popular science of phrenology, the theory that different parts of the brain governed different

---

24. On the African-American clothiers of Boston and their brushes with the law, see Peter P. Hinks, *To Awaken My Afflicted Brethren: David Walker and the Problem of Antebellum Slave Resistance* (University Park: The Pennsylvania State University Press, 1997), 66–68.

25. Nicholas Biddle, *An Ode to Bogle* (Philadelphia: Privately printed for Ferdinand J. Dreer, 1865); R. H. Small, *Philadelphia; or, Glances at Lawyers, Physicians, First-Circle, Wistar Parties, &c, &c.* (Philadelphia: R. H. Small, 1826), 81–82. See also Henry W. Minton, *The Early History of the Negro in Business in Philadelphia, Read Before the American Negro Historical Society, March 1913* (Nashville, Tenn.: AMESS Union, 1913), 11–12.

FRANK JOHNSON.

Published at the Arch St. Gallery of the Daguerreotype, Philadelphia.

PRINTED BY WAGNER & M^cGUIGAN

1816.

Frank Johnson. Lithograph by Robert Douglass Jr. from a daguerreotype. Printed by Wagner & McGuigan, 1846. (Courtesy of the Dreer Collection, Historical Society of Pennsylvania). Like the celebrated black caterers of Philadelphia, musician and composer Frank Johnson (1792–1844) was a fixture at upper-class white entertainments. He and his band performed in various American cities and in Europe. This lithograph was done by another talented member of the African-American community, Robert Douglass Jr. Joseph Willson knew Johnson, who was a member of his church, and Douglass, whom he mentioned in *Sketches*.

mental faculties, and that the shape of the skull determined an individual's character and abilities. He even authored a treatise on the subject. Medicine might be an individual's secondary rather than their primary occupation. For instance, Charles Nash was a bleeder and a skilled cabinetmaker. John Purdy could draw blood, but he could also make shoes.[26] Then there were the African-American women who were seamstresses and laundresses but also acted as midwives. At a time and in a place where many people, irrespective of race, lacked the means to hire a licensed physician, such individuals provided basic medical care. Their fees were lower, and their services often earned them the respect of their patients—a respect that transcended race.

With sixteen black churches by 1838, Philadelphia had a cadre of African-American ministers. Willson singled out the minister of his own church, William Douglass, as a man who coupled learning with piety, although he acknowledged there were others equally deserving of praise. The pulpit brought men of real talent to Philadelphia. Even so, few earned the kinds of salaries that enabled them to dispense with a second job. They taught school, made shoes, and turned their hand to anything that would enable them to support their families.

Although poverty was pervasive in black Philadelphia, there were men and women of considerable wealth, and Joseph Willson came to know most of them. Grocer Littleton Hubert had accumulated $3,800 in real estate and $2,000 in personal property by 1847, when the Quakers conducted a survey of the African-American population. In 1838 barber and hairdresser Robert Douglass Sr. was worth $8,000. Sailmaker James Forten was worth almost $100,000 by the early 1830s. The astute barber turned moneylender Joseph Cassey left an estate estimated at $75,000. If not quite in the same league as Forten and Cassey, Jacob C. White did very well as a barber, bleeder, store-owner, and eventually the proprietor of an African-American cemetery. Then there were the people who had inherited their wealth. Joseph Willson was one such fortunate heir. Another was Robert Purvis. Purvis received a legacy of over $100,000 from his British-born father, a successful South Carolina cotton factor, and increased it by his own skill as a real estate speculator and entrepreneur.

Wealth was very unevenly distributed in the black community, as it was in the larger white community. Theodore Hershberg has calculated that

26. PAS, *Register of Trades*.

during the 1830s and 1840s the poorest 50 percent of the African-American population possessed only 5 percent of the total black-owned wealth in the city. The top 10 percent owned almost 70 percent, and the top 1 percent owned a staggering 30 percent.[27] The distribution may in fact have been more uneven, since some of the richest people in the community, including James Forten, his son, Robert B. Forten, Robert Purvis (who was married to one of Forten's daughters), and William Douglass, declined to disclose the full details of their wealth. The compilers of the Pennsylvania Abolition Society census of 1838 could learn nothing from Purvis and the Fortens about their property holdings. When the Friends took their own survey in 1847, Joseph Cassey told them he had $2,000 in personal property, but said nothing about his real estate, although the deed books for Philadelphia and Bucks Counties indicate he held title to a number of valuable properties. As for the Rev. William Douglass, he apparently sent the census-taker away with a flea in his ear. The man took a guess at the minister's wealth, noting: "[R]efused any information whatever. This was obtained without his knowledge."

Indisputably, despite the success of a Robert Purvis, a James Forten, or a Joseph Willson, poverty was endemic in Philadelphia's African-American community. Poverty restricted choices, especially when it came to housing. In a pamphlet they published in 1849, the officers of the Pennsylvania Abolition Society quoted at length from a former coroner, who had had ample opportunity to inspect the hovels of Moyamensing, where so many blacks and whites lived and died in squalor. "Many are found dead in cold and exposed rooms and garrets, board shanties five and six feet high, and as many feet square, erected and rented for lodging purposes, mostly without any comforts, save the bare floor, with the cold penetrating between the boards, and through the holes and crevices on all sides; some in cold, wet and damp cellars, with naked walls, and in many instances without floors; and others found lying dead in back yards, in alleys, and other exposed situations."[28] This was a far cry indeed from the comfortable parlors of the African-American elite, or even the modest but scrupulously clean dwellings of the "middling sort," and that was

---

27. Theodore Hershberg, "Free Blacks in Antebellum Philadelphia: A Study of Ex-Slaves, Freeborn, and Socio-Economic Decline," in Joe William Trotter Jr. and Eric Ledell Smith, eds., *African Americans in Pennsylvania: Shifting Historical Perspectives* (University Park: The Pennsylvania State University Press, 1997), 127.

28. *A Statistical Inquiry into the Condition of the People of Colour in the City and Districts of Philadelphia* (Philadelphia: Kite and Walton, 1849), 34.

something the compilers of the report wanted to emphasize. Despite all the barriers thrown in the way of black conomic advancement, their investigation showed "a population, to a considerable degree, sober, industrious, and independent. . . . The degradation and wretchedness which mark the infected district in Moyamensing, are foreign to the real character of our colored population, to whom it would be doing a gross injustice, not to point out clearly the broad line of separation."[29] That was precisely the point Joseph Willson was trying to make in his book.[30]

By 1833, when the Willsons decided to make their home in Philadelphia, Pennsylvania's Gradual Abolition Act of 1780 was more than half a century old. True, freedom had come slowly under the provisions of the act, but freedom, whether inherited, purchased, granted under the law, or seized through flight, was the prevailing condition of black people in Joseph Willson's Philadelphia. But what did "freedom" mean? What it meant depended on whom one asked.

Philadelphia might have the reputation as a haven of liberty and equality, but the image was far removed from the reality, at least by the 1830s. True, people of color did not need a license to live in the city, as they did in some southern cities, but that "solution" to the perceived problem of a growing African-American presence in the state of Pennsylvania as a whole, and in Philadelphia in particular, had been debated on more than one occasion.[31]

During the two decades he lived in Philadelphia, Joseph Willson saw a steady erosion of African-American freedom. The arguments used to bolster each restriction were illogical in that some ran directly counter to others. Black people were lazy, preferring to steal or beg rather than work. Black people were competing too successfully in the job market and taking work away from whites. Black people preferred to live in squalor, threatening the health and well-being of their white neighbors. Black people were doing rather too well, acquiring property and thinking themselves as good as white people. Black people were ignorant and vicious in their

29. Ibid., 39.
30. Frank J. Webb would make the same point in his 1857 novel, *The Garies and Their Friends* (London: G. Routledge & Co., 1857; reprint, New York: Arno Press, 1969). While his main theme was the pernicious nature of racial violence, Webb, who had grown up in a middle-class black family in Philadelphia, tried to describe for his white readers the home life of the African-American elite and that of the "middling sort."
31. Julie Winch, *Philadelphia's Black Elite: Activism, Accommodation, and the Struggle for Autonomy, 1787–1848* (Philadelphia: Temple University Press, 1988), 17–20, 132–34.

habits. They needed whites to exercise strict control over them for their own good. However, these same people would do splendidly if they were colonized in Liberia or some other suitably remote spot far away from the presence of white people.... The arguments ran on and on, unanswerable by African Americans because none of their detractors really cared to listen to their answers.

The sense of being marginalized and of losing rights they had once enjoyed was all the more galling because black Philadelphians could not see what they had done to deserve such treatment. Again and again, in petitions and pamphlets, in speeches and letters to officials, in statements in the press, African-American leaders pointed out the basic integrity and worthiness of themselves and those on whose behalf they spoke. There was black crime. They acknowledged that and pledged to bring lawbreakers to justice, but they noted that proportionately more crimes were committed by whites, and their criminal offenses tended to be much more serious.[32] There were black men and women in the almshouse, but they insisted the African-American community tried to take care of its own poor through a network of mutual benefit societies and charities. Were African Americans unpatriotic? How could that be when they and their fathers had rallied to the general defense when the city was threatened by the British during the War of 1812? Were they uncaring? Had their parents and grandparents not nursed the sick during the great yellow fever epidemic of 1793 with a commendable disregard for their own safety? Why had the majority community, with the exception of a few selfless friends, apparently turned its back on them? In the words of one group of Philadelphians, who petitioned the state legislature in 1832: "We claim no exemption from the frailties and imperfections of our common nature. We feel that we are men of like passions and feelings with others of a different color.... But we think that in the aggregate, we will not suffer by a comparison with our white neighbors."[33]

At least as far as legislative action was concerned, an especially heavy blow fell in 1838, when the state constitution of 1790 was revised so that blacks lost the right to vote. As a substantial property owner and a member of the African-American upper class, Joseph Willson was directly af-

---

32. On efforts by those in the African-American "higher classes" to combat black crime, while at the same time pointing to the extent of white criminal activities, see *Poulson*, March 3, 1822.

33. James Forten, Robert Purvis, and William Whipper, *To the Honourable the Senate and House of Representatives of the Commonwealth of Pennsylvania* (Philadelphia, 1832), 6–8.

fected by that. He had just reached the age of majority, and he was about to lose a precious right. There were some, of course, who maintained that he and others like him—men of color over twenty-one who paid taxes on a certain amount of property and had established residency in a given county—had never been "freemen" under the terms of the state's 1790 constitution. Their argument was that "freeman" was not synonymous with "free man," and that no man of color could qualify as a voter. To be a "freeman" one had to be white. Lawyers, politicians, white abolitionists, and African-American citizens wrangled for decades over that question.[34] It was resolved once and for all by the Reform Convention of 1837–38, which rewrote the constitution in such a way that far more white men were permitted to vote, but black men, regardless of wealth and status, were disfranchised.

Actually, most black Pennsylvanians who could meet the property qualification to be "freemen" had never been able to exercise the right they believed they had, either for fear of violence or because election officials refused to accept their votes, but some had gone to the polls and cast their ballots, although apparently not in Philadelphia County. Now there was no doubt about their access to the ballot box. The framers of the new constitution had spoken, and the white voters quickly ratified the results of their deliberations. In the words of the members of Philadelphia's "higher classes" who drew up the *Appeal of Forty Thousand* (the supposed number of eligible black voters under the old constitution), African Americans had lost "their check on oppression, their wherewith to buy friends." John Joseph Gurney, a British Quaker, reported hearing a story that may have been apocryphal, but certainly summed up public sentiment. "I was told that a white boy was observed seizing the marbles of a coloured boy in one of the streets, with the words, '*You have no rights now.*'"[35]

Writing three years after the Reform Convention had done its work, Joseph Willson angrily rejected the criticism that black people were lazy about improving their situation and blind to the difficulties that beset them. "Never have any people, in proportion to their means of operation, made greater efforts for their entire enfranchisement." They could not

34. Winch, *Philadelphia's Black Elite*, 134–37.
35. Robert Purvis, *Appeal of Forty Thousand Citizens, Threatened with Disfranchisement, To the People of Pennsylvania* (Philadelphia: Merrihew and Gunn, 1838), 4. John Joseph Gurney, *A Visit to North America, Described in Familiar Letters to Amelia Opie* (Norwich, England: Joseph Fletcher, 1841), 102.

vote, and "consequently, in all matters relating to their interests, which involve legislative action, they must appear . . . in the attitude of suitors; and show themselves very humble in the exercise of even that prerogative." Few politicians would act on their behalf when they had no votes to give at election time.

What long-term black residents may not have realized, any more than the newly arrived Joseph Willson, was that by the early 1830s Philadelphia was a city in decline. That decline led to a host of social and economic tensions. Once the nation's premier Atlantic port, Philadelphia had long since ceded that position to New York and was struggling not to fall into third place behind her rival to the South, Baltimore. New jobs were being created, notably in manufacturing and the textile industry, but the city and its people would face lean times as the decade wore on.[36] The Panic of 1837, and the failure of the Bank of the United States, would cause a wave of business failures and throw many hundreds out of work.

Philadelphia was also trying to cope with a flood of immigrants, most (although by no means all of them) from Ireland. Like many others cities, Philadelphia was beset by ethnic and religious animosities that on occasion led to rioting. It also experienced overcrowding, lawlessness, and outbreaks of epidemic disease, including cholera. City services were strained to the breaking point. Political turmoil was a fact of life. All those tensions affected in one way or another the lives of black citizens.

As the city's African-American population grew, so did the level of white animosity. Racial violence was nothing new. Sporadic outbursts had long been part of the social scene. People of color were assaulted in the streets with impunity by whites, who considered them legitimate targets on whom to vent their frustrations.[37] The kind of "spree" William Otter described participating in sometime in 1807—the invasion of a black church in the Northern Liberties and the beating of worshipers as they tried to escape the mayhem—was all too common.[38] However, during the

36. It is significant that African Americans were unable to find work in the factories that were springing up in and around Philadelphia.
37. See, for instance, *Relf's Gazette*, November 24, 1809.
38. Richard B. Stott, ed., *William Otter, History of My Own Times* (Ithaca: Cornell University Press, 1995), 58–59. On the contest between African Americans and whites over the use of the streets as "public space" in Philadelphia, see Nash, *Forging Freedom,* 176–77, 181. For a discussion of the situation throughout the North, see Shane White, " 'It Was a Proud Day': African Americans, Festivals, and Parades in the North, 1741–1834," *JAH* 81 (June 1994), 13–50.

1830s and 1840s violence occurred on a much larger scale. Perpetrated generally by the "lower sort," it seemed to have the sanction of many of the more "respectable" whites.

The Willsons had been in Philadelphia only a matter of months before the "Flying Horses" riot broke out in August 1834. Although the flashpoint was a dispute between black and white youths over a carousel in South Street, tensions had been simmering for some time. It would take special constables, the militia, and a company of infantry to restore order.[39] The following year there was trouble when a West Indian servant attacked his employer. In 1837 the cause was the murder of a white watch-

"A cry at once arose that a white man was shot, and the attention of the mob was directed to the California House, at the corner of Sixth and St. Mary street."—page 30

"A cry at once arose," from *Life and Adventures of Charles Anderson Chester* (Philadelphia, 1850). (Courtesy of the Library Company of Philadelphia). This illustration depicts the California House race riot of 1849, which occurred less than six blocks from the Willsons' home at Ninth and Shippen.

39. On the 1834 outbreak, see John Runcie, " 'Hunting the Nigs' in Philadelphia: The Race Riot of August 1834," *PA Hist* 39 (April 1972), 187–218; Bruce Laurie, *Working People of Philadelphia, 1800–1850* (Philadelphia: Temple University Press, 1980), 62–66; and Lapsansky, " 'Since They Got Those Separate Churches,' " 54–55, 61, 64, 73.

man by a mentally disturbed African-American man.[40] In 1838 the target was Pennsylvania Hall, the new meeting-place abolitionists had built for themselves. Rumors of "race mixing," of men and women, black and white, parading about the city arm in arm, proved too much for hundreds of white citizens, who converged on the "Temple of Liberty" and burned it to the ground.[41] In 1842 violence ensued when an African-American temperance parade came uncomfortably close to an Irish enclave. The marchers' banner was deemed highly offensive. Supposedly it showed a city burning and slaves running amok. When it was eventually displayed in court, it was found to show a kneeling slave with his manacles broken and the rising sun in the background. Its motto was:

> How grand in age, how fair in truth
> Are holy Friendship, Love, and Truth

Hardly an incitement to bloody rebellion![42]

Plenty of other riots broke out during the same period, sparked by rivalries among different groups of whites. Those outbursts completely bypassed the black community, but it was small comfort to know that one was not *always* the target. African Americans were singled out often enough to feel both threatened and abandoned. After the 1842 riot, which was directed as much against the "higher classes" as against the black "lower sort," Robert Purvis wrote of his sense of powerlessness: "I am convinced of our utter and complete nothingness in public estimation. . . . [D]espair black as the face of Death hangs over us—And the bloody Will, is in the heart of the community to destroy us."[43]

Despite all the threats to them—from legislators and from rioters—by the 1830s people of color in Philadelphia had created a viable and complex community. At the center of that community were the churches. These were the institutions that gave the community its strength and in a sense

---

40. Winch, *Philadelphia's Black Elite*, 146.
41. Ibid., 146–48; Nash, *Forging Freedom*, 277.
42. *Public Ledger*, August 2–4, 1842, quoted in Sam Bass Warner Jr., *The Private City: Philadelphia in Three Periods of Its Growth* (Philadelphia: University of Pennsylvania Press, 1968), 141. For an overview of the riots of the 1830s and 1840s, see Warner, *Private City*, 125–57.
43. Robert Purvis to Henry C. Wright, April 22, 1842, BPL.

helped define its very existence. African-American churchgoers had their choice of sixteen churches by 1841—Episcopal, Methodist, African Methodist Episcopal (AME), Lutheran, Presbyterian, and Baptist. Only the AME was an independent black denomination. The other congregations enjoyed varying degrees of autonomy within a predominantly white hierarchy. Some of Willson's contemporaries opted to remain in fellowship with white congregations, despite frequent displays of discriminatory treatment like that witnessed by English visitor William Chambers.[44] Unlike some other cities, such as New Orleans and St. Louis, Philadelphia had few black Catholics. They accounted for a mere 3 percent of African-American churchgoers in 1838.[45] There was no strong tradition of black Catholicism in Philadelphia, and the Catholic church was increasingly identified as the church of the Irish immigrants, who were so often at odds with black residents over everything from job opportunities to temperance.

Some black migrants, including the Willsons, had been drawn to Philadelphia by the promise of educational opportunities. A network of schools—public, charitable, and private—existed in the city for African-American children. The public schools were woefully inadequate, but they were free. However, plenty of parents were obliged to keep their children away because they could not clothe them properly (a problem African-American women in the "higher classes" tried to address through their charitable societies) or because they needed to send them out to work. Charity schools generally requested that parents pay what they could afford, although tuition was free to the poorest pupils. As for private schools, including the Pennsylvania Abolition Society's Clarkson School, which the Willsons attended, they were beyond the means of most families. Despite their limitations, Philadelphia's African-American schools must have looked appealing to people like the Willsons, who had moved to the city from a state where the education of black children, free and slave, was illegal.[46]

44. William Chambers, *American Slavery and Colour* (London: W. & R. Chambers; New York: Dix and Edwards, 1857), 129.
45. PAS census, 1838; PAS MSS, HSP.
46. On the education of African Americans in Philadelphia, see Harry C. Silcox, "Delay and Neglect: Negro Education in Antebellum Philadelphia, 1800–1860," *PMHB* 97 (October 1973), 444–64; William C. Kashatus III, "The Inner Light and Popular Enlightenment: Philadelphia Quakers and Charity Schooling, 1790–1820," *PMHB* 118 (January 1994), 98–99; Lapsansky, "'Since They Got Those Separate Churches,'" 59, 69; and Nash, *Forging Freedom*, 203–5, 208–9.

White critics liked to point to the prevalence of ignorance and "vice" (a term that encompassed everything from unemployment to criminal activities) among people of color in the city, and certainly there were those in the community who preferred street life to the schoolroom, but education clearly mattered to the vast majority of black Philadelphians. Many parents made financial sacrifices to send their children to school. Children who worked during the week often attended Sabbath schools. Classes for adults offered in the evenings by the various African-American churches or by white charitable groups had no shortage of pupils. People would turn up ready to study after a long day's work. Willson emphasized again and again in *Sketches of the Higher Classes* the yearning for education on the part of all sectors of the community. He observed, though, that it was love of knowledge for its own sake that drove them on. They understood the harsh realities of their situation. "The educated man of color, in the United States, is by no means . . . the *happiest* man. He finds himself in possession of abilities and acquirements that fit him for most of the useful and honorable stations in life . . . but . . . can he ever with reason anticipate their . . . being . . . appreciated and rewarded?" One could master reading and writing, but what then? So often the various branches of higher education were off-limits to people of color. Willson could and did name talented and highly educated men and women in the community. That there were not more, he attributed to prejudice.

> The machinery of the watch will not fulfill its intent, unless the impulse of the spring be applied; and, though things inanimate are not to be compared with the human soul, yet, neither can a man be expected to rise to eminence in a given department, where . . . there is not only an absence of all encouragement . . . but from the exercise of the legitimate functions of which . . . he would be absolutely excluded! He may indeed reach the base of the hill of science; but when there . . . what does he behold? Brethren ready to extend the hand of greeting and congratulation, when he hath made the ascent? No; not so with the man of color: need I say what reception *he* would be most likely to meet with?

Inevitably, the knowledge that learning was unlikely to bring anything but personal satisfaction led some to abandon the struggle. Philadelphia had many attractions, and plenty of African-American residents found grog-shops and gambling dens every bit as appealing as their white neighbors did. The community did indeed have a vibrant street culture. However, many black Philadelphians—and not just the affluent and well educated—shunned that culture. They pooled their often meager resources and pushed ahead, forming libraries, literary societies, and debating groups. Belonging to a literary society might say less about one's level of education than about one's aspirations. Men with the inclination to do so could seek enlightenment and entertainment at a host of societies, from the venerable Philadelphia Library Company of Colored Persons to the newly established Demosthenian Institute. Women were more limited in their choices, but by the mid-1830s they had three literary societies. Only one organization, the Gilbert Lyceum, broke with tradition by admitting men and women.

It was important that the African-American community organize its own lectures and debates, since black citizens could never be sure when they would be excluded from supposedly "public" events. Joseph Willson was proud of the intellectual endeavors of the people of color in his adopted home. He challenged whites who harbored notions of black intellectual inferiority to set aside their prejudices for an evening or two and attend meetings of African-American literary and debating societies, listen to young black women play the piano or recite poetry they had written, look at the paintings they had produced, take part in the well-informed discussions and the refined conversation that graced the drawingrooms of the black "better sort."[47] Then they might begin to appreciate those men and women they had shunned for so long as idle, useless, and quite unworthy of their notice, let alone their friendship.

Some of Joseph Willson's white contemporaries were quite willing to acknowledge that a black "better sort" did indeed exist in Philadelphia.

---

47. On the social and intellectual life of the "higher classes of colored society" in Philadelphia, see Emma J. Lapsansky, " 'Discipline to the Mind': Philadelphia's Banneker Institute, 1854–72," *PMHB* 117 (January 1993), 83–102; Julie Winch, " 'You Have Talents—Only Cultivate Them': Philadelphia's Black Female Literary Societies and the Abolitionist Crusade," in Jean Fagan Yellin and John C. Van Horne, eds., *The Abolitionist Sisterhood: Women's Political Culture in Antebellum America* (Ithaca: Cornell University Press, 1994), 101–16; Salvatore, *We All Got History*, 51–73; Donald Yacovone, ed., *A Voice of Thunder: The Civil War Letters of George E. Stephens* (Urbana and Chicago: University of Illinois Press, 1997), 7–9. On the various musical societies and concerts organized by African Americans in Philadelphia, see Eileen Southern, *The Music of Black Americans: A History*, 2nd ed. (New York: W. W. Norton, 1983), 99–110, 113–16.

Red bud on stem with leaves, from Mary Ann Dickerson Album. (Courtesy of the Library Company of Philadelphia). This painting in the album of another member of the "higher classes" is signed A.H.H. and may well be the work of Ada Howell Hinton. She was related to Joseph Willson by marriage. (Willson's sister, Elizabeth, was Ada's stepmother.)

Butterfly watercolor by Sarah M. Douglass, from the Album of Amy Matilda Cassey. (Courtesy of the Library Company of Philadelphia). This delicate painting is another example of the work of teacher Sarah M. Douglass. The album belonged to Amy Matilda Cassey, the wife of affluent barber and money-lender Joseph Cassey. Both Douglass and the Casseys are mentioned by Willson in his *Sketches*.

Calligraphed title page from the Album of Martina Dickerson. (Courtesy of the Library Company of Philadelphia). This example of decorative handwriting was done by James Forten Jr. in 1840 for the album of a friend. Forten was the eldest son of sailmaker and businessman James Forten Sr.

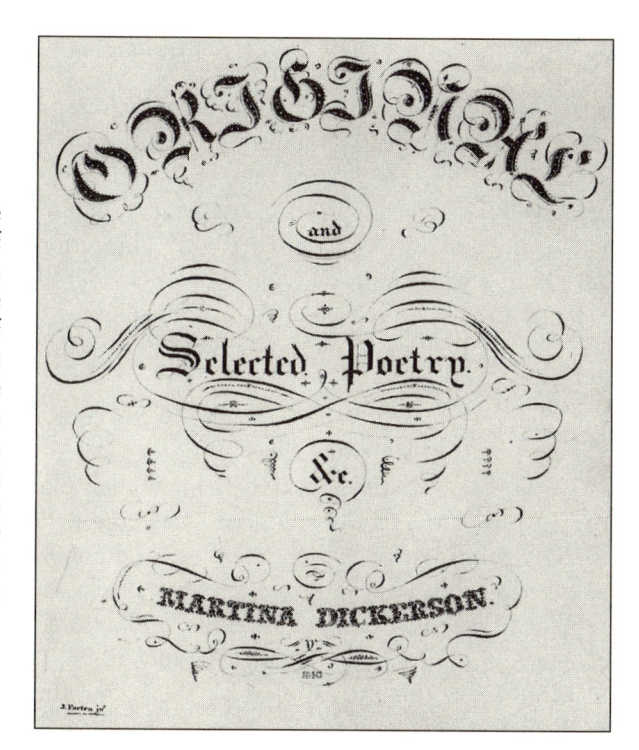

Vase of flowers, from the Album of Amy Matilda Cassey. (Courtesy of the Library Company of Philadelphia). The poem that accompanies this picture is signed "Margaretta." The painting and the poem may well be the work of James Forten Jr.'s sister, teacher Margaretta Forten.

After an 1832 visit to the city, during which he spent most of his time in the African-American community, abolitionist William Lloyd Garrison declared: "There are colored men and women, young men and young ladies, who have few superiors in refinement, in moral worth, and in all that makes the human character worthy of admiration and praise." Two decades later, a white minister from New York, identified only as A.H.B., was amazed at what he saw on a trip to Philadelphia. "Never in [his] life" had he "seen *gentlemen* of more elegant and unassuming manners than some colored men [he] . . . met."[48]

Others were far less enthusiastic. In his *Annals of Philadelphia*, John Fanning Watson lamented the passing of "the good old days" when the city's African-American residents "knew their place." "In the olden time, dressy blacks and dandy coloured beaux and belles, as we now see them issuing from their proper churches, were quite unknown. . . . Once they submitted to the appellation of servants, blacks, or negroes, but now they require to be called coloured people, and among themselves, their common call of salutation is—gentlemen and ladies."[49]

Members of the "higher classes" also found themselves the targets of a particularly vicious series of cartoons. Edward Clay's "Life in Philadelphia" series, published in the late 1820s and reprinted not only in Philadelphia but in London, proved immensely popular. Upwardly mobile African Americans, those who "aspire[d] too much," were depicted as addicted to the most exaggerated white fashions. Uncouth and incapable of putting together a coherent sentence, they gave themselves airs and paraded around the city in their finery, to the merriment of all who saw them.[50] It is hardly surprising that Willson should have felt the need to state in the preface that his book was *not* full of "burlesque representations." Probably more than one white reader looked at the title, *Sketches of the Higher Classes of Colored Society in Philadelphia by "A Southerner,"* and opened the book expecting to find it full of "darky" caricatures and dialect jokes. If so, they were disappointed.

It is significant that one of the reasons John Fanning Watson offered for

---

48. Garrison to Ebenezer Dole, June 29, 1832, in Walter M. Merrill, ed., *The Letters of William Lloyd Garrison* (Cambridge, Mass.: Belknap Press of Harvard University Press, 1971), vol. 1, 155. A.H.B., quoted in Yacovone, ed., *Voice of Thunder*, 7.

49. John Fanning Watson, *Annals of Philadelphia* (Philadelphia, 1830), in Lapsansky, "'Since They Got Those Separate Churches,'" 62.

50. Nash, *Forging Freedom*, 254–59; Lapsansky, "'Since They Got Those Separate Churches,'" 64–68.

"Is Miss Dinah at home?" by Edward W. Clay, from *Life in Philadelphia* (Philadelphia: William Simpson, 1828). (Courtesy of the Library Company of Philadelphia). Willson wrote of genteel members of the African-American community exchanging visits and leaving their calling-cards. This is how Edward Clay lampooned what he and many of his white contemporaries viewed as their foolishness in attempting to emulate the behavior of the white "higher classes."

"Dat is bery fine, Mr. Mortimer," by Edward W. Clay, from *Life in Philadelphia* (Philadelphia: S. Hart, 1830). (Courtesy of the Library Company of Philadelphia). Willson described decorous musical evenings at the homes of members of the African-American elite, while Clay poked fun at the whole notion of black refinement and gentility.

"Abroad," by H. Harrison after Edward W. Clay, from *Sketches of Character at Home and Abroad* (London: W. H. Isaacs, c. 1833). (Courtesy of the Library Company of Philadelphia). Clay's "burlesque representations" found a ready market in Britain as well as in the United States, and, as this cartoon demonstrates, he had his British imitators.

the inflated notions people of color had of themselves was the growth of "separate churches." Churches, the hubs of African-American life and the very visible symbols of a strong black presence in the city, were the targets in every outbreak of racial violence. As Emma Lapsansky has noted, destroying the churches was somehow equated with destroying the community. With assaults on the churches came assaults not just on the black poor but on the African-American upper and middle classes. In a very real sense, people of color who were property owners, who had skilled jobs or even operated their own businesses, were far more threatening to the white community than the dispossessed and the economically marginalized. At the lower end of the economic ladder, white unskilled laborers certainly did clash with their black rivals. However, well-dressed, ambitious, and affluent people of color presented a far more serious and subtle challenge to white notions of black people's appropriate station in life.[51]

How did Joseph Willson tackle the intertwined issues of race and class, and what role did he think those in the "higher classes" should play? Willson approached the problem of defining an upper class as a serious social scientist. To begin with, he refused to see elite status as somehow bound up with Euro-American ancestry. Although he himself was half-Irish and light-skinned—census-takers sometimes described him as white—he considered such matters as complexion and hair texture unimportant. One either fit his definition of a member of the "higher classes"—socially committed, responsible, determined to work for the betterment of the whole community—or one did not. Those in his "higher classes" included individuals such as Robert Purvis, who could have "passed" had he chosen to do so, and the dark-skinned Rev. William Douglass, whom Willson praised as a man of great learning and an ornament to the pulpit.

Did wealth matter to Willson? To a certain extent it did, in that he knew someone living a hand-to-mouth existence lacked the time, the energy, and the resources to become involved in efforts for community advancement. Without at least some disposable income, one could not, for instance, subscribe to a black newspaper, such as the *Colored American*. One could not pay the entrance fee and weekly or monthly dues to be a member of a literary society. One could certainly not absent oneself from work for days at a time to travel to Harrisburg, or even to New York or

51. Lapsansky, " 'Since They Got Those Separate Churches,' " 71–72.

Boston, for a black convention or an antislavery meeting, as some of the wealthier members of the community did. However, money alone was not a prerequisite for membership in the "higher classes"—at least as Willson defined them. There was always room for individuals like John L. Hart. Hart, an ex-slave, never graduated beyond the humble trade of porter, but his integrity, and his hard-won literacy, qualified him to become a vestryman at prestigious St. Thomas's African Episcopal Church and secretary of no fewer than five benevolent societies. Willson's inclusion of Hart and others like him spoke directly to *his* notion of the role of the people in the "higher classes." Those who used their wealth to separate themselves from the rest of the African-American community, instead of trying to serve that community, had no place in Willson's "higher classes."

Willson knew how white commentators judged whether or not an individual in the majority community belonged to the upper classes. "The chief grounds of distinction among men, are founded upon wealth, education, station, and occupation," but the familiar landmarks did not pertain to "colored society." "I have not the foundation of wealth; because the number who may be permitted to come under that denomination are too limited, to be justly made the standard of the men and manners of the whole body.... I cannot make moral worth ... the standard; for in that case it might be necessary to exclude a number of those who are denominated wealthy!" He finally settled on "that portion of colored society whose incomes, from their pursuits or otherwise (immoralities or criminalities ... excepted), enable them to maintain the position of householders, and their families in comparative ease and comfort." Could Willson have said precisely how many people constituted the elite of Philadelphia's black community? Probably not, but by his definition about 100 to 150 families—at most perhaps 5 percent of the total black population—made up the "higher classes."

Although Willson hedged on the question of "moral worth," he did in fact require that individuals subscribe to a certain standard of behavior. He was distressed by the conduct of some of the young women he encountered. Being a "womanly woman" meant being above reproach, and not scheming to ruin the reputations of others. A "lady" should be cultured, refined, and unassuming. It went without saying that she should be virtuous. Black female virtue, so often sneered at by whites as a contradiction in terms, related directly to the virtue, the intrinsic moral worth, of all people of color. Her life should be bound up in her family, but it was also permissible, and indeed praiseworthy, for her to develop her mind, and

Unidentified man, from Dickerson Family Collection of daguerreotypes. (Courtesy of the Library Company of Philadelphia)

In stark contrast to the Clay cartoons, these carefully posed portraits from the 1850s show affluent and genteel members of Philadelphia's African-American community. Edward Venning Jr., a carpenter, was a Philadelphia native. He and his family worshiped at the same church as the Willsons.

Photograph of unidentified man, possibly Edward Venning, from Dickerson Family Collection. (Courtesy of the Library Company of Philadelphia)

become involved in everything from antislavery societies to sewing circles. He even suggested that women introduce "systematic debates" into their literary societies, something other African-American men often regarded as their prerogative.[52]

As for the men in the "higher classes," Willson emphasized that personal ambition must give way to concern for the general welfare. He deplored "the constant competition among the 'leading men' to take *the* lead in all matters of concern. . . . There are too many men, who . . . [would] not take part in forwarding any scheme, however well intended on the part of the original movers, unless they themselves were components of that original." All too often, "Blustering, loud speaking and unlimited denunciation, are substituted for reason and common sense." Public meetings were "frequently made the scenes of personal disputes and quarrels, totally irrelevant to the matter for which they were assembled."

Willson was very critical of what he regarded as the unproductive and positively harmful factionalism within the "higher classes." Feuds, some of them dating back a generation or more, are "carried into most of the relations of life, and in some cases are kept up with the most bitter and relentless rancor." He observed: "I do not intend to represent, that there is always an open hostility kept up; it may appear dormant for the while, but favored by the time and the occasion . . . it seldom fails to develope [sic] its existence. It is the personification of true revenge." He believed feuding poisoned relations within the community. "The influence of such a course of conduct upon those who are subject to its operation, is easily perceptible. Suspicion and distrust very naturally usurp the place of confidence—without mutual reliance the one upon the integrity of the other, no circle of society can long exist together in unbroken harmony."

The problem was not that disagreements existed. After all, one had the right to choose one's friends. But Willson was deeply troubled about the effectiveness of a leadership that was divided within when the task ahead of it, namely, the winning of equal rights, was so great. He deplored the practice of "introducing private piques, preferences and antipathies into . . . public assemblages." It drove "many useful men" out of public life.

---

52. For discussions of "appropriate" behavior for African-American women, see James O. Horton, "Freedom's Yoke: Gender Conventions Among Free Blacks," in Horton, ed., *Free People of Color: Inside the African American Community* (Washington, D.C.: Smithsonian Institution Press, 1993), 98–120, and Anne M. Boylan, "Benevolence and Antislavery Activity Among African-American Women in New York and Boston, 1820–1840," in Yellin and Van Horne, eds., *The Abolitionist Sisterhood*, 119–37.

Unidentified young girl, from Dickerson Family Collection of daguerreotypes. (Courtesy of the Library Company of Philadelphia). This charming portrait of a child from the well-to-do Dickerson family of Philadelphia probably dates from the 1850s.

Unidentified young woman, from Dickerson Family Collection of daguerreotypes. (Courtesy of the Library Company of Philadelphia)

These two women epitomize Joseph Willson's notion of female decorum. Both are dressed fashionably but not flamboyantly. The books in the portraits suggest education and refinement.

Unidentified woman, from Dickerson Family Collection of daguerreotypes. (Courtesy of the Library Company of Philadelphia)

"Respecting themselves,—having no taste for contention and strife,—they very properly keep aloof." Willson had nothing but contempt for those "blustering Sir Oracles" who gave the impression of having "been educated in a pigstye" and never to have heard the words "honor, courtesy, [and] self-respect."

Joseph Willson was not the first to decry internal wrangling. A decade earlier, Presbyterian minister John Gloucester Jr. had declared:

> [T]here is nothing in this world so fatal in its consequences as that prejudice which exists among the coloured [sic] population; it raises up a battery against the interests of society, and threatens to give to the winds the most hopeful blossoms. It leads man gently on to the infectious fountains of partiality, there to drink incurably deep of the spirit of party prejudice; it gives to men the lead, who have never employed themselves for the benefit of mankind. That prejudice which exists among us, generally forms a dislike of our most promising men, and recommends one man to the good opinion of another, for the sake of supporting a party.[53]

It was true that African Americans did not have a monopoly on infighting. One need only look at white politicians to see that unanimity was seldom achieved even *within* parties, let alone *among* parties. As for the sacrifice of one's personal feelings for the good of the whole, that was rare indeed. However, what Willson and Gloucester were saying was not that their community had no right to its differences, but that those differences were positively dangerous when they were allowed to divide an already oppressed and marginalized population. The forces ranged against the people of color in Philadelphia demanded a united and well-coordinated response.

Willson had more advice to offer about the need for unity than he had about the best way to bring about change. Frankly, he was ambivalent about the nature of community activism. Black Philadelphians "never let a subject of peculiar importance to them . . . pass without a public expression of their views and opinions in regard to it. Their inability to act with efficiency . . . makes but little difference with most of the leading men. A meeting they must have." The fact that they were interested in their own

---

53. John Gloucester Jr., *A Sermon, Delivered in the First African Presbyterian Church in Philadelphia, on the 1st of January, 1830, before the Different Coloured Societies of Philadelphia* (Philadelphia, 1830), 5.

welfare was "certainly very praiseworthy," but "the character of their proceedings are [sic] frequently very objectionable." Simply insulting those who sought to abridge their rights would not achieve anything positive. It was one thing to abuse hostile legislators (although Willson did not really approve of that), but quite another to attack anyone who crossed them, "in matters of far less importance than is here supposed." It was hardly likely to influence anyone, however richly the insults were deserved. Politicians knew perfectly well they had nothing to lose by alienating people of color, since they could not show their displeasure at election time.

One is prompted to ask what course of action Willson advocated in place of public meetings. He admitted the power of people of color to effect change was limited without the franchise. In essence, his "higher classes" were trapped. They could and did work for the betterment of their community. Perhaps Willson placed his faith in that. Perhaps he hoped whites would be won over by obvious signs of the dedication of the African-American "better sort" to reform. And yet he acknowledged the depths of white prejudice.

> The exceedingly illiberal, unjust and oppressive prejudices of the great mass of the white community, overshadowing every moment of their existence, is enough to crush—effectually crush and keep down—any people. It meets them at almost every step without their domiciles, and not unfrequently [sic] follows even *there*. No private enterprise of any moment,—no public movement of consequence for the general good,—can they undertake, but forth steps the relentless monster to blight it in the germ. But in the face of all this, they not only bear the burthen successfully, but possess the elasticity of mind that enables them to stand erect under their disabilities, and present a state of society of which ... none have just cause to be ashamed.

If he had a solution to the painful reality of prejudice and discrimination, Willson did not explain what it was. Perhaps it consisted of simply "bear[ing] the burthen" with quiet courage and dignity. Essentially, the men and women in his "higher classes" were condemned to be leaders without the power to bring about change where it was most desperately needed. They could transform their own community through devotion to "good works." They could preach the virtues of thrift and education, sound morality, and hard work. What they could not do was oblige whites to value their efforts, to see that a transformation had taken place and act accordingly by accepting people of color as worthy of their respect and deserving of all the rights of citizens.

As for their ties to the rest of the African-American population in the city, there they also faced difficulties. Not everyone subscribed to the values and beliefs of the "higher classes." Theirs was a perennial problem. How could any one section of a community exert moral stewardship over the whole of that community? Being a member of the "higher classes"—in effect a minority within a minority—did not automatically entitle one to the respect of the "lower sort." And respect, even when it was forthcoming, did not necessarily translate into obedience or authority.[54]

How was *Sketches of the Higher Classes of Colored Society* received when it appeared in the summer of 1841? Some whites did take notice of it. The editor of the *Pennsylvania Freeman* did so because, as an abolitionist, he was interested in developments within the African-American community and was fairly often in contact with members of the "higher classes." While he admitted he had only glanced at the work, he observed: "Its outward appearance is creditable, and the style of a few paragraphs, which we have read, show[s] ability on the part of the writer." Lest there be any doubt about the matter, he added: "The author . . . is himself a colored man."[55]

The Philadelphia *Public Ledger* also made mention of the book. However, the editor saw only half of Willson's purpose: the call for reform among the "higher classes." "From a glance at its pages, we should deem it an interesting and useful work to that class of the community for whom it is immediately intended. It is well written, moderate, and candid in tone, and is careful to point out errors wherever they exist. We have no hesitation in saying that if properly consulted, it is a little work calculated to do much good."[56] The editor completely missed the point that the book was written for white Philadelphians, as well as their black neighbors, and that Willson considered his message about the injustices perpetrated against

---

54. For a discussion of the issues facing the African-American elite by the time of the Civil War, see Emma J. Lapsansky, "Friends, Wives, and Strivings: Networks and Community Values Among Nineteenth-Century Philadelphia Afroamerican Elites," *PMHB* 108 (January 1984), 4.

55. *PF,* September 8, 1841. In a subsequent issue (October 27, 1841) he named the author as "our talented young friend Joseph Wil(l)son."

56. *PL* in *PF,* September 8, 1841.

people of color to be every bit as important as his criticisms of the quarrels and mistaken policies of the "higher classes of colored society."

As for the response in the African-American community, from New York Charles B. Ray, the editor of the *Colored American*, wrote: "This work is . . . on a delicate subject, and we should think it required more than an ordinary share of moral courage, even in an anonymous author, to handle it." Ray had had his own differences with Philadelphians over the years, and he was quite capable of magnifying their faults while overlooking those of their counterparts in New York. Moving from the subject matter of the book to its literary merits, he observed: "It is written rather in good style, and adds to the number of our authors, and we presume will find a ready sale, from curiosity to read it."[57] According to another source, there were certain individuals who were indeed "quite . . . strong in their disapprobation."[58]

Various members of the "higher classes" might not have appreciated what Willson had to say, but he was not forced into exile. His book appeared in 1841 and not until 1854 did he decide to move on, abandoning Philadelphia for Cleveland. In fact, in the years following the publication of *Sketches of the Higher Classes* he strengthened his ties with the "higher classes" and with the larger African-American community. In the late 1840s Willson relocated from Spring Garden to Shippen Street in Moyamensing. The move put him on the fringe of the South Street corridor, the heart of African-American community life, and close to a host of black churches, schools, and meeting places. It brought him closer to other people like himself, the very people who constituted the "higher classes." And it brought him closer to the squalor, the poverty, and the crime that characterized the lives of the poorest of the black poor. He was only a block or two away from scenes of true misery and wretchedness. His decision to buy a house so close to the South Street corridor also exposed him to the risk of racial violence, for South Street and its immediate vicinity had been the scene of every one of the race riots the city experienced through the 1830s and 1840s.[59]

If Willson was not driven into exile for having had the temerity to speak out, it should also be noted that he probably changed few minds. His message to whites about respect for their black neighbors fell on deaf ears.

57. *CA*, September 25, 1841.
58. *PF,* September 8, 1841.
59. Lapsansky, " 'Since They Got Those Separate Churches,' " 58–59.

Those whites most likely to be sympathetic to what he had to say were already involved in antislavery and outreach activities. He was preaching to the converted. As for those in the "higher classes," quarreling and factionalism persisted long after Willson had left the city. True, the African-American upper class in Philadelphia was more open than the white upper class.[60] Talented women and men who were relatively new to the city could earn the approbation of Philadelphia natives and move into positions of authority. Had Joseph Willson returned to Philadelphia in 1861, he would have found constituting the "higher classes" some of the people he had written about in 1841, and their children, but he would also have seen new faces and heard new names.

As for the subsequent history of his book, it has been reprinted only once in the hundred and fifty years since its initial publication. So completely was *Sketches of the Higher Classes of Colored Society in Philadelphia* forgotten, even during Willson's lifetime, that it was not mentioned in his various obituary notices. Apparently he never wrote anything else, and that in itself is a pity because he was a talented and perceptive writer. *Sketches of the Higher Classes* offers us a glimpse into a world that few of his contemporaries knew. In his witty and yet penetrating analysis of race and class, Willson cut to the heart of what he saw as the dilemma facing America. Tragically, it is a dilemma that is still unresolved.

Joseph Willson, "Our Talented Young Friend"

Most of the members of Philadelphia's "higher classes of colored society" knew the identity of the anonymous "Southerner" who had been so bold as to write about them. He had lived among them for the better part of ten years. He worshiped with some of them at the elite St. Thomas's African Episcopal Church. He was a member of various of their intellectual and charitable institutions. In the year or so before his book appeared, he had been asking questions, seeking information, interviewing people. Some probably thought young Joseph Willson had abused their hospitality. Others took a measure of pride in his learning—so abundantly displayed in his book—and welcomed this relative newcomer's appreciation of their refinement, their social activism, their role as an elite of talent as well as privilege. But what did they really know of Joseph Willson and his family?

---

60. Lapsansky, "Friends, Wives, and Strivings," 13.

What had brought this articulate and obviously wealthy young man to live among them? Perhaps only a handful of intimates knew his story, for it was a complex one. To begin with, Joseph Willson had not always been Joseph Willson....

The author of *Sketches of the Higher Classes of Colored Society in Philadelphia* had been born Joseph Keating in Augusta, Georgia, on February 22, 1817. His father, John Willson Jr., was a prosperous Scots Irish Protestant from the village of Ballygallon in Londonderry, and his mother, Betsy Keating, was a free woman of color.[61] Joseph Willson (his mother eventually took her lover's last name) may have assumed Betsy Keating was a Georgia native. That was what he told the census-taker in 1880. In fact, Betsy had been born in South Carolina and had come to live in Augusta in 1801 or 1802, when she was about ten years old.[62]

Betsy Keating may never have told her son the full story of her ancestry, and how and why she came to Augusta and into John Willson's household. She may not have known it herself. Betsy's story began in the late 1760s or early 1770s, when Edward Keating, a prosperous farmer in Edgefield County, South Carolina, in the rugged Ninety-Six District, took the slave Rose to live with him as his "house wench" (his description of her). Rose eventually bore him five children: Mary, Billy, Charles, Moses, and Aaron. When Edward Keating drew up his will in 1790, he tried to ensure the freedom and prosperity of his slave family. Rose and the children were to be set free, and they were to be given a herd of cattle, fifteen cows and fifteen calves, to help them set themselves up as farmers. The rest of the estate, including another two dozen slaves, went to Richard Keating Jr., Edward's nephew, with Richard Sr., Edward's brother, as executor.[63]

So much for good intentions. Perhaps the Keating estate was encumbered and all the slaves had to be sold to pay off Edward Keating's debts, or perhaps young Richard Keating and his father balked at losing six good slaves and a fine herd of cattle to an old man's whim. In any event, at some point over the next decade Edward Keating's children (or at least some of

---

61. *Washington Bee*, September 7, 1895. Richmond County, Georgia, Will Book A, 204. Willson may actually have been born in 1816, not 1817. He was listed as three years of age in the registration of free people of color in 1819. Chris Nordmann, "Georgia Registrations of Free People of Color, 1819," *NGSQ* 77 (Dec. 1989), 298.
62. Nordmann, "Georgia Registrations," 298. U.S. census (1880), Ohio, Cuyahoga County, Cleveland, Ward 6, 23.
63. Edgefield County, Will Book A, 88, in James E. and Vivian Wooley, eds., *Edgefield County, SC Wills, 1787–1836* (Greenville, S.C.: Southern Historical Press, 1991), 25. U.S. census (1790), South Carolina, Edgefield County, 96th District.

them) found themselves the property of John Willson Sr., one of the wealthiest merchants in Augusta.

John Willson Sr. had come to British North America from Ireland in 1759, when he was twenty years old. His elder brother, Joseph, had inherited the family estate in Londonderry, and he and another brother, Hugh, had chosen to emigrate rather than labor for Joseph. Hugh and his wife, Sibey, had headed for Pennsylvania, while John had made his way south.[64]

The decision to leave Ireland proved a wise one. John Willson adapted quickly to his new environment and set about investing the capital he had brought with him in real estate and slaves. A bachelor, he also provided himself with a "house wench." In 1812, when he made his will, he freed "my good and faithful Servant Mary Keating on account of her care and attention to my domestic concerns." He left her several houses and a valuable city lot. His executors were directed to provide her with a suit of mourning clothes. He also freed "My little Girl Maria," perhaps his daughter by Mary, or perhaps the result of a liaison with one of her predecessors.[65]

In principle, the possession of slaves did not much trouble Willson. He had bought various "parcels" of bondsmen and women over the years.[66] However, he was concerned about one particular group of slaves, Mary's kinfolk. Perhaps he learned from her of her father's intentions and how they had been thwarted. Perhaps, when he made his own will, he acted out of a sense of basic fairness, or perhaps he was rewarding Mary for her years of companionship with more than just *her* freedom. Whatever his motives, he freed her and provided for her, and then he did what he could for her family. In his will he wrote: "[A]s I am well convinced, it was never the intention of Edward Keating, that any of his unfortunate Children should be Slaves to any Person whatever. . . . I do therefore pronounce Charles Keating, Aaron Keating, Jenny Keating the Wife of the late William Keating, with her three Children Polly, Betsy and Martha and her Mother Polly, to be free and total[l]y emancipated from slavery." He also left them real estate. He had learned from Edward Keating's example. He stipulated that his other heirs would lose every cent of his bequests

---

64. Georgia Society of Colonial Dames of America, *Some Early Epitaphs in Georgia* (Durham, N.C.: The Seeman Printers for the Society, 1924), 352. Will of John Willson Sr., Richmond County, Georgia, Will Book A, 95.

65. Will of John Willson Sr.

66. For his various purchases of slaves, see Richmond County, Georgia, Deeds, Book F, 96, 97, 327, 328; Book G, 293, 317, 318, 319.

to them if they meddled with the Keatings and tried to deprive them of their freedom and their inheritance.[67]

Willson died in 1813. The principal beneficiary of his will was his nephew, John Jr. Lacking legitimate heirs, John Sr. had written to his relatives in Ballygallon at some point and invited his nephew (like him a younger son) to join him in Augusta. John Jr. patterned his life on his uncle's. He proved to be a shrewd man of business. And he modeled his household on that of John Sr., bringing over from Ireland two of his sister's sons, and taking as his companion Betsy Keating. She was not "little Betsy," Jenny and William's child. She was a cousin to that Betsy Keating, the child of Mary, Charles, Aaron, or Moses Keating.[68]

Judging by the ages of the children their relationship produced, John Willson Jr. began his liaison with Betsy Keating around 1808, when she was sixteen or seventeen. Given the dearth of church records and vital records for Augusta in the early nineteenth century, his age cannot be determined, but he was probably many years older than Betsy. At some point before the birth of their first child, he freed her. Since children followed the condition of their mother, all of her children were born free. The law in Georgia with regard to the freeing of slaves was constantly changing and becoming more restrictive. Delay on Willson's part might have made it impossible for him to manumit his children if they had been born slaves.[69]

Betsy Keating and John Willson had five children—Caroline (born in 1808 or 1809), Emily (born in 1811 or 1812), Eliza (born in 1813 or 1814), Joseph, and John (born in 1820). When he drew up his will, John Willson was a very wealthy man. He had improved considerably on his inheritance from his uncle. The bulk of his estate went to his white family—his father, his elder brother, his six sisters, and his various nieces and nephews. But he also left his "housekeeper" and her children well provided for. In return "for her faithful services rendered me," Betsy Keating was to receive two hundred shares in the Bank of Augusta, which Willson and his uncle had helped found, as well as other sums of money from his estate. Since the law made it impossible for free people of color to administer their

67. Will of John Willson Sr.
68. On Betsy Keating's dealings with her Keating kin, Aaron, Polly or Mary, and "little Betsy," dealings that extended well into the 1830s and long after she had left Georgia, see Richmond County, Georgia, Accounts, Book D, 255, 325, 354; Book G, 368.
69. Edward F. Sweat, "The Free Negro in Ante-bellum Georgia" (Ph.D. diss., Indiana University, 1957), chap. 1.

affairs and hold property of any kind in their own name, Willson appointed guardians for Betsy and the children. If they chose to remain in Augusta, the guardians were to see that they had a house rent-free, with "suitable household and Kitchen furniture and an adequate number of male & female Servants to wait upon them." Willson recognized that it might not be possible for them to stay in Georgia, and he provided for that contingency. "[I]n the event of its becoming necessary . . . to remove the said Betsy Keating and her Children," the guardians were to make sure they had the means to live comfortably elsewhere. Willson also imposed certain restrictions on Betsy. She would lose her legacy and custody of her children if the guardians determined she was "behaving herself improperly or treating [the children] with cruelty and inhumanity." If she married she would forfeit half of her inheritance.[70]

John Willson died in the summer of 1822, and Betsy Keating and her children remained in Augusta for the next eleven years.[71] John P. King, the principal guardian Willson had chosen for them, proved a faithful steward of their property. King, a Kentucky native, had not long qualified for the Georgia Bar when he became the Keatings' guardian, but he already had a promising law practice. He would become a powerful voice in Georgia politics over the next two decades and would go on to serve in the United States Senate.[72] If anyone could protect the interests of Betsy Keating and her children, it was a man with King's connections and influence.

The Keatings lived quietly but comfortably in Augusta. King made regular payments to them from John Willson's estate and helped Betsy get her children an education—no simple task for a free black parent in the Georgia of the 1820s. Her daughters were probably tutored privately in

---

70. Will of John Willson Jr., Richmond County wills, Book A, 204. On the restrictions on the ownership of property by free people of color in Georgia, see Schweninger, *Black Property Owners*, 65.

71. The 1830 census lists two free women of color by the name of Betsy Keating as heads of household. Only one of those households corresponds in size and composition to that of John Willson's mistress. It includes four slaves, indicating that Willson's executors had done as he instructed and provided Betsy and the children with a domestic staff from among his "people." U.S. census, Richmond County, Georgia, City of Augusta, Ward 1, 253. Numerous slaves are referred to by name in the accounts John P. King submitted to Richmond County authorities in connection with his trusteeship—Adam, Bacchus, Binah, Bob, Charlotte, Elsey, Harry, Jacob, Quamine, Squash, and Tom. Several were hired out, but the others probably waited on the Keatings. In 1823 King sold twenty-five slaves belonging to the estate. Richmond County, Georgia, Accounts, Book D (1823–28), 26–28, 137.

72. Charles C. Jones Jr., *Memorial History of Augusta, Georgia* (Syracuse, N.Y.: D. Mason and Co., 1890), 235.

Augusta.[73] Joseph was sent out of state for his early schooling. King arranged for him to board for a time in Huntsville, Alabama, with the family of Andrew D. Veitch. Veitch bought and sold slaves, but apparently he treated his young charge well.[74]

By the early 1830s, though, the Keatings and their guardian had to reconsider their future in Georgia. The laws governing the lives of free people of color in the state seemed to be becoming harsher by the year.[75] If Joseph Willson and his siblings were to continue their education, if they were to find suitable marriage partners, if they were to enjoy any of the privileges their father had sought to guarantee them, it would have to be in another state. With King's help, they assessed their options.

To use the money they had inherited to purchase a plantation somewhere in the Lower South was one possibility, but it was one with limited appeal. Betsy Keating and her children were not cut from the same cloth as South Carolina's William Ellison or Louisiana's Andrew Durnford. Augusta might not be a large city, but it was a city nonetheless, and the Keatings were urban dwellers with no experience in operating a plantation.[76] And city life brought other advantages in terms of schools, churches, a viable and hopefully vibrant community life with other affluent people of color.

Of the cities of the Lower South, the Keatings' choice was really restricted to two, New Orleans and Charleston. The Crescent City had a sizable free colored population—11,500 in 1830—and free people pursued an impressive range of occupations. But the Keatings had no ties of kinship or friendship with members of that city's mulatto elite. The Keatings'

---

73. It is not clear whether Betsy was literate, but she certainly valued education for all her children, and not just her sons. For an example of daughter Emily's poetry, see "Original and Selected Poetry of Amy Matilda Cassey," LC.

74. Richmond County, Georgia, Accounts, Book D, 137. Veitch died in 1828. On Veitch and his business interests, see Edward Chambers Betts, *Early History of Huntsville, Alabama, 1804 to 1870* (Montgomery, Ala.: The Brown Printing Co., 1916), 55, and Pauline Jones Gandrud, *Alabama Records*, vol. 124, 20.

75. For the restrictions on the education of free people of color, for instance, see Sweat, "The Free Negro," 122, and Whittington B. Johnson, "Free Blacks in Antebellum Augusta, Georgia: A Demographic and Economic Profile," *RCH* 14 (1982), 15.

76. On the cotton planter Ellison, see Michael P. Johnson and James L. Roark, *Black Masters: A Free Family of Color in the Old South* (New York: W. W. Norton, 1984). On Durnford, a Louisiana sugar planter, see Schweninger, *Black Property Owners*, 101, 105, 107–8, 119, and Berlin, *Slaves Without Masters*, 264, 274–75, 276, 280. Augusta, although relatively small, was a bustling center of trade in the 1820s and 1830s. Its population in 1845 was 7,500. Jones, *Memorial History of Augusta*, 174.

European antecedents were Irish and Protestant rather than French and Catholic. As for Charleston, that was not an especially congenial setting in the early 1830s. In the wake of the Denmark Vesey conspiracy, free people from out of state were decidedly unwelcome, and the Keatings had no influential white friends in Charleston to help safeguard their interests.[77]

Among the cities of the Upper South, there was Washington, D.C., with more than 3,000 free people of color in 1830, or possibly Richmond or Petersburg, Virginia. By far the most attractive choice, at least in terms of numbers of free black residents, was Baltimore, with more than 14,500.[78] Ultimately, though, the Keatings would look north of the Mason-Dixon line, perhaps fearful that restrictions along the lines of those they were facing in Georgia would be imposed anywhere that slavery was legal and free people viewed as a threat to the "peculiar institution."

In terms of the Midwest there were few options. Cincinnati was clearly a city to be avoided after the racial turmoil of 1829 and the mass exodus of African-American citizens. Chicago's black community was so small at this point as to make it not worth considering. Pittsburgh might have lured the Keatings had they been making their move a decade later, but in 1830 it had fewer than five hundred black residents. While Cleveland would attract at least one of the Keatings in the 1850s, its appeal was limited in the early 1830s.[79]

Assuming the Keatings wished to remain in the United States—and Canada or Britain might have beckoned, as they certainly did to some of their contemporaries—that left the major urban centers of the Northeast. Although Boston's black population numbered less than 2,000 in 1830, its network of community institutions and its growing reputation as a bastion of antislavery activism drew other free people of color from the South,

---

77. On New Orleans, see Schweninger, *Black Property Owners*, 71, 81, and Berlin, *Slaves Without Masters*, 108–32. On Charleston, see Michael P. Johnson and James L. Roark, eds., *No Chariot Let Down: Charleston's Free People of Color on the Eve of the Civil War* (Chapel Hill: University of North Carolina Press, 1984), and Marina Wikramanayake, *A World in Shadow: The Free Black in Antebellum South Carolina* (Columbia: University of South Carolina Press, 1973).

78. For the populations of various cities in 1830, see Curry, *The Free Black in Urban America*, 244–45, 250. On Baltimore, see Christopher Phillips, *Freedom's Port: The African American Community of Baltimore, 1790–1860* (Chicago: University of Chicago Press, 1997).

79. On Pittsburgh, see R. J. M. Blackett, "'Freedom or the Martyr's Grave': Black Pittsburgh's Aid to the Fugitive Slave," in Trotter and Smith, eds., *African Americans in Pennsylvania*, 149–51. On Cleveland, see Kenneth L. Kusmer, *A Ghetto Takes Shape: Black Cleveland, 1870–1930* (Urbana and Chicago: University of Illinois Press, 1976), 10.

most notably David Walker.[80] Joseph Keating would spend a year or two in Boston in the mid-1830s, but the family rejected it as a permanent home. That narrowed their choice to Philadelphia or New York City. What considerations moved them to opt for Philadelphia one can only guess at. Abolition had come much earlier in Philadelphia than in New York.[81] Perhaps the Keatings had the image of Philadelphia as truly a city of brotherly love, where opportunities for black people existed in abundance and where racial prejudice, if not unknown, was not endemic. They may well have believed it was the stronghold of Quaker benevolence, or they may have drawn a sense of assurance from its recent history. Black Philadelphians had spoken out, and were continuing to do so, on a host of issues of concern to the African-American community as a whole—everything from slavery to African colonization, from the kidnaping of free people of color to the provision of public education for black children.

Philadelphia was the headquarters of the African Methodist Episcopal Church. Although the Keatings were Episcopalians, that may still have created a favorable impression. Black national conventions met regularly in Philadelphia, drawing delegates from all over the North and the Upper South. The black population of the city numbered in the thousands, and included people of wealth and influence. If the Keatings had to leave Augusta, Philadelphia seemed an attractive city in which to start anew.

How and when the move to Philadelphia was accomplished is not clear, but John P. King's accounts for 1833 indicate he was making payments on behalf of Betsy Keating and her children to one Joseph Cowperthwaite. Cowperthwaite, a Philadelphia merchant, was a cashier of the Bank of the United States. He had undertaken to see that the Willsons were suitably lodged and that Joseph was enrolled in one of the schools for children of color, probably the Pennsylvania Abolition Society's Clarkson School, the school other family menbers also eventually attended.[82]

Apparently what they saw of Philadelphia in their first months in the

---

80. On black life in antebellum Boston, see James Oliver Horton and Lois E. Horton, *Black Bostonians: Family Life and Community Struggle in the Antebellum North* (New York: Holmes and Meier, 1978), and Hinks, *To Awaken My Afflicted Brethren*, 66–90.

81. On New York City's antebellum black community, see Anthony Gronowicz, *Race and Class Politics in New York City Before the Civil War* (Boston: Northeastern University Press, 1998), and Shane White, *Somewhat More Independent: The End of Slavery in New York City, 1770–1810* (Athens: University of Georgia Press, 1991), chap. 6.

82. Richmond County, Georgia, Accounts, Book F, 69–72. On Joseph Cowperthwaite, see Philadelphia directories, 1830, 1833, 1839; U.S. census (1850), Philadelphia County, Northern Liberties, Ward 1, 50.

city satisfied the Keatings and they decided to settle there permanently. In his own name, but with the Keatings' money, John P. King bought a house on Morgan Street in Spring Garden, one of Philadelphia's unincorporated "liberties" or suburbs. Faithful to his charge, he had a deed drawn up explaining that the property was only nominally his, and that the true owners were Betsy Keating and her children.[83]

John Willson's estate provided money to furnish the house in a suitable style, and the Keatings moved in toward the end of 1833. The household at 10 Morgan Street was a complex one. Betsy Keating had refused to leave behind in Georgia her grandson, Joseph Greenfield McClendon. Daughter Caroline had apparently died young, leaving one child. Betsy had taken him in and was raising him. There was also her own child, Henry Edward Hart. Although he was sometimes referred to as Henry Willson, he was not John Willson's son. Betsy had had another lover after Willson's death, and their union had produced Henry, who was born in 1826. If her lover was white, under Georgia law he could not have married Betsy Keating, even had he been willing to do so. If the mysterious "Mr. Hart" was a man of color, Betsy had every reason to refuse an offer of marriage, had one been forthcoming, since she would have forfeited half of her inheritance under the terms of John Willson's will.[84]

The Keatings lived quietly and comfortably in their new home. Betsy Keating enrolled her two younger sons and her grandson in the Clarkson School.[85] The family quickly put down roots in Philadelphia. They "belonged" in a way they never had done in Augusta. Philadelphia, with its thousands of free people of color, offered them a degree of sociability, a level of opportunity, they could have found in few other cities. At the school they attended, at the church they joined (St. Thomas's African Episcopal Church), at the various mutual improvement societies they frequented, Mrs. Elizabeth Willson (as Betsy Keating now styled herself) and her children met and socialized with members of the city's "higher classes of colored society."

One of the people who befriended the Willsons soon after their arrival was Frederick Augustus Hinton. Like the Willsons, he was a Southern emigré. (He was from Raleigh, North Carolina.) He had done well in Phil-

---

83. Philadelphia County Deeds, SHF, Book 17, 510, PCA.
84. Betsy Keating acknowledged in her will that Hart was her son and McClendon her grandson. See will of Elizabeth Willson, alias Betsy Keating, Philadelphia County Wills, Book 19, 407, #208, PCA. I have been unable to find any record of Caroline's death.
85. Clarkson School Roll Book, 1836–37, PAS MSS, HSP.

"A Sunday Morning View of the African Episcopal Church of St. Thomas in Philadelphia, taken in June 1829." Lithograph by William L. Breton. (Courtesy of the Historical Society of Pennsylvania). The Willsons joined St. Thomas's African Episcopal Church shortly after their arrival in Philadelphia. This lithograph shows the elegance and refinement of many of the congregation, although St. Thomas's had its share of less affluent members.

adelphia. A barber and perfumer, he was the proprietor of the fashionable "Gentleman's Dressing Room." He had married into Philadelphia's African-American elite. He was a prominent lay member of the socially prestigious St. Thomas's African Episcopal Church. More to the point, Hinton's contacts with white reformers put him in a position to help young Joseph Willson. Frederick A. Hinton was a zealous abolitionist who numbered among his friends antislavery editor William Lloyd Garrison. In fact, Hinton was one of the agents for Garrison's *Liberator*. When Joseph Willson left school, he tried, without success, to get an apprenticeship. However, no white employer would take him on. He communicated his disappointment and frustration to Hinton, who wrote Garrison and his business partner, Isaac Knapp, on Willson's behalf. Willson, "a young gentleman of great respectability," was planning to come to Boston "for the purpose of learning a trade." Hinton added that he was "a particular friend" of the Willson family, and therefore felt "a great interest in [Joseph's] well being."[86] Although he did not spell it out in so many words, Hinton was giving the two white reformers the chance to live up to their professions about racial equality and the advancement of African Americans. They were quick to condemn white employers for not taking on young men of color as apprentices and teaching them skilled trades. *They* were employers. They operated a printing office. What would *they* be willing to do for Joseph Willson?

Garrison and Knapp apparently rose to the challenge. Joseph Willson moved to Boston and spent the next couple of years mastering the printing trade.[87] Then he returned to Philadelphia. In 1838, when the Pennsylvania Abolition Society conducted a census of Philadelphia's African-American population, he was living with the rest of the family at 10 Morgan Street and working as a printer.[88]

Frederick A. Hinton continued to help Joseph Willson in his quest for financial stability and membership in Philadelphia's "higher classes of colored society." The friendship between the two men became even closer when, on January 11, 1837, Hinton, widowed just over a year earlier and left with two children to raise, married Willson's sister, Elizabeth.[89] Hinton drew his new brother-in-law into the abolitionist movement. Willson became a member of the Philadelphia Young Men's Anti-Slavery Society. (Hinton was one of its founders.) Elizabeth Willson Hinton joined the Philadelphia Female Anti-Slavery Society.[90]

It had always been an article of faith with Hinton, as with other members of the Northern black elite, to reject the notion of emigrating to Liberia. Throughout the 1830s he was in the vanguard of opposition to the

86. Frederick A. Hinton to William Lloyd Garrison and Isaac Knapp, December 10, 1833, BPL.
87. *Washington Bee*, September 7, 1895.
88. PAS census (1838), PAS MSS, HSP.
89. *Lib*, January 21, 1837. For the marriage settlement, see Philadelphia County Deeds, SHF, Book 7, 395.
90. Philadelphia Young Men's Anti-Slavery Society roster, n.d.; Philadelphia Female Anti-Slavery Society Records, 1845–48; PAS MSS, HSP. Both Elizabeth and Emily Willson were active in the antislavery cause before Elizabeth's marriage. See *Lib*, November 28, 1835.

Advertisement for Evans, Card and Fancy Printer (1859). (Courtesy of the Library Company of Philadelphia). As a skilled printer turning out everything from handbills to business cards, Joseph Willson would have been very familiar with a press of this sort.

"Philadelphia Fashions, 1837," by Edward W. Clay. (New York: H. R. Robinson, 1837). (Courtesy of the Library Company of Philadelphia). This may be a satirical rendering by Clay of the fashionable wedding of Joseph Willson's elder sister, Elizabeth. In January 1837 she married well-to-do barber Frederick Augustus Hinton in a ceremony at St. Thomas's Church.

American Colonization Society, condemning it as a tool of the slave-holding interest. However, by 1840 he was wavering. Disheartened by racial violence in Philadelphia, by the fragmentation of the antislavery movement, and by the failure of African Americans to achieve civil and social equality in the United States, he began to talk with the agents of the ACS. And he involved his brother-in-law in those discussions. A local ACS recruiter reported to the organization's headquarters in Washington that he had high hopes of getting Hinton and Willson to become commission merchants in Liberia. Rumors about their intended move reached a friend in Liberia, who wrote to beg them to reconsider. The colony was very unhealthy, and opportunities for making money legally (as opposed to involving oneself in slaving or the rum trade) almost nonexistent.[91]

Ultimately, neither Hinton nor Willson left the United States. Hinton turned to promoting emigration to Trinidad, and Willson gave himself up to literary pursuits. In 1841 he published his *Sketches of the Higher Classes of Colored Society in Philadelphia by "A Southerner."* Try as he might to hide his authorship, Willson soon discovered that the identity of the writer of *Sketches* was an open secret.[92] Apparently, though, he suffered no repercussions for what some might have regarded as a breech of hospitality (he was not, after all, a Philadelphian!), or worse, as an unwelcome washing of dirty linen in public.

In the mid-1840s Joseph Willson married. Elizabeth Harnett was from a background very similar to his own. Her mother was a free woman of color from Georgia and her father an immigrant from Scotland. She was herself a Georgia native.[93] Perhaps the Willsons and the Harnetts were old friends. It is also possible that Joseph met Elizabeth while on a visit to Georgia to take care of Willson family investments there. Whatever the case, the two married and Willson returned with his bride to Philadelphia. Although his mother was still living, Joseph now assumed control of the Willson household. In 1847, when the Society of Friends took a census of African Americans in the city and "liberties" of Philadelphia, the Willsons were still at the home on Morgan Street. Joseph was listed as a printer

---

91. Benjamin Coates to Samuel Wilkeson, June 17, 1840; ACS Papers, Correspondence Incoming, June 1–30, 1840, LibC. *PF,* November 12, 1840. On the range of responses to Liberian emigration within the African-American community, see Wilson Jeremiah Moses, ed., *Liberian Dreams: Back-to-Africa Narratives from the 1850s* (University Park: The Pennsylvania State University Press, 1998).

92. See, for instance, *PF,* October 27, 1841, and "Pencil Pusher's Notes," in *Tribune,* May 11, 1912.

93. U.S. census (1900), Indianapolis, vol. 45, e.d. 41, sheet 1.

and his brother, John, as a clerk. There was a young child—Joseph and Elizabeth's baby son, Leonidas. As for Willson's mother and unmarried sister, they continued to live in the family home and occupy themselves with "domestic duties." Financially the Willsons were doing very well. Their home was worth $2,800, and they had $20,000 in personal property, $16,000 of it in Georgia.[94]

Over the next few years life changed dramatically for the Willson family. Elizabeth Willson, alias Betsy Keating, died in 1847, soon after the census was taken. She had settled her affairs two years before, and her executors arranged to have her will probated in Philadelphia and in Augusta, where most of her assets were.[95] Her death was not unexpected, but Frederick Hinton's death was a shock to his Willson in-laws. Hinton died in the cholera epidemic of 1849. Thirteen years Joseph Willson's senior, he had been not merely his sister's husband but his friend, his adviser, in some respects his elder brother or even the substitute for his long-dead father. His death left a void in the younger man's life.[96] But there were more positive changes. Joseph Willson abandoned the printer's trade for dentistry. It proved a good career move, especially as his growing skill enabled him not merely to fill or pull teeth but to perform routine surgical procedures, such as bleeding.[97] He also remained active in the community, and may well have been the "J. Wilson, M.D., of Philadelphia" who attended the Colored National Convention of July 1853 in Rochester, New York.[98]

Soon after his mother's death, Joseph Willson moved out of the house on Morgan Street. Elizabeth Willson had stipulated in her will that the

---

94. Society of Friends census (1847), PAS MSS, HSP. The $16,000 referred to was probably the value of the 200 shares in the Bank of Augusta that John P. King was managing for the family. See Jones, *Memorial History of Augusta*, 335.

95. Philadelphia County Wills, Book 19, 407, #208. Richmond County, Georgia, Will Book A, 226.

96. Philadelphia Board of Health Records. There may have been family tensions in the months before Hinton's death. In June 1848 the Philadelphia Guardians of the Poor ordered him to support the child one Mary Edmondston was carrying. There is no evidence of how this proof of Hinton's adultery affected his relationship with his wife's family. Jefferson M. Moak, comp., *Philadelphia Guardians of the Poor: Bonds for the Support of Illegitimate Children and Other Indigent Persons, 1811–1859* (The Chestnut Hill Almanac, Genealogical Series, Publication #3, 1996), entry for June 27, 1848.

97. Willson's skill as a dentist is noted by Martin R. Delany, *The Condition, Elevation, Emigration, and Destiny of the Colored People of the United States* (Philadelphia: The Author, 1852; reprint, New York: Arno Press, 1968), 131.

98. *Proceedings of the Colored National Convention, Held in Rochester, July 6th, 7th and 8th, 1853* (Rochester: At the Office of Frederick Douglass' Paper, 1853), 29.

house was to be sold and the proceeds divided among her children. Joseph could have bought out his siblings, but he chose not to. Instead, he and his wife purchased a three-story house, 347 Shippen Street in Moyamensing, from African-American plasterer Peter Glasgow and his wife, Elizabeth, a couple they may well have known from various community endeavors they were involved in, for the Glasgows were, like the Willsons, members of the "higher classes." The house doubled as the Willsons' home and Joseph Willson's dental surgery.[99] It was there that two more children were born, Emily in 1852 and Josephine in 1853.

The decision to move to Moyamensing had far-reaching implications. It also revealed something of the Willsons' sense of self-identification. To begin with, it was on the other side of Philadelphia from Spring Garden. For years the Willsons had headed across the city to attend church and to socialize. Now Joseph and Elizabeth had opted to relocate to be nearer to so many of the community institutions around which they had built their social, spiritual, and intellectual lives. They had also chosen to move into a neighborhood that was decidedly "blacker" than Spring Garden and one that had a history of racial violence.

"Southeast and southwest corners of Ninth and Lombard." Watercolor by David Johnson Kennedy, 1839. (Courtesy of the Historical Society of Pennsylvania). In the late 1840s Joseph and Elizabeth Willson moved to a home two or three blocks from this location and into a house very similar to those depicted here.

99. Philadelphia County Deeds, RDW, Book 52, 111. Willson also bought an adjoining piece of land. Ibid., GWC, Book 85, 217. U.S. census (1850), Philadelphia County, Moyamensing, Ward 3, 389. Philadelphia directories, 1850–52.

Shippen Street was on the edge of the South or Cedar Street corridor, the area historian Emma Lapsansky has identified as the heart of Philadelphia's African-American community.[100] The Willsons could walk to any number of black churches and institutions much more easily from Shippen Street than from Spring Garden. However, there were other matters than proximity to one's church and one's friends to consider. Elizabeth Harnett Willson was a relative newcomer to Philadelphia, but Joseph had spent well over a decade there. He knew the South Street corridor was the scene of repeated outbursts of racial violence, something Spring Garden had been spared.

The South Street corridor was home to many more black Philadelphians than Spring Garden, but it was still a racially diverse neighborhood. Although more African Americans were moving into the South Street neighborhood, there was no accompanying "white flight." As for the economic profile of the neighborhood, the Willsons would not have had to go far to witness real human misery. The Society of Friends' 1847 census noted: "On Shippen Street between 7–8 there are some very respectable colored people, but for the most part, those miserable creatures are in the majority.... [T]he number is alarming." However, their block of Shippen, the ninth, was pleasant enough. Their neighbors were white tradespeople, and immediately next door lived John Henderson, a twenty-nine-year-old mulatto from Virginia with an estate worth $30,000.[101]

For all its social problems, all the assaults by angry mobs on black churches and black-owned houses in the neighborhood during the 1830s and 1840s, the African-American community in the South Street corridor had a sense of permanence, and perhaps that was what the Willsons found so appealing.[102] Churches and homes were rebuilt or repaired after each outbreak of rioting, and, as Lapsansky has demonstrated, members of the "higher classes," instead of abandoning the area, were actually moving there.[103] The Willsons were part of that influx. They could easily have stayed in Spring Garden. Joseph's brother, John, did so. It is significant that the census-taker in 1850 categorized the light-skinned John Willson, who had money and was living in a predominantly white neighborhood,

---

100. Lapsansky, " 'Since They Got Those Separate Churches,' " 58–59.
101. Society of Friends census (1847), Southwark and Moyamensing, 25, in Emma J. Lapsansky, *Neighborhoods in Transition: William Penn's Dream and Urban Reality* (New York: Garland, 1994), 97. U.S. census, Moyamening, Ward 3, 389.
102. Lapsansky, " 'Since They Got Those Separate Churches,' " 58–61.
103. Ibid., 74–75; Lapsansky, *Neighborhoods in Transition*. 149–50.

as white. Across town, his brother was described by another census-taker as mulatto.[104] Of course, one does not know what criteria the two white officials used to make their determination, and there are no known portraits of John and Joseph Willson to indicate whether one was lighter-skinned than the other. However, it is at least possible that Joseph, by choosing to move to the South Street corridor, was making a statement about how he saw himself. Although half Irish, he was perhaps choosing to be counted as a man of color.

In fact, the sojourn on Shippen Street did not last long. Some months after Josephine's birth, Joseph and Elizabeth decided to leave Philadelphia and move to Cleveland. They sold their home in Moyamensing at a profit to Richard T. Tompkins, an aspiring black restauranteur from Virginia, and bought a house at 27 (later renumbered 228) Perry Street, in Cleveland.[105] The house was big enough to serve as both a family home and Joseph Willson's surgery. Two more children were born after the family's move to Cleveland—Mary in 1854 and Victoria in 1856.[106]

What made Cleveland more attractive than Philadelphia? To begin with, it had a reputation not merely as a center of antislavery agitation but as a place where significant numbers of white residents were willing to speak out against laws that limited the rights of their African-American neighbors—to the amazement and annoyance of whites in other parts of Ohio.[107] The black population of Cleveland, if not large, was at least growing. The 1850 census recorded 224 African Americans in the city, or 1.3 percent of the total population. By 1860 that figure had risen to 799, or 1.9 percent.[108] The Willsons were not naive enough to suppose that racism was totally absent, but they clearly believed Cleveland offered advantages they could not hope to find in Philadelphia. For one thing, Cleveland's public schools were integrated. With their children to consider, that was almost certainly a major factor in their decision to relocate.[109]

---

104. U.S. census (1850), Philadelphia County, Spring Garden, Ward 3, 15, and Moyamensing, Ward 3, 389. John, his wife, Hannah, their young son, Albert, and an older woman who was probably Hannah's mother, were all described as white.
105. Philadelphia County Deeds, RDW, Book 52, 111. U.S. census (1850), Moyamensing, Ward 2, 266. Cleveland directories, 1854, 1855.
106. The 1860 census incorrectly gives Victoria's age as two. She was, in fact, four.
107. Kusmer, *A Ghetto Takes Shape*, 6–7, 9.
108. Ibid., 10.
109. Ibid., 16. For an overview of the situation of African Americans in antebellum Cleveland, see Russell H. Davis, *Black Americans in Cleveland* (Washington, D.C.: The Associated Publishers, 1972), chaps. 2–3.

The Willsons' hopes for a bright future in Cleveland were justified. Joseph's dental practice flourished. He attracted both black and white patients, and word of his skill spread. He and his family joined the predominantly white congregation of St. Paul's Protestant Episcopal Church. The Willsons' prosperous middle-class lifestyle, Joseph's professional standing, and their mixed racial ancestry probably led some of their neighbors to consider them as white. In 1860 the census-taker described them as white, although they were designated as "Negroes" a decade later.[110] They socialized with the "colored aristocracy" of Cleveland as they had with "the higher classes of colored society" in Philadelphia, joining the Social Circle, "a club organized in 1869 'to promote social intercourse and cultural activities among the better educated people of color' in Cleveland."[111]

The Willsons enrolled their children in the public schools. When Leonidas graduated, he opted for a career in the law. He started out as a copyist or law clerk. By 1872 he had passed the Ohio Bar examinations and become a full-fledged lawyer, one of the first African-American attorneys in the state. He went into partnership with a white lawyer, a Mr. Sykora, and married a white woman, Ina L. Dustan, the sister of another lawyer.[112]

Emily left school in 1870 and became a music teacher. Josephine graduated from Cleveland High School a year later and secured an appointment as a teacher at the Mayflower School, a public grammar school. Eventually Mary and Victoria followed in the footsteps of their elder sisters and became teachers. They taught a range of subjects, but all at some point taught music. Elizabeth Harnett Willson was an accomplished musician and presumably gave her daughters their early training.[113]

The Willsons were people who valued their privacy. (Some in the African-American community claimed they were far too exclusive.) In 1878, though, they suddenly became "news." Josephine Willson, so newspaper readers across the United States learned, was engaged to marry Blanche K. Bruce, one of the first African-American men to serve in the United States Senate. The story was replete with romantic elements. Born a slave in Virginia, Bruce had struggled to gain his freedom, had put himself through Oberlin College, and after the war had headed south to Missis-

110. U.S. census (1860), Ohio, Cuyahoga County, Cleveland, Ward 6, 29.
111. Gatewood, *Aristocrats of Color*, 4.
112. The marriage took place on July 3, 1873. Church of Jesus Christ of Latter-Day Saints, International Genealogical Index.
113. Cleveland directories, 1870–85.

Advertisement for Snowden & Brother, dental and surgical instrument manufacturers, from Wenderoth, Taylor & Brown, *Gallery of Arts and Manufactures* (1871). (Courtesy of the Library Company of Philadelphia). As a skilled dentist and surgeon, Joseph Willson would have used the kinds of instruments shown here.

sippi, where he entered political life. Handsome, talented, wealthy, and politically well-connected (newspaper readers were assured that he was very much the gentleman), he had looked around for a wife. His choice had fallen on a young lady from Cleveland. Tragically, she fell ill and died a matter of weeks before their wedding. The heartbroken senator had continued to visit Cleveland. He remained close to the family of his fiancée and also owned real estate in the city. On one of his visits, someone had introduced him to Josephine Willson, who was described as accomplished and "quite beautiful." *New York Times* readers learned that "it requires much more than usual attention to notice that she has any African blood. She appears to be a common brunette, but close scrutiny will reveal her origin in her peculiar lips and hair."[114]

The Willson-Bruce wedding afforded an eager public a glimpse into the world of the "colored aristocracy," a world few of them knew anything about. However, the Willsons were not eager to flaunt their wealth and elite status or to have their privacy invaded. They arranged to have the wedding not in a church but in their Perry Street home. There were no formal invitations. Joseph and Elizabeth Willson simply called on their friends a few days before the wedding was to take place (on the evening of June 24, 1878) and asked them to attend. Eager onlookers could see carriages pulling up outside the Willson home and elegantly dressed guests, many of them white, entering the home. They could see no more. Not Josephine in her gown of white silk and satin, the creation of a New York couturier. Not the wedding gifts, including the set of silver flatware from the bride's parents. Not the waiters scurrying to and fro, serving the elegant wedding supper. Not the couples dancing to the music of one of the city's finest orchestras. The heavy velvet drapes at 228 Perry were shut tight. If the eager public wanted more, they must turn to the newspapers.[115]

As the newlyweds left on a special train for New York and a long honeymoon in Europe, calm descended once more on Perry Street. The Willsons continued to entertain their friends. Elizabeth Willson was a gracious hostess. Joseph Willson, "a man of gentle and agreeable manners," was well liked in his social circle. He was "well informed in books and current events, and a good conversationalist, though modest and reticent."[116] The Willsons took pleasure in their family. Daughter Emily mar-

114. *NYT,* June 23, 1878.
115. Gatewood, *Aristocrats of Color,* 6.
116. *Washington Bee,* September 7, 1895.

ried respectably, if not with quite the social *éclat* of Josephine, and moved to Louisiana with her husband.[117] There were visits from Josephine and the senator, and their young son, Roscoe Conkling Bruce. Ina and Leonidas had moved out and purchased a home of their own, but they and their two daughters, Laverne and Leona, were frequent visitors to the house on Perry Street.[118]

In the mid-1880s Joseph Willson's health began to deteriorate. He and Elizabeth decided to leave Cleveland. Mary and Victoria had settled in Indianapolis and were principals in that city's public school system. Joseph Willson made his will before he moved to Indianapolis. Elizabeth was to have the right to the Perry Street property during her lifetime, and to allow their unwed daughters to live there if they wished. A year after Elizabeth's death, the property was to be sold and the proceeds shared among all five Willson children. Everything else went to Elizabeth, with the exception of a fine piano that had been a gift to daughter Emily.[119] Willson used some of his capital to buy a house on College Avenue in Indianapolis, and he and Elizabeth spent the rest of their days there living with Mary and Victoria.

Joseph Willson died in his home in Indianapolis on August 21, 1895, of complications from diabetes. He was seventy-eight years old. After a service at St. Paul's Protestant Episcopal Church, the predominantly white church the Willsons had attended since their arrival in Indianapolis, he was laid to rest in a lot he had purchased in fashionable Crown Hill Cemetery.[120]

Joseph Willson's widow and their two unmarried daughters lived on in the College Street home for many years. Elizabeth Willson died in 1907, Mary in 1929, and Victoria in 1936.[121] As for Leonidas, his first wife died in 1886. Two years later he married again. His second wife was Anna L. Foote, a native of the District of Columbia, and "one of the Washington, D.C. colored teachers."[122] Leonidas was in poor health in his later years.

---

117. Ibid. Emily married a Mr. Harang of Lafourche Parish, Louisiana. I have been unable to learn more about him.
118. U.S. census (1880), Cleveland, Ward 4, 281.
119. Will of Dr. Joseph Willson, Cuyahoga County Wills, vol. 31, 289, #13411.
120. *Indianapolis News*, August 21, 1895; *Washington Bee*, September 7, 1895. Crown Hill Cemetery, Indianapolis: Burial Records.
121. Crown Hill Cemetery, Burial Records. On Mary and Victoria Willson, see Gatewood, *Aristocrats of Color*, 37.
122. Cleveland Necrology, Western Reserve Historical Society. *Cleveland Gazette*, July 14, 1888. U.S. census (1900), Cleveland, vol. 29, e.d. 57, sheet 11.

DR. JOSEPH WILSON'S DEATH.

FATHER-IN-LAW OF B. K. BRUCE—CAREER AND CHARACTER.

Dr. Joseph Wilson died last Monday morning at half past 4 o'clock at the family home, No. 449 College avenue. He had been an invalid for several years. The immediate cause of his death was diabetes. He was born at Augusta, Ga., February 22, 1817, and was educated in Philadelphia and Boston. In early life he learned the printer's trade, after which he followed a number of pursuits, and finally became a dentist, in which occupation he continued for many years in Cleveland, O., whence he removed to Indianapolis nine years ago. Since he has lived here he was, by failing health, unable to continue the practice of his profession.

Dr. Wilson was a man of gentle and agreeable manners, well informed in books and in current events, and a good conversationalist, though modest and reticent. He leaves a widow and five children. The children are Leonidas A., of Cleveland, O., Mrs. Emily F. Harang, of La Fourche Parish, Louisiana; Mrs. Blanche K. Bruce, of Washington, D. C., and two unmarried daughters, Mary A. and Victoria A., who for several years, have been teaching in the public schools of this city. Ex-Senator Bruce, who is a son-in-law was here recently and saw Dr. Wilson in his last illness.

Dr. Wilson was a member of the Protestant Episcopal Church, and the funeral sermon was preached by Rev. G. A. Carstensen, of St. Paul's. He was buried at Crown Hill Cemetery.

Mrs. Senator Bruce, who left the city a few days ago to be with her father in his last illness, returned to the city last Saturday.

Miss Victoria Richardson, who is a teacher in Livingston College, N. C., is in the city, the guest of her brother Dr. G. H. Richardson.

Joseph Willson's obituary, as it appeared in the September 7, 1895, *Washington Bee*

His law practice declined, and he died in sadly reduced circumstances. When he came to write his will he left all he had to Anna. In his eyes this was a matter of simple justice. "[M]y second marriage was unfortunate on account of my broken health; my wife was naturally and justly disappointed; yet in the last few years while I have suffered from distressing infirmities she has stood by me as a ministering angel." His elder daughter, Laverne, was dead, although she had a young son, Betram Willson Shaw, who lived in Detroit. Daughter Leona "has a good husband [Frank Kuzel] & is better provided for than I am." Leonidas died in Cleveland in 1901.[123]

123. Cuyahoga County Wills, vol. 48, 579, #27030. Cleveland Necrology.

As for Josephine Willson Bruce, she distinguished herself as a gracious Washington hostess during her husband's time in the Senate. Widowed in 1898, she dedicated herself to public service, involving herself in the work of the NAACP, the Women's Christian Temperance Union, and the National Association of Colored Women. A friend of Booker T. Washington and an admirer of his educational work, she was for three years the "lady principal" at Tuskegee. She died in 1923 in Kimball, West Virginia, at the home of her son, who was a school principal in Kimball.[124]

---

124. Willard B. Gatewood, "Josephine Beall Willson Bruce," in Darlene Clark Hine, Elsa Barkley Brown, and Rosalyn Terborg-Penn, eds., *Black Women in America, A Historical Encyclopedia* (Bloomington and Indianapolis: University of Indiana Press, 1993), vol. 1, 187–88. I could find no information on Joseph and Elizabeth Willson's fifth child, Emily, beyond the fact of her marriage and her removal to Louisiana.

SKETCHES

OF

THE HIGHER CLASSES

OF

COLORED SOCIETY

IN PHILADELPHIA.

BY A SOUTHERNER.

PHILADELPHIA.
MERRIHEW AND THOMPSON, PRINTERS.
No. 7 Carter's Alley.
1841.

The title page from the 1841 edition of Joseph Willson's *Sketches of the Higher Classes of Colored Society in Philadelphia by "A Southerner."* (Courtesy of the Library Company of Philadelphia)

Contents

Preface   79

CHAPTER I.
Introductory Observations—General Characteristics of Colored Society   81

CHAPTER II.
Remark—The Higher Classes of Colored Society Defined—State of Education—Young Ladies, and their Accomplishments—Isolated Instances Avoided   85

CHAPTER III.
General Remarks—Divisions among the Higher Classes of Colored Society—Causes which lead thereto—Disreputable Conduct of Parties—Insincerity of Young Ladies toward each other—Breaches of Confidence—Detraction—Slander—"Northerners" and "Southerners"—Another bad feature—Miscellaneous Observations   90

CHAPTER IV.
Social Intercourse—Visiting—Evenings at Home—Amusements and Conversation—Evening Parties—Guests—Hours of Retirement—Habits of Temperance at private Parties—General Remarks   97

CHAPTER V.
Political rights—First National Convention of People of Color—Character of Proceedings—Names of Delegates—Improvement of the People of Color—Public Meetings, Men and Measures—Contentions at Public Meetings, Rivalry, Opposition, &c.&c.   102

CHAPTER VI.
GENERAL REMARKS—LITERARY SOCIETIES—PHILADELPHIA LIBRARY COMPANY OF COLORED PERSONS—RUSH LIBRARY COMPANY AND DEBATING SOCIETY—DEMOSTHENIAN INSTITUTE—MINERVA LITERARY ASSOCIATION—EDGEWORTH LITERARY ASSOCIATION—GILBERT LYCEUM—NEW ASSOCIATION CONTEMPLATED   111

Preface

In presenting this little volume to the public, a few words prefatory may not be amiss. Its author does not pretend to have entered fully into the general condition of colored society in Philadelphia; but has merely glanced at some of the chief characteristics with the design, first, to remove some of the unfounded prejudices from without; and secondly, to correct certain abuses which are known to exist among themselves.

The idea of "Higher Classes" of colored society is, it must be confessed, a novel one; and will, undoubtedly, excite the mirth of a prejudiced community on its annunciation. Nevertheless, it is perfectly correct and proper—and is only objectionable in its connexion here, because the definition given of the "higher classes" is too liberal in its construction, and may be made to embrace a far greater number than it is intended to include. This, however, could not be well avoided—it was found a difficult case to decide intelligently otherwise—and a proper discrimination left to the intelligent reader.

Others again, there are, who like to see their neighbors' merits caricatured, and their faults distorted and exaggerated,—will expect burlesque representations, and other laughter exciting sketches, and probably be thereby led to procure this little volume for the purpose of gratifying their *penchant* for the ludicrous. Now, while I desire not to put any thing in the way of its *sale*, be the motive for purchasing what it may, yet all such are informed—but they must first procure it before they can possess the information!—that they will find upon perusal, that they had indulged in a very erroneous impression.

As to the colored classes themselves, they will at once discover that none but the best of feelings throughout, has had any influence in guiding the pen of their humble servant,

THE AUTHOR

Philadelphia, June 22, 1841

SKETCHES
OF
COLORED SOCIETY, & C.

CHAPTER I.

INTRODUCTORY OBSERVATIONS—GENERAL
CHARACTERISTICS OF COLORED SOCIETY

The subject of men and manners has ever been one of interest and popularity with almost every class of readers. Our own evil dispositions naturally prompt us to ferret out the faults and foibles of others, seemingly as an apology or justification of our own. Weak and irresolute ourselves,—prone to inconsistency, instability, and absurdity,—it seems to afford a relief to the mind to have the follies and short-comings of our neighbors elaborately canvassed, under the vain impression that in the general shout that may be raised over the exposed parties, our own misdeeds will be kept entirely out of view.

Although these remarks may not be justly applicable to all the world, yet it is most unquestionably true, that they are well deserved by the far greater portion of mankind. They are evidenced in the insatiable desire which pervades the reading classes, for productions of a defamatory character, as the "Journals," "Diaries," &c., of those writers who visit countries foreign to their own, for the purpose of collecting together a worthless compilation of ridicule and personal abuse, for retail among their countrymen on their return home.[1] It is well known, that if the fruits of such labors were not of the calibre [sic] that is generally seen, their authors would be but poorly rewarded for the time, labor and expense consumed in their preparation; but they are well acquainted with the tastes—it may be said the wishes—of those for whose entertainment they may have exerted themselves, and keeping in strict accordance therewith, their reward is certain. They well know that their patrons will expect ridicule, abuse, fault-finding, and all manner of idle gossip; and, beside large draughts upon the imagination, they fail not to probe every vulnerable point, in order to comply therewith in the fullest measure. Their book, once completed, is sought with voracity, and if found to be well spiced with such ingredients as named, is highly approved, by no small portion of the monster public.

A yet more pointed and pertinent consideration, in sustenance of the position here approached, may be adduced from the fact, that when a work, of the character under notice, reaches the country of those who form or constitute its subject, it is speedily republished, and readily acquires a circulation, scarcely surpassed by the reception given it at the point of its original publication! This may arise from a pardonable curiosity to know what the author has said upon the various topics he may have chosen; but it evinces something more. It shows that such is the anxiety of many persons for readings, as well as *hearings* of the kind, that rather than suffer deprivation of them, they will contribute to the encouragement of their own defamers!

Though fully aware, that there is ample field and abundant material for so doing, yet it is not for the purpose of administering to this depraved taste, that the writer of these pages has undertaken the censorship of the manners and morals of a certain class of the population of Philadelphia. This class, more for perspicuity, than for the purpose of originating any invidious distinctions in the body at large, I shall divide into and denominate the *higher classes* of colored society. In pursuit of this object, I disclaim all intention to make false representations, to administer wanton and undeserved ridicule, or to excite it in others. If correct principles did not place me above this, I think some assurance might be gleaned from consanguinity! While I shall not be forward to magnify the good or to extenuate evil, yet still, I would not have "aught set down in malice."[2]

The prejudiced reader, I feel well assured, will smile at the designation "higher classes of colored society." The public—or at least the great body, who have not been at the pains to make an examination—have long been accustomed to regard the people of color as one consolidated mass, all huddled together, without any particular or general distinctions, social or otherwise. The sight of one colored man with them, whatever may be his apparent condition, (provided it is any thing but genteel!) is the sight of a community; and the errors and crimes of one, is [sic] adjudged as the criterion of character of the whole body. But the first of these considerations is far from being correct; the latter, too openly palpable to command a moment's attention. Compared in condition, means, and abilities, there are as broad social distinctions to be found here, as among any other class of society; aye, and, it may be added, with as much justice, too;—for what are all human distinctions worth, founded otherwise than in virtue? True, it is readily admitted, they have not, to any great extent, the customary grounds which have always obtained, for marking their lines of separation with distinctness; but this is the fault of circumstances—the offspring of existencies [sic] which they had no agency in producing—and which they have never been able to surmount.

Taking the whole body of the colored population in the city of Philadelphia, they present in a gradual, moderate, and limited ratio, almost every grade of character, wealth, and—I think it not too much to add—of education. They are to be seen in ease, comfort and the enjoyment of all the social blessings of this life; and, in contrast with this, they are to be found in the lowest depths of human degradation, misery, and want. They are also presented in the intermediate stages—sober, honest, industrious and respectable—claiming neither "poverty nor riches,"[3] yet maintaining, by their pursuits, their families in comparative ease and comfort, oppressed neither by the cares of the rich, nor assailed by the deprivation and suffering of the indigent. The same in these respects that may be said of any other class of people, may, with the utmost regard to truth, be said of them.

They have their churches, school-houses, institutions of benevolence, and others for the promotion of literature; and if I cannot include scientific pursuits, it is because the avenues leading to and upholding these, have been closed against them.[4] There are likewise among them, those who are successfully pursuing various branches of the mechanic arts; tradesmen and dealers of various descriptions, artists, clergymen, and other professional gentlemen; and, last of all, though not the least, men of fortune and gentlemen of leisure.

Their churches embrace nearly all the Christian denominations, excepting the papal, and those which may be considered *doubtful*, as I am not aware that there is any Universalists' society among them.[5] Whether this arises from a determination to keep on the sure side here, and enjoy the benefit of others' doubts, if realized, hereafter, it has never occurred to me, till now, to inquire! The Methodists are by far the most numerous, and next to these, in numerical order, may be named the Presbyterians,

Baptists and Episcopalians.[6] There is in existence, I believe, a Unitarian society; but their house of worship, for the want of competent support, has, for some time past, been relinquished.

Mutual Relief Societies are numerous.[7] There are a larger number of these than of any other description, in the colored community. They are generally well sustained, to the great advantage of those who compose them. There are also one or more others, strictly devoted to objects of out-doors benevolence. The last mentioned are chiefly composed of females.[8]

I pass by here the several literary associations, proposing to make them a distinct subject in another place.

In addition to the public, or common schools supported by the commonwealth—for the continuance, and prosperity of which, much interest and solicitude has of late been manifested—there are also three or four private schools, male and female, conducted by colored teachers. The great facilities afforded by the first mentioned of these, has had the effect greatly to decrease the numbers in the private schools; nevertheless, the latter class still present a favorable condition—particularly the female—from the superior excellence of their government, and attention to the general deportment of the pupils.[9]

In addition to this brief random glance at some of the more prominent features which distinguish colored society at large, the annexed statistical account is added for the convenience of those who desire accuracy on the subject. It is gleaned from a statement "showing the progress and present state of the colored population," compiled by the "Board of Managers of the American Moral Reform Society,"[10] and published in their first annual report, which latter was kindly furnished me, by the chairman of said Board, Mr. John P. Burr.[11] Though the statement referred to, bears [a] date as far back as 1837, yet it is presumable that no very remarkable changes, in most instances, have occurred since then; and as there has been no later enumeration in this wise, it is adopted, leaving the reader to form his own judgment in regard to more recent advancements.

For the City and County of Philadelphia, is given as the

Number of Churches		15
" Clergymen		34
" Day-schools		21
" Teachers		6
" Sabbath-schools		17

"	S. School Teachers	125
"	Literary Societies	3*
"	Debating	3
"	Mutual Relief or Benevolent Societies	64
"	Moral Reform	1
"	Temperance	4
"	Lyceums	1†

*There has been some change in the character of one of these.
†Since formed.

In the same tabular view, the number of mechanics for this city, are set down at 78; and real estate owned, and taxes, rents, &c., paid, at $850,000. In what manner this eight hundred and fifty thousand dollars is portioned among the population, rising nineteen thousand inhabitants, it is difficult to determine; although it appears to be undoubtedly true, that but a small number are actual freeholders, when compared with the whole body.

Thus much for generalities. The succeeding sketches, will be chiefly confined to that portion of colored society, which shall hereafter be indicated.

CHAPTER II.

Remark—The Higher Classes of Colored Society Defined—State of Education—Young Ladies, and their Accomplishments—Isolated Instances Avoided.

It is with caution and timidity that I approach the principal subject of the present chapter. Like, in all matters of similar application, where distinctions and comparisons are involved, the greatest difficulty to the sensitive mind and feeling heart, arises from the indisposition to give offence [sic]. If one should approach a crowd of persons, point out a certain number, and pronounce them "gentlemen," those who might be neglected in the designation, would be very apt to feel a little incensed toward the individual who made it. They would at least consider that he had given a negative opinion against *their* gentility. But this is not necessarily the case. Opinions are founded upon investigation, and a knowledge of facts. If upon examination, it is found that a certain portion of any given class of persons have attained to particular positions in society—which also may be the aim, and within the probable reach of all of that class—in giving a statement of the fact merely, it is not to be inferred, that any opinion is passed upon the merits of those who may not have yet arrived at the supposed point.

> "Order is Heaven's first law; and this confest,
> Some are, and must be, greater than the rest—
> More rich, more wise."[12]

In the present case, however, it must be confessed, that the difficulty of establishing, successfully, a distinguishing line of separation is very great. The embarrassment arises altogether from the absence of those landmarks, which have always obtained in fashionable society, and which many may consider indispensable to make plain to others that which is sufficiently obvious to those who are aware of the facts. I am to present a boundary between a class of persons whom the great body of the public have been accustomed to consider so closely allied to each other, as to render it very improbable, if not impossible, that any social differences could be held in recognition among them. This is a great error, it is true, but it does not much lesson [sic] the difficulty. The chief grounds of distinction among men, are founded upon wealth, education, station, and occupation. In other countries, birth, or family connexion [sic], will go a great way towards promotion; but unattended by either of the former, it is soon forgotten—it will not stand alone. But here are none of these, to an extent which would warrant their, or either of them, being made the point of departure. I have not the foundation of wealth; because the number who may be permitted to come under that denomination are too limited, to be justly made the standard of the men and manners of the whole body. Beside this, there are other objections—objections which will be discernible when it is known that I cannot make moral worth, strictly speaking, the standard; for in that case it might be necessary to exclude a number of those who are denominated wealthy! Neither may I erect [sic] upon education, nor occupation; as among the higher classes—unless an unjust and illiberal contrast is sought—there is no very remarkable difference any where to be found.

Having thus, then, exhibited the difficulty of my situation, it will be seen that in determining the higher classes of colored society, it will be necessary to glean the materials from persons of all grades of moderate possessions, education, moral worth, (as outwardly adjudged,) and whose occupations generally present but little difference. What, therefore, I would have the reader understand by the designation "higher classes," as here applied, consists of that portion of colored society whose incomes, from their pursuits or otherwise, (immoralities or criminalities of course excepted,) enables them to maintain the position of house-holders, and their families in comparative ease and comfort. This definition probably includes a greater number than will come within the scope of my sketches, and it may be that a few who are eligible, will be by it excluded. It is, however, the best that can be given—the exceptions are unavoidable. It would likewise seem to be liberal enough to suit the most captious!

The education of this class is by no means so limited as the uninformed are accustomed to imagine. The seniors, it is true—or most of them—appear not to have enjoyed the great advantages of early training of the mind; but they possess a practical education—a general knowledge of all important matters—and an intelligence which fit them for the occupancy of all the useful stations of life, wherein an extensive knowledge of letters is not required. They turn their experience to good account—look forward to no extraordinary changes in this life—and so govern themselves, as, at least, to maintain the position at which they may have arrived, if they do not improve it. Having often had occasion to feel the necessity of a good education themselves, they have thereby been led to spare no exertion for securing the same to their children; so that the young men and young ladies of their generation, present, in this wise, quite a different aspect.[13] They have enjoyed many of those advantages of which their parents were deprived; and it may be said, without exaggeration, that the most of them have equalled [sic], and many far surpassed, the best opportunities afforded them. It must be borne in mind that they are opposed by many and varied restrictions and discouragements, at almost every step in the pursuit of knowledge—that it is almost impossible for them to obtain, in an open, honorable way, a thorough classical education here, whatever may be their ability for entering the pursuit—and they are therefore, after completing an ordinary school course, thrown mainly upon their own, and such other resources for further advancement, as they may privately gather about them. But even in this irregular way, and in the face of all embarrassments, some of the young men have attained to a degree of intelligence and general information, which, with a little instruction in regard to details, fit them for any and all of the useful stations in life; and to the highest of which, were they otherwise situated, they might with great propriety aspire.

If it be asked why the young men do not give greater exhibition of the truth of this assertion, it is answered that they are but men—endowed with the same human nature that characterizes any other division of the human family—and more should not be expected of them, than of any other class similarly circumstanced. The machinery of the watch will not fulfill its intent, unless the impulse of the spring be applied; and, though things inanimate are not to be compared with the human soul, yet, neither can a man be expected to rise to eminence in a given department, where, as is the case with men of color, there is not only an absence of all encouragement—all impulse—all definite motive to cheer him onward—but from the exercise of the legitimate functions of which, even were he fitted therefor, he would be absolutely excluded! He may indeed reach the base of the hill of science; but when there, casting his eye upward, what does he behold? Brethren ready to extend the hand of greeting and congratulation, when he hath made the ascent? No; not so with the man of color: need I say what reception *he* would be most likely to meet with?

But the young men of color do give many evidences of their intellectual acquirements and worth. They are confined to a narrow fold; and hence those who would be convinced, must seek them on their own premises. The literary associations among them must be visited; their debating societies must be scanned; the talent which they exhibit in acting upon all public matters, of immediate concern to them, must be taken into consideration; and the result will be, that no unprejudiced mind will have cause to depart in disappointment of the realization of any just expectation. The wonder, indeed, will be most likely to turn upon the fact that they have arrived at the point of intelligence and refinement, which they already evidence on such occasions, and in such matters. True it is, the body may be destroyed; but the mind—the immortal mind—will rise above the flesh; it cannot be entirely crushed.

"Mind, mind alone, bear witness earth and heaven!
    The living fountain of itself contains
Of beauteous and sublime";[14]

and these qualities, wherever existing, will, in greater or less[er] degree, sooner or later, burst forth and show their paternity.

In the departments of the lighter accomplishments, likewise, the higher classes of colored society show much advancement and proficiency. The young ladies, especially, are deserving of notice in this respect. In addition to the usual branches of education, many of them show much taste and skill in painting, instrumental music, singing, and the various departments of ornamental needlework, &c.. They, too, have their literary associations for mutual improvement. The order of their exercises in these, consists, principally, of readings and recitations of appropriate compositions, both original and selected. It has not transpired, that the ladies' associations have yet introduced the form of systematic debates. If such an introduction were made, there is little cause to doubt, but that great improvement would result therefrom. It would at least be the means of promoting conversational powers; and ease and fluency, in this respect, is an accomplishment certainly well worthy the aim of all.[15]

In thus speaking of the state of education among this class, it is by no means my aim, or even my remotest desire, to claim for them more than they actually deserve. It is not my purpose, to endeavor to excite the belief that they possess qualities and attainments, which, upon examination, would prove to be otherwise. My intention is to render credit for that alone for which it is due, and for nothing more.

Had a different course been chosen, more than here appears might probably have with justice been said. But isolated instances have been avoided. The professional men—the educated ministry—the physicians—the artists[16]—have not been made the theme; but society in a body, as it would be found by a stranger visiting. And let none say that these instances do not exist. There are one, two, three, or more colored ministers in this city, who would do honor, if it may so be spoken, to any pulpit, not only for their exemplary piety, but because of the intellectual ability they evidence in their calling.[17] Will it be set down as a disparagement of the merits of the others, if among these, the liberty is taken—pardonable, it is hoped—of naming the Rev. WILLIAM DOUGLASS,[18] Rector of St. Thomas' Protestant Episcopal Church? No such invidious comparison is intended; none, it is hoped, will be inferred. As to the physicians, there are several of them; in practical anatomy and surgery, they may be deficient; and though they may not have drunk so deep at the fountain of classical lore as some of their contemporaries, still, in the great end of the practice of physic—the healing of the sick—they would not suffer by comparison with a large number who have enjoyed such advantages.[19] For the artists, there is at least one, whose progress has no doubt been fully equal to his most favorable opportunities.[20]

In contrast with the favorable view here presented, I shall proceed, in the next chapter, to give an exposition of some of the follies and vices, which corrupt the social intercourse, and furnish a great obstacle to the further mutual improvement of the higher classes of colored society.

CHAPTER III.

General Remarks—Divisions among the Higher Classes of Colored Society—Causes which lead thereto—Disreputable Conduct of Parties—Insincerity of Young Ladies toward each other—Breaches of Confidence—Detraction—Slander—"Northerners" and "Southerners"—Another bad feature—Miscellaneous Observations

If men generally would but contemplate how vain, how ridiculous, and oftentimes how silly, are the various pretences [sic] to superiority, which one class of men frequently set up over another, surely, in very shame for past errors, we should all be speedily brought back to the only true and just standard—the MIND;—the *mind*, as developed in the goodness—the virtue—of its possessor. If it be "by the color of the soul" that "we shall be judged at last,"[21] why are we not content now to make this the standard of our decision, in passing upon our fellow-creatures? He that is least disposed to dishonor the image of his Maker—why not give him precedence in determining who is most worthy to be taken into companionship? But no: this equitable role of the Creator, will never serve the purposes of the poor, weak creature, man. He is too well aware, that if the trite couplet of poor Richard should be held in strict observance, and be carried into practice, many who now, in perfect assurance, wear the dignity of "men," would soon be reduced and compelled to bear the title merely of "fellows."[22] Hence it is necessary for such, in order to sustain their elevation, to call in accidental or adventitious circumstances to their aid; and where "worth" is wanting, if something from the catalogue of these may be read in its place, the difficulty is at once adjusted—the scale is at once poised in their favor. This is the ground, above all others, that obtains among men, in regulating and adjusting distinctions in society; upon such foundation have they ever rested; and, until the advent of some happier period—patiently looked for, but yet to dawn upon us—we have no reason to apprehend any very beneficial change. The religious world has never exhibited a tithe of the horror at its unreserved and indiscriminate intercourse with the sinners—the sheep, the goats, and the wolves of the human family—that one class of these same worldlings are seen to manifest at the idea of contact with another!

The sources of divisions in society here referred to, have no certain and fixed boundaries, but are purely arbitrary. They are common among all classes—the exclusives and the excluded—each establishing its own standard of government and adherence; and as they are traced downward, the primary rule seems to be—"that there are none so low, but others may be found a link beneath them."[23]

The higher classes of colored society in Philadelphia, are amenable to a liberal share of animadversion,[24] on account of the numerous divisions which exist among them. However they may appear to the eye of the casual observer to be resolved into one unbroken link, yet, he who is acquainted with their social relations, well knows that this seeming unity is quite contrary to the actual existence, and true state of things, in this respect. There are numerous distinct social circles, even among those equally respectable and of equal merit and pretensions, every way; and if these were confined within proper and legitimate limits—as each has the undoubted right to choose his or her private friends—there is certainly nothing in the fact to excite surprise or call forth censure. But they are not thus confined. They are carried into most of the relations of life, and in some cases are kept up with the most bitter and relentless rancor—arising, however, in such extreme cases, from ancient feuds or personal disagreements, which have descended perhaps from father to son, and so been perpetuated! I do not intend to represent, that there is always an open hostility kept up; it may appear dormant for the while, but favored by the time and the occasion, and often when the occasion would seem loudly to forbid, it seldom fails to develope [sic] its existence. It is the personification of true revenge,

> "—patient as the watchful alchymist,
> Sagacious as the blood-hound on the scent,
> Secret as death."[25]

Secret—until the opportunity offers of making its victim feel its presence. But where those personal dislikes or hates do not exist—when the social separation springs solely from the exercise of the unquestionable right, to choose one's private associations and companions—the case is widely different; and in all other relations, they meet each other on terms of apparent amity and good will.

The separations, however, in all cases, are seen to produce rivalry between the different circles; and in settling the claim to precedence and superiority, the character and reputation of one or the other of the parties, is almost sure to suffer, that being the first thing aimed at. An effort of this description, when set on foot, involves the basest of means for carrying it forward, and frequently nothing is left undone that malignant mischief can invent, for destroying the peace, happiness, and success of any one party or individual, who or which may become obnoxious to another.

The chief causes which lead to divisions in the society of the colored classes, are, in turn, the very result of these divisions. They are not to be found in any real pride of self-conceited superiority; for they well know that any pretension of this kind, founded otherwise than in personal good qualities, would never avail them aught beyond their own immediate pale, and among those who know them, would be laughed to scorn. They lie deeper or nearer the surface, as the reader pleases. There is an unhappy disposition, untiring and ever constant, to detract the one from the merits of the other; and if possible to thwart every plan or scheme, by which a few may be benefitted, unless it is made more than obvious, that all may equally partake of such benefit. The motto is changed from "live, and let live," to "let *me* live *first*, and you afterwards." This reprehensible disposition, it may be truly said, is carried into nearly all the relations of life. The more determined in its practice, will disregard every honorable consideration, whenever they set themselves about to arrest the career of some one of their acquaintances, who may appear to be more successful in some particular department than themselves. Instead of following the example of their more industrious neighbors—of letting the good fortune of these furnish a motive to their own laudable exertions—their first efforts are directed to discredit and to destroy. Thus, because they either will not, nor cannot move themselves, they stand ready to grasp, and to hold back, all those who would advance. In this way many lose more time—waste more anxiety—than would be required to make them all they could reasonably wish to be. And what are the means of success, usually resorted to in such cases? Falsehood the most vile, slander, the most opprobrious, hypocrisy, violated faith, social traitorism,—these, with their sub-divisions and concomitants, furnish the chief weapons for keeping up the odious strife.

The influence of such a course of conduct upon those who are subject to its operation, is easily perceptible. Suspicion and distrust very naturally usurp the place of confidence—without mutual reliance the one upon the integrity of the other, no circle of society can long exist together in unbroken harmony. Division after division, must necessarily be the consequence, upon the discovery of each new conspiracy, by any aggrieved party; for surely no person of common sense, would a second time repose full confidence in those who, without provocation, had, by the use of the basest of means, shown themselves so eminently unworthy of it. And such discoveries, unfortunately, are too frequently made—quite too frequent, for the general good and improvement of colored society!

Those who are always the greatest sufferers from the shafts of envy and malice, aimed at their destruction, are those young ladies who are so *unfortunate*—so it may be regarded in many instances!—as to become objects of jealousy to their associates. Be the cause of offence real or imagined, and never so trifling—and though the newly appointed victim may have had no direct agency in producing it—still it makes no difference with her inexorable persecutors. The late, perhaps, bosom friend, is now an object of aversion in the circle of her sex in which lately she moved and appeared to be esteemed, and must fare according to the usage which, with them, in such cases governs. This not being the kindest or most sisterly, is not always to be coveted!

This insincerity in the conduct of the young ladies toward each other, is remarkable in various other ways, and to an extent almost incredible. If a young man makes his appearance in society, whose position and prospects render him worthy of being sought for as a prize, by any or all of the marriag[e]able ladies of a circle, you may rest assured that if he chooses at all, the one so decided upon will be marked out by her companions—her dear, confidential friends!—as one whose character must speedily be blackened, in order, if possible, to prevent any consummated results! They may probably first "sound" (as the vulgar phrase goes) the young lady on the subject—first "feel her pulse well"—and if they find she is likely to make a "case" of the gentleman's proposal, they will leave nothing available untried to make a *case* of her!

Suppose those who engage in such crusades are successful in their design, what but a fiendish satisfaction, can it afford? The satisfaction of having been instrumental in destroying, perhaps, for ever the happiness of a fellow creature!—that fellow creature an innocent young lady!—that young lady late you proclaimed your friend! Is there any thing in nature more heartless and inhuman?

It is known that young men!—start not reader!—it is known that those who *call* themselves MEN, have been engaged in similar noble exploits against innocence and virtue!—but for the honor of our common nature, they are passed by!

I could give numerous instances, to prove the correctness of these representations, if it were deemed proper. But I am additionally deterred from so doing because of the personal references it would necessarily involve; and a charge of this nature, I desire not to incur. I can, however, scarcely refrain from referring to a case in point, which has occurred within two or three weeks of the present writing. An instance of a more unprincipled and fiend-like attempt, to blast the fair fame of an innocent and harmless young lady, and that, too, by her *ci-devant*[26] FRIENDS, is rarely to be met with. It is not likely, however, that she will ever suffer much inconvenience from the vile imputations which have been so wantonly and so unjustly cast upon her. Falsehood, it is true, may travel a great way while truth is preparing for the journey; but the latter, though slow, never fails most effectually to do its office of obliterating error, and of shielding the innocent from the vultures of our species, who are ever seeking to prey upon their happiness.

Think me not ungallant, ladies!—think me not ungallant for thus spreading before the world, some of the vices, which, wherever they obtain among you, are calculated so thoroughly to degrade your character—to

> "—blight your fair fame
> As whirlwinds nip the tender buds of spring."[27]

and render you worthy of being shunned by all who have once discovered their existence. It is for your good that I have done so; 'tis that you may view their odious character and reform the heinous abuses; and that, in your mutual intercourse, you may pursue those dictates only, that are commendable of virtue. Banish envy—banish jealousy—banish hypocrisy and deceit; and with these will be banished that hateful spirit of destruction and slander, which now renders each one of you a terror to the other, and makes such sad havoc with the reputations of all who come within the reach of the blighting influence. "Faithful are the wounds of a friend";[28] and it is alone in friendship that I thus openly rebuke you. If it shall be found to result in your improvement—if, to any extent, you are led to think seriously of the matter, and are thus benefitted—I shall be more than rewarded for the disagreeable task of here giving it record.

There are other causes of disaffection and disunion among the higher classes of colored society, which might have been before noticed; but they are either so limited or intricate as to command but little attention. Among these might be named those which arise from real or pretended sectional preferences. The prejudices said to exist in some instances between the natives and the southern families that have located among them, are of this character. I do not think the "northerners" have any just cause of complaint against the conduct of the "southerners" in this respect. The latter are true and faithful in their friendships, while they find a like reciprocation; and it is not to be wondered at, that they should be equally faithful to themselves, in resisting further intercourse, whenever and wherever they discover opposite qualities on the part of the former. But instances of this kind, as before intimated, are but limited; the southerners are held in esteem by the northerners, generally; and notwithstanding some young ladies "can't bear the southerners," it does not appear likely that either party will ever suffer much from the prejudice.

Another bad feature in the circles of the higher classes of colored society, is that which requires of those who obtain admission in any particular one, a total surrender of their independence to the whims or caprices of the majority who compose it. In fact one must make up his mind to be governed entirely by their feelings—their affections and aversions;—love those whom they love—hate those whom they hate—slander those whom they slander—and laud those whom they speak well of. Any exhibition of the right of opinion, in such matters, is very apt to beget for him who had the boldness to show it, the indifference of the other members of the circle—excite in their bosoms suspicions of his attachment to them—and thereupon he is very apt to find his society suddenly "cut," before, perhaps, he is fully aware of the cause! It may be, however, that they have "searched the scriptures" for this rule of their government, and are determined to consider all who are "not with them," to the utmost extent required, as being decidedly "against them."

Although I have here spoken in terms of general application, in recounting some of the more prominent vices, that are in practice among the higher classes of colored society, yet I would by no means have it understood that they are all equally vulnerable in this respect. There are exceptions—honorable exceptions—in the ranks of both male and female. There are young ladies, whose virtues, purity of mind and strict moral worth, render them in no wise amenable to my censures,—who are as incapable of the practices adverted to, as any to be found in any other division of society;—but whose misfortune it is to be brought in[to] social contact with those to whom this exception cannot justly apply.

Those therefore whom it will fit, will readily recognise [sic] the garment—and it is hoped will endeavor to repair it;—and such as it would illy become, will concur heartily in the most unlimited denunciation of its wear.

The vices of the higher classes in all countries, are no less those of the better informed, and more wealthy portion of those who form the subject of these sketches. The vulgar and indecent practices which obtain foothold among them, and which would perhaps for ever soil the fame of any one of the plain, unostentatious, unpretending members of pleb[e]ian society in the estimation of his associates, are by them termed "fashionable foibles," and he or she who is not an adept in such matters, is looked upon as a "simpleton," or a "flat"; or is otherwise regarded in the light that one would be who should appear in a ball-room and offer to lead in the dance, with brogans[29] upon his feet—a grossly ignorant and unfashionable fellow! It is not of course for the want of education or of better information, but in truth the very possession of these, which they consider—conjoined with wealth—confers upon them the privilege of establishing and adhering to just whatever regulations and practices, under the name of "fashion," their corrupt fancies may lead them to. So with many of those at whose vices I have aimed. Their demeanor in the eyes of the world is by no means in consonance with such conduct.* They are as fully sensible of the importance of "keeping up appearances," as any that can be named, and are as equally successful in maintaining them.

---

*Let it be here distinctly understood, that I design not to impute any greater criminality or grosser immorality, than has been distinctly designated.

The succeeding chapter will serve in some measure to show the ability of the higher classes of colored society to maintain social intercourse, on terms as creditable and honorable as the most fastidious could desire, and to the satisfaction of the most pungent and carping of moralists.

CHAPTER IV.

Social Intercourse—Visiting—Evenings at Home—Amusements and Conversation—Evening Parties—Guests—Hours of Retirement—Habits of Temperance at private Parties— General Remarks

The prejudiced world has for a long time been in error, in judging of what may be termed the *home condition*, or social intercourse, of the higher classes of colored society, by the specimens who in the every day walks of life are presented to their view as the "hewers of wood and the drawers of water."[30] This rash mode of judgment—the forming an opinion of the beauty of the landscape merely by the heavy shading in the fore-ground of the picture, has long been the source of many groundless and unjust aspersions against their general character, and one which common justice requires should be removed. It is equally erroneous to adjudge all to be saints, because of the few good; as to suppose all are in a state of servitude and degradation, because it is not denied that the majority are in close approximation to that condition. With the latter, however, I profess not to concern myself here; but may say with great propriety, in passing, that many of those even who are usually regarded in this light, are far more "sinned against, than sinning";[31] and if their homes could be visited, they would be seen to present an air of neatness and the evidences of comfort which would be quite astonishing, when compared with their limited advantages for securing them.

Among the higher classes there is no want of a knowledge of the good things of this life, or of the ability so to arrange the means at their disposal, as to make them productive of the most substantial good, present and prospective. Unlike fashionable people of other communities, they mostly live within their incomes, from whatever resources derived; and hence, if they do not appear to make very rapid advances in the road to wealth, they manage well to maintain even appearances, and support such comforts, conveniences and luxuries, as they appear to have for a long period been uniformly accustomed to. In this way they avoid many of the embarrassments that are common to those whose sole claim to "fashion" consists in the success they may meet with in making a commanding "show" on particular occasions. They keep up, apparently, an even tenor at all times,—seeming very wisely to consider that it is quite as proper for themselves to enjoy the fruits of their possessions or exertions, as that strangers should come in and have all heaped upon them. Not that I would represent them as being less hospitable than other people in this latitude: it does not appear that they are. Probably if trial were made—means compared—the scale in this respect at least would turn in their favor.

It will not, it is believed, be expected of the writer, in speaking of the ability of the higher classes of colored society to maintain social intercourse on terms of respectability and dignity, to give an elaborate statement or inventory of the furniture in their dwellings—its quality and cost;—the size of their market-baskets (an article, by the way, not to be lost sight of in making up the sum of a happy home!) and the usual character of their contents;—it will not be necessary to say that their parlors are carpeted and furnished with sofas, sideboards, card-tables, mirrors, &c. &c.,[32] with, in many instances, the addition of the piano forte. These, with other relative matters, governed by no particular standard, the reader is left to form such an opinion of, as he may deem most correct! I will say, however, that usually, according to pecuniary ability, they fail not to gratify themselves in this wise, to the extent and after the manner that gains observance among other people.

Visiting *sans ceremonie*[33] does not obtain to a very great extent with the higher classes of colored society. Even among those who are otherwise intimate acquaintances, the order of unceremonious visits is but limited. They are mostly by familiar or formal invitation, or in return for others previously received. This latter observance is most rigidly adhered to by many. Such as are its more determined votaries, will not attend upon a friend, even by particular invitation, unless their last call has been acknowledged by like return.[34] The intimacy in such instances, however, as may be readily imagined, is not very great; and it seems rational to suppose there is very little care to continue that which may exist.

The period of paying and receiving visits, is mostly confined to the evening; among the gentlemen almost entirely so. Many circumstances combine to render this arrangement most convenient and agreeable to all parties; and as the same observance is respected in nearly all conditions of society in our money-seeking country, the chief cause of its adoption will be found too obvious to require particular reference.

Casual visiting with the young men is very common. Their attendance upon the ladies is mostly confined to visiting them at their dwellings. Very little out-door amusement is resorted to, as walking or riding excursions; but the reason of the non-observance of these, and one which is quite sufficient to prohibit them, is readily traceable to its proper source.[35] With the young ladies at home they pass their evenings agreeably if so disposed. It is rarely that the visitor in the different families where there are two or three ladies, will not find one or more of them competent to perform on the piano-forte, guitar, or some other appropriate musical instrument; and these, with singing and conversation on whatever suitable topics that may offer, constitute the amusements of their evenings at home. The love of music is universal; it is cultivated to some extent,—vocal or instrumental,—by all; so that it is almost impossible to enter a parlor where the ear of the visitor is not, in some sort or other, greeted therewith. It is consequently made a prominent part of the amusements on all occasions of social meeting together of friends. The character of the conversation is usually varied, interesting and instructive. All the current topics of the time, appropriate and of sufficient interest, are elaborately discussed in a mild, dignified and becoming manner, in which the ladies mostly take part and contribute their full quota. The degree of promptness and ability often displayed on such occasions, is far surpassing the common opinion on this subject. The best informed persons could not but be pleasingly entertained, provided they could command sufficient courage to enable them to lay aside, for the time, the music of prejudice, (if blinded by it,) so as to be competent to take a just and an impartial view.

If prejudiced persons were to be governed more by positive knowledge—actual demonstration—than they are by rash, hasty, groundless conclusions, very different views than at present generally obtain, would soon be formed, respecting the degree of refinement and cultivation to be found among the higher classes of colored society. The ease and grace of manner with which they are capable of bearing themselves in company— their strict observance of all the nicer etiquettes, proprieties and observances that are characteristic of the well-bred—render their society agreeable and interesting to the most fastidious in such matters; and speak loudly against the injustice that is done them, in refusing to accord to them any knowledge, possession or practice of those qualities or accomplishments.

On occasions of appointed entertainments, which are usually in the form of evening parties, the greatest order and neatness of management is observed. There is always a first and second table,[36] both appropriately and well stored, and in a manner generally unexceptionable. The guests at the parties consist only of such individuals or families as are accustomed to entertain their host or hostess, for the time, in a similar manner in their turn. Those who are all things in reception and nothing in return,—strangers, agreeable, entertaining and *eligible* bachelors, and sojourners in the city at *board*,[37] always of course excepted,—are considered detrimental to the harmony of social intercourse; and, consequently, are very apt to be neglected in the list of invitations, that may be issued! In this way they manage to collect a very agreeable company, all perhaps on terms of perfect agreement and intimacy. The amusements of the evening are much the same as before noticed,—music, conversation, &c.,—with the addition of exchanging "mottoes" taken from the "secrets' papers,"[38] which are to be found in plenteousness at all the regular evening parties.

The hours of retirement from the evening entertainments, are usually from ten to eleven o'clock—rarely beyond eleven. Many of the visitors leave as early as ten; and after the first movement, it is not long before the entertainers are in full and quiet possession of their parlors, recounting, as it is imagined, the incidents of the evening, and determining among themselves how every thing "passed off."

The observance of abstinence at the parties of the higher classes of colored society—total abstinence from all that has a tendency to intoxicate—is worthy of remark. So far as my observation has extended, the only drinks that are presented—if indeed there are any others seen than the pure, unadulterated ale of our first parents—may consist of lemonade, or some pleasant and wholesome syrup commingled with water. No wines of any description—not even the lightest and mildest—are ever brought forward. Whether this arises from a pure love of temperance or a disposition to avoid unnecessary expenditure, either of which is commendable, I shall not pause to inquire.[39] But certain it is that the visitors at such times and places, who neglect to carry "merry hearts and laughing eyes"[40] with them, will find nothing in the way of distilments to excite them after they get there. It is not intended to insinuate that there are no worshippers at the shrine of Bacchus[41] among this class. It is to be feared there are. It will be observed, however, that I have spoken solely in relation to private entertainments, or social parties, where both sexes are present.

Enough has been said, it is conceived, on the subject of the social condition of the higher classes of colored society, to convey to the mind of the stranger reader, a sufficient outline of the actual position they occupy. They are, indeed, far in advance of the peculiar circumstances by which they are surrounded. The exceedingly illiberal, unjust and oppressive prejudices of the great mass of the white community, overshadowing every moment of their existence, is enough to crush—effectually crush and keep down—any people. It meets them at almost every step without their domiciles, and not unfrequently [sic] follows even *there*. No private enterprise of any moment,—no public movement of consequence for the general good,—can they undertake, but forth steps the relentless monster to blight it in the germ. But in the face of all this, they not only bear the burthen successfully, but possess the elasticity of mind that enables them to stand erect under their disabilities, and present a state of society of which, to say the least, none have just cause to be ashamed.

Yet I would not have them lose sight of the numerous evils existing among themselves, (adverted to in a preceeding [sic] part,) which have the effect greatly to retard their still further progress in the walks of cultivation and refinement. They have the elements among themselves—regardless of obstacles from without—for a more general and more uniform advancement; and it becomes them, peculiarly, to banish all those low-minded traits, as jealousy of each others' success, envy of advancement or conceived superiority; and to endeavor to uphold and sustain, rather than to pull down and destroy all that any portion may not have yet attained to. The habit of detraction—of undermining each the other's worth and attainments—must be entirely banished. The effect of this practice often furnishes those whose minds are predisposed to unfavorable judgments, with a fruitful source of forming additionally derogatory opinions. Those who indulge in it to an extent which leads to this, little think, in their anxiety to laud themselves, that they are aiming at their own best interests, in attempting to strike down the prosperity of those with whom they are so closely linked in destiny. Let, then, such unworthy considerations be entirely banished; and the general improvement of all will be seen to be two-fold greater than at present.

It is not my desire to be understood as an advocate of universal social union. Far from it. Such a union would not only be impracticable, but even could it take place, would, to say the least, be highly injudicious and prejudicial. If the virtuous and exemplary members of society should not keep aloof from the vicious and worthless, they would furnish no example to the latter to strive to make themselves reputable, and of like consideration. By associating with such persons we not only thereby give countenance to their doings, but we degrade ourselves to their level, and are adjudged accordingly. Hence, distinctions and divisions on this ground, are in every respect commendable, proper and just; but it should be borne in mind, that this is the only just foundation—the condition of the mind and heart—upon which they can be made; and the only one that should govern the discrimination of the higher classes of colored society, particularly, in regulating their intercourse with each other.

CHAPTER V.

POLITICAL RIGHTS—FIRST NATIONAL CONVENTION OF PEOPLE OF COLOR—CHARACTER OF PROCEEDINGS—NAMES OF DELEGATES— IMPROVEMENT OF THE PEOPLE OF COLOR—PUBLIC MEETINGS, MEN AND MEASURES—CONTENTIONS AT PUBLIC MEETINGS, RIVALRY, OPPOSITION, &C., &C.

Among the very erroneous opinions that are formed, respecting the people of color, is the one that supposes them indifferent to the state of things by which they are surrounded, and that they make little or no effort for their relief. But this arises from the want of closer observance of their situation, and the nature and character of their disabilities. If the truth, which should be the aim of all, is faithfully sought, it will be found in the very reverse of this supposition. Never have any people, in proportion to their means of operation, made greater efforts for their entire enfranchisement. It should be kept in view, that in Pennsylvania, particularly, and also in some other of the non-slaveholding states, they are almost, if not entirely, deprived of political rights and power;[42] and that, consequently, in all matters relating to their interests, which involve legislative action, they must appear altogether in the attitude of suitors; and show themselves very humble in the exercise of even that prerogative. They cannot say to legislators, "If you fail to act for us, we shall not fail to act against you, when called to exercise the function of electors"; they expect not, as yet, to be called to that exalted purpose; and this the former being well aware of, they take particular care to proceed in such manner only, as they deem best calculated to further their popularity with those who do possess and exercise that power. When a certain Secretary of State was asked "Why he did not promote merit?" he promptly replied, "Because merit did not promote me!" This anecdote (which I have somewhere read,) presents the precise situation of our legislators. "Why do you not act for colored men?" "Because colored men did not act for me!" (And may not another question in this connexion [sic] be with propriety asked? *"Who hindered them?"*) Thus it is necessary for the people of color to keep up an incessant *begging* of their *rulers* to legislate in their behalf; and with what effect is well known to all.

The first national movement of any importance among the people of color in this country, for the improvement of their general condition took place in 1831.† A call for a National Convention was issued by a society then in existence in Philadelphia, and the people in five states (three of which were, and are at present slaveholding,) responded thereto. The smallness of the number of states represented, and a part of those lying South of this, will be wondered at by some; but is easily accounted for, in various ways, which need not, however, be noticed here. The people were represented in the States of New York, Pennsylvania, Delaware, Maryland and Virginia. Nothing is said in the minutes (from which I gather the information,) of any representation North or South of these. The delegates met in the city of Philadelphia on the 6th. of June, and continued their sessions five days—probably intending to give each of the states represented, a day to itself![43] It was hardly to be expected that under the auspices of a first annual assemblage, and that so meagrely [sic] attended, much good could be immediately effected; but the minutes show, that

---

†An effort was made the year previous by "The American Society of Free Persons of Color, for Improving their Condition," &c., &c., to organize a National Convention, but in consequence of a want of extensive notice in time, there was but a small representation, and consequently nothing of importance was transacted—saving to recommend Conventions annually thereafter. Hence this may be considered the first regularly organized National Convention. The credit of its *origin*, is however, due to the "American Society," &c., of which the RT. REV. RICHARD ALLEN was *President*, and William Whipper the *Corresponding Secretary*.

important improvements were contemplated, the most advantageous part of which, however, has never yet been carried into execution. Among the plans for future improvement, decided upon, was the establishment of a College or Manual Labor School in New Haven, Ct., in accordance with suggestions made to the Convention by three well known philanthropists, who in person attended upon its sittings. The plan submitted by those gentlemen‡ to a committee of conference, appointed by the convention, estimated the cost of the College at about twenty thousand dollars, one thousand of which amount was conditionally subscribed by a gentleman on the spot, and agents appointed to collect the remainder. Nothing more at this time is heard of the contemplated Manual Labor School, so that it is now presumable that the difficulties in the way of its establishment were too great to be surmounted.[44]

Since the period of the meeting of the first Convention—though only ten years—the condition of the people of color has undergone a great and beneficial change. The result of that movement was to resolve upon similar meetings annually, and so they have, in some form or other, been continued up to the present time.[45] Measures were also taken to secure a more numerous and general attendance. Meetings were called and auxiliary societies formed in nearly all the states, cities and towns, where it was found practicable; and as soon as the people were aroused to the importance of the measure, it met with most hearty concurrence and support. "Persecution," says the first conventional address, "was the cause of our Convention"; and this same spirit and practice of persecution has not been wanting since then to keep the people on the alert in regard to their rights. But to the "first annual Convention" certainly belongs the credit of having blown the first great blast, by which the people were awakened to the importance of their own united and energetic action, in removing their disabilities and securing equal rights with other men. I, therefore, cheerfully take pleasure in doing what little I can towards crowning with immortality the names of the delegates who composed it.

NAMES OF THE DELEGATES

Who composed the First National Convention of the People of Color, held by adjournments in the City of Philadelphia, from the sixth to the eleventh of June, 1831.

‡Messrs. A. Tappan, S. S. Jocelyn, and W. L. Garrison.

Philadelphia

JOHN BOWERS,[46] Pres't of Convention
DR. BELFAST BURTON[47]
JAMES CORNISH[48]
JUNIUS C. MOREL[49]
WM. WHIPPER,[50] Secretary

Carlisle, Penn.

JOHN PECK[51]

Maryland

REV. ABNER COKER[52]
ROBERT COWLEY[53]

New York

REV. WM. MILLER[54]
HENRY SIPKINS[55]
THOMAS L. JENNINGS,[56] Assist. Sec'ry.
WILLIAM HAMILTON[57]

Long Island

JAMES PENNINGTON[58]

Delaware

ABRAHAM D. SHAD[D],[59] Vice President
REV. PETER GARD[I]NER[60]

Virginia

WM. DUNCAN,[61] Vice President

There are other names [sic] mentioned in the "Minutes" as having taken part in the proceedings, but their names do not appear in the list of delegates. Among these are noticed the Rev. CHARLES W. GARDNER,[62] and the Rev. SAMUEL TODD,[63] who were appointed Chaplains to the Convention. I do not profess, in this brief notice, to give a connected history of the Convention, or the more immediate causes which gave rise to it; but only to notice such facts as are in this place deemed appropriate.

The ten years that have elapsed since the period to which I have adverted, have witnessed a great change in the condition and prospects of the people of color in Philadelphia.§ You could not find here now, as was the case then, a committee of intelligent men submitting to one of their meet-

§This is not said in disparagement of the people elsewhere.

ings or other public bodies, in unqualified terms, "the necessity of their deliberate reflection on the . . . dissolute, intemperate, and ignorant condition of the colored population"; because the facts would by no means warrant the indiscriminate and sweeping assertion. The higher classes, at least, who form the subject of these sketches, are as chaste and as temperate as any other body of the population; and, it may be added, as intelligent as thousands who have had better facilities afforded them.

The usual mode of expressing the popular will, in all free countries, by public assemblages of the people, obtains to the fullest extent with the people of color at the present time. They never let a subject of peculiar importance to them, that may be agitated in the community, pass without a public expression of their views and opinions in regard to it. Their inability to act with efficiency in the premises makes but little difference with most of the leading men. A meeting they must have. The sin of failing to remonstrate against any scheme, that may be turned to their disadvantage, they are determined never to let rest upon their shoulders. This is certainly very praiseworthy, of itself considered; but the character of their proceedings are frequently very objectionable. Measures denunciatory are too often resorted to, which—especially when directed against those who will not be moved, by even the ordinary dictates of common right, where the people of color are concerned—are most assuredly calculated to defeat, rather than to achieve, the end desired. Instances of this description are to be found on any occasion of legislative attempt to abridge or deprive [them] of existing rights. At such times, as is very natural, the proceedings of the Legislature are scanned with more than ordinary interest; and as soon as the cast of parties in the matter is ascertained, those who are found to be in adverse to their interests, are, without more ado, set up as targets to be "abused at," (no better term is deserved,) instead of being selected for convincement and consequent conviction of their error.

This misguided course is often resorted to, in matters of far less importance than is here supposed, and likewise of altogether a different tenor and bearing. But in all such cases and, it may be added, with saints and sinners, very nearly the same effect is produced. No man likes to be abused into, or out of any measure. He is by such a course put on the defensive, and driven to take stronger measures to sustain himself. Whether in the right or in the wrong, it would be apt to make but little difference; and even were it possible to convince him by senseless railing, he would be very slow to acknowledge it. It is left to metaphysicians to inquire into the nature of the courage by which he would be most likely to be prompted, but this we do know, that such is degenerate man. And how is it when such a one finds that his assailants are composed of those whom he is already inclined to hold in contempt?—from whom, politically—without imputing any higher motive—he has nothing whatever to fear, and therefore, if he heeds them at all, it is with derision and scorn? What folly, then, for men of color thus to "offer war where they should kneel for peace";[64]—to attempt to coerce, where the only mode left is to sue the way to consideration and favor?

I should not neglect to state in this connection, that however severe the people of color may be in assailing their opponents, they are no less forward in expressing their gratitude to those who, on such occasions exert themselves in their behalf.

Among the evils which operate to produce the mode of proceeding, to which I have adverted, the constant competition among the "leading men" to take *the* lead in all matters of concern may be mentioned as one of the principals. The absence of discipline of mind and want of mature reflection, undoubtedly has a large share in it;—so hath oppression, which "maketh a wise man mad";[65]—but if momentary self-exaltation were a little less thought of, and the general good more, they would have ample time to provide themselves in these respects with the necessary qualifications for wiser and more deliberate action. There are too many men, who might otherwise be useful, who desire to be considered the leaders and the chiefs in every matter of interest that is agitated. They will not take part in forwarding any scheme, however well intended on the part of the original movers, unless they themselves were components of that original. This begets rivalry and contention in the public meetings. Rivalry must be sustained; and in order to do this, impeachment of motive and other personal assaults of words are resorted to. If these fail to produce the end desired—of settling the question of precedence—attention is at last turned to the object the meeting may have been called to pass upon. Then, if the subject happens to be of the character before supposed, where "our dearest rights" are involved, the batteries are opened upon those who are known to be adverse to them. In this, nearly all the "leaders" and would-be leading men, are apt to join. Blustering, loud speaking and unlimited denunciation, are substituted for reason and common sense; and he who is most proficient in this respect and gains the loudest plaudits of the moment, thinks himself fairly entitled to the consideration he aimed to secure—of being the smartest and wisest of all his competitors! And this the thoughtless crowd—as is apt to be the case among every class of persons—too often award to no greater deserts. Thus is the general good made subservient to private ends; and thus, too, in the pursuit of those ends, is the very object defeated which it was ostensibly the sole aim of all to effect.

The public meetings are likewise frequently made the scenes of personal disputes and quarrels, totally irrelevant to the matter for which they were assembled, and of no possible consequence to any but those directly engaged in them. In such cases the most ridiculous, vulgar and unmanly—not to say ungentlemanly!—exhibitions are often presented. A quarrel between two school boys is magnanimous when compared with it! Undoubtedly they do appear ridiculous in the eyes of the juveniles, who may at such times be looking on! But the parties themselves, in their enraged moments, are not in a condition to enter into the feelings of the calm, reflecting auditor. Of this I am well aware; and it is for this reason, that I have here taken occasion to help them to a picture of themselves, that they may see its defects and amend them. The belligerents in these windy combats, surely know what belongs to decency,—or so much, at least, in charity must be allowed; and if they have no self-respect, they ought certainly to pay a little regard to the feelings and rights of those upon whom they intrude such scenes.**

This evil of introducing private piques, preferences and antipathies into the public assemblages, convened for acting upon matters of the general good, operates badly in every way; and not among the least of its results is the effect it has of driving many useful men entirely out of the way of exerting themselves for the public good, by direct co-operation with others in matters of general interest that may command attention. Respecting themselves,—having no taste for contention and strife,—they very properly keep aloof, and thereby save themselves from unpleasant feelings, and the discouragements which such disorderly proceedings are apt to engender. There are several who could be pointed out—men of sound judgment and mature minds—who are rarely seen to appear upon the platform of public action. This undoubtedly excites the wonder of some who know them, but who are not aware of the causes which, in this respect, keep them apparently silent. But if such were pressed for a reason, there is no doubt they would reply something to this effect—that they have no objec-

---

**I have learned, recently, that certain moderate and discreet men of the community, having become disgusted with the frequency of the scenes here referred to, have determined to thrust out the participators therein, on all future occasions when attempts shall be made to bring them forward at the public meetings.

tion to visit a menagerie occasionally, for the sake of gratifying their love for natural history; but that they do not desire to enter an arena where the voracious animals are permitted, uncaged, to roam at large, and prey upon whom they please! This would be a severe figure; but is it wholly void of application?

Besides those gentlemen who keep away from the public meetings, or go merely as spectators, there are others who do co-operate in this wise, but are not justly amenable to the charges of disreputable conduct adverted to. Their only culpability consists in giving a moment's heed to the impotent, harmless assaults of those who endeavor to gain importance by provoking a reply. They present themselves at a meeting with the best intentions in the world; they offer a suggestion in the same spirit; when forthwith, up starts some blustering Sir Oracle,[66] to give, gratuitously, an unfailing indication of his own vulgar mind and dishonest heart, by questioning the purity of the mover's intentions. He pauses not for examination or explanation; it is sufficient for him to know that the proposition comes from one, against whom he cherishes personal ill-will;—and that is the key to all his opposition—that with him is sufficient to outweigh all other considerations! The only alternate [sic] left then, is for the former to withdraw from the proceedings, or take upon him the hangman's duty of applying the scourge; and this it may truly be said, has sometimes been done, and with an effect that has operated to the no small discomfiture of the assailing party! But why not visit the impeachment with contempt, and proceed peaceably and in order? This may be answered by saying that our Sir Oracle may be one of those beings so insensible to refined feelings, or so puffed up with his own imagined consequence, that such treatment would defeat the object intended; that mistaking contemptuous silence for fear, he might grow more obstreperous than before!—so that in either event contention and general disorder is quite unavoidable. Thus are well and peaceably disposed persons in a manner forced into the degrading scenes; and are, therefore, to a greater or less extent excusable.

Now what is the effect of all this? Does any individual grow better or wiser by it? Who is aided or whose interests are promoted by such proceedings? Surely a more unwise course—one more certainly calculated to retard or defeat any beneficial undertaking—could not well be pursued!

If the standard of courtesy—since duelling is out of fashion!—was somewhat more elevated, much of the dissension which now divides the energies of men of color in Philadelphia, might be avoided. There are one or more "public men," who, in this respect, are sadly at fault. They are not at all backward in laying claim to "all the decency" and all the good sense; and yet to witness their conduct on almost all public occasions, one would be led to think that they had been educated in a pigstye [*sic*]! The words honor, courtesy, self-respect, they seem never to have heard; or hearing, could never properly comprehend their import! So much at least is said in charity: for if they have heard and do comprehend, they are most assuredly of a nature debased past reclaiming!

I have said that from a spirit of rivalry or some other cause, one class of the "leading men" in the colored community will not fall in with the suggestions or plans of another, unless they themselves were part to the original movement. This is true to an extent which renders it almost impossible for the people to proceed together in unanimity on any given subject, however directly important to them, may be the issue. Instances have occurred, wherein the wishes of the majority have been totally misrepresented before the public, by an alteration of their proceedings, before sending them for publication, to gratify the private feelings of parties who may have been disappointed in the original results! Probably these individuals may have got themselves appointed on a committee to attend to publishing the proceedings;[67] and have taken advantage of the appointment to violate the trust reposed in them!

No one, of course, expects unanimity in all matters of policy among any people. Differences are expected and will always arise. But it is expected that those differences will be marked by an open, manly and honorable course of procedure, and not by low scheming and chicanery, if not positive dishonesty. It is hardly necessary to add, that those who merit reproach for indulgence in the last named practices, are always the very first to pounce upon and impeach the motives of their neighbors! I will do them the favor to say, however, that the error of judging mankind by their own standard does not rest alone with them. The virtuous and good sometimes repose great confidence in persons totally unworthy of the trust, because they are too pure in mind to adjudge evil without testimony not to be mistaken; and it is nothing extraordinary to see the reverse of the proposition exemplified by those who are themselves of questionable worth!

It is certainly to be hoped that the young men—and there are many of them—who are just entering the stage of public action, in behalf of their fellow men, will guard against the rocks and shoals upon which their senior contemporaries have nearly wrecked all hopes of ever being able to do any permanent general good. Had they, instead of striving with and endeavoring to destroy each other, united their energies and labored for the mutual benefit of all, they might have presented a state of society which would have been an invincible argument against the tyrannical act‡ of the ever memorable "Reform Convention,"[68] and perhaps secured for their posterity all of the "rights, privileges and immunities" enjoyed by other citizens of the Commonwealth. The young men may, therefore, building upon past results, rest assured, that until they learn to respect themselves, and the rights, feelings and interests of their brethren, they can never hope to gain the respect of others, or attain to any remarkable point of political consideration, or private worth.

CHAPTER VI.

GENERAL REMARKS—LITERARY SOCIETIES—PHILADELPHIA LIBRARY COMPANY OF COLORED PERSONS—RUSH LIBRARY COMPANY AND DEBATING SOCIETY—DEMOSTHENIAN INSTITUTE—MINERVA LITERARY ASSOCIATION—EDGEWORTH LITERARY ASSOCIATION—GILBERT LYCEUM—NEW ASSOCIATION CONTEMPLATED

The number and character of the institutions for the promotion of literature in any community, may be justly regarded as an unfailing indication of the tastes and morals of its components. It would be vanity here to attempt to illustrate the effects of education upon society, or to describe the superior worth and prosperity of communities in which it is generally diffused among all classes, over those where the majority of the people remain in comparative ignorance. The aspiring disposition that education imparts to its possessor—the continued, insatiable desire for more, more, the farther he progresses—is of itself sufficient to show its inestimable

††Disfranchisement.

worth in fitting us for the high stations in the scale of being, designed by the Creator that we should occupy. He who implanted the mind and endowed it with certain capabilities and faculties of developement [sic], hath also placed in our power the *means* thereof; and happy is he who makes the best use of them.

Among no people, in proportion to their means and advantages, is the pursuit of knowledge more honored than among the colored inhabitants of Philadelphia. The exalted standard in the world of letters, which characterizes the favored class, is by them seconded to the utmost extent in their power. Many of them seem, in this respect, to have fully entered into the spirit of taste and refinement of those by whom they are surrounded; and their success is seen to be such, as of which they have no reason to be ashamed. The actual standard of literary acquirements, it is true, even among the best informed class, is nothing extraordinary of itself considered; they have engaged in the pursuit of knowledge more for its own sake—the adornment which it gives them—than from any relative or collateral advantages which could be expected; they have not been stimulated and encouraged to seek education as a *trade*, which would well repay their assiduity and the pecuniary cost to the pursuit: and, therefore, in the absence of all those cheering motives which impel others, to expect a higher state of advancement than they at present exhibit, would be illiberal if not unjust.

The educated man of color, in the United States, is by no means, so far as he may be affected by exterior circumstances, the *happiest* man. He finds himself in possession of abilities and acquirements which fit him for most of the useful and honorable stations in life, where such qualities are requisite; but does he find—can he even with reason anticipate—their ever being in like manner appreciated and rewarded? If there was nothing in education to recommend *itself*, well might reason be construed against the utility of the man of color's entering its paths; aye, well might *he* conclude within himself, that with the people of color "ignorance *is* bliss!" and for them it is, therefore, "folly to be wise!"[69] "He that is robbed, let him not know it, and he is not robbed at all."[70]

But education possesses its own intrinsic worth, which it imparts to those who enter its pursuits. Of this, colored Philadelphians seem to be fully aware, and as one important avenue towards further advancement and perfection, they have established numerous literary associations, the most prominent of which it is here proposed briefly to notice.

Among the earliest established of these institutions, stands first—

"THE PHILADELPHIA LIBRARY COMPANY OF COLORED PERSONS"[71]

This Company was instituted January 1st., 1833. The number of persons present at its formation, and who signed the Constitution, were nine; whose names are here given:—Messrs. Frederick A. Hinton,[72] James Needham,[73] (now *Treasurer*, and who kindly furnished these particulars,) James Cornish,[74] Robert C. Gordon, junr.[75], John Dupee[76] [sic], William Whipper,[77] J. C. Bowers,[78] Charles Trulier,[79] Robert Douglass, junr.,[80] and James C. Mathews;[81]—who may be considered the founders of the first successful literary institution of this description, established by the colored classes in Philadelphia.

The object of the Company, as its title implies, was the collection of a library of useful works of every description for the benefit of its members, who might there successfully apply, without comparatively any cost, for that mental good which they could not readily obtain elsewhere. This enterprise met with great encouragement, both in the way of donations of books, pamphlets, maps, &c., and otherwise; so that in a short time a large and valuable collection was made. A systematic order of reading was then adopted by the members, to the very great advantage of those who persevered therein. In connexion [sic] with this, a system of debates was introduced, for the purpose of stimulating the members to historical and other researches, and for practising [sic] them in the arts of elocution and public speaking.

Soon after the establishment of the Library Company—their numbers having greatly augmented—application was made to the Legislature for an act of incorporation. In this they also met with speedy success—corporate existence having been granted them in the early part of 1836. From this period the Company rapidly increased in numbers and usefulness, until at the present time the roll book presents the names of about one hundred (including a number of honorary) members; all of whom have partaken of its benefits.

The debating department has of late greatly improved in regard to the intelligence and ability of those who usually participate therein. Discussions of interesting subjects take place on Tuesday of each week.

The Library at present contains nearly six hundred volumes of valuable historical, scientific and miscellaneous works, among which are several Encyclopaedias [sic], and is a source of great mental profit to the members of the Company. Among those who took an interest in, and contributed towards the collection of the Library, was the late Right Reverend Bishop WHITE, of the Protestant Episcopal church.[82]

The fee of admission to membership of the institution, is such as to place it within the reach of every one disposed to connect themselves therewith. It is *one dollar*; and the monthly assessment thereafter, *twenty-five cents*.

The Company, at the present time, holds its meetings in the basement of St. Thomas' Episcopal Church, South Fifth street, where persons, so disposed, are at liberty to visit and judge for themselves of its probable character.

The progress of this institution has been marked by evidence of the most gratifying character—gratifying to all who delight to witness the progress of knowledge and refinement among their fellow-men. Many a young man of color in this community, who previous to the establishment of "The Philadelphia Library Company of Colored Persons" never dreamed of rising before a public auditory to make an address, or engage in a debate, is now enabled to do so with little or no embarrassment, and in a manner highly creditable.

The next, in the order of its formation, comes—

"THE RUSH LIBRARY COMPANY AND DEBATING SOCIETY OF PENNSYLVANIA"[83]

This Society was formed on the 16th of December, 1836; and, as will be seen, is several years younger than its predecessor. Present at its formation there were seven persons, as follows:—Messrs. John L. Hart[84] (now the *President*—and to whom I am indebted for these particulars,) William D. Banton,[85] Littleton Hubert,[86] Harrison R. Sylva,[87] James Bird,[88] and Charles Brister.[89] In about two months after this beginning, the list of its members had increased to twenty-two; at which period an act of incorporation was granted by the Legislature, bearing date March 1, 1837.

The object aimed at, by the founders of the "Rush Library Company and Debating Society," was the same as that of the one first noticed. They have succeeded in collecting a handsome library, at the present time numbering two hundred volumes, and gradually increasing. Its contents are, of course, of a miscellaneous character; but all of the books are useful, and among them many valuable works. From this source the members have derived great advantages.

The debating department is also maintained with spirit—many of the members evidencing much ability in the discussion of the various questions that are brought before them. This is likewise, to the members, a source of great improvement in elocution and public speaking.

The roll book of the Rush Library Company, at the time this is written, (June, 1841,) numbers thirty members, with occasional additions. Its place of meeting is at "Salters' Hall," Elizabeth street.[90]

Those best acquainted with the affairs of this institution, are of opinion that it is "one of the most really useful, of its kind, among the colored classes, in the city";—that others may equal it in regard to the benefits derivable therefrom, but none surpass. This opinion is, in all probability, nothing more than is justly due. If the energy and enterprise of its President may be taken as a sample of the spirit that characterizes the body of its members, there is no doubt but that "The Rush Library Company and Debating Society of Pennsylvania" will eminently keep pace, in the onward march of improvement, with the best of its contemporaries.

I shall now proceed to notice an institution which was originally composed of young men in their minority, and who were thereby excluded from the membership of those previously established. It was this exclusion, if I am correctly informed, which chiefly gave rise to the now flourishing—

"DEMOSTHENIAN INSTITUTE"[91]

This association was formed January 10, 1839, at the home of Mr. John P. Burr; at which time and place, the following named young men were elected its officers:- John E. Burr,[92] President; David Gordon,[93] Vice President; Benjamin Stanley,[94] Secretary; William Jennings,[95] Treasurer; G. W. Gibbons,[96] Librarian; Lewis B. Meade,[97] E. Parkinson,[98] Zedekiah J. Purnell,[99] A. F. Hutchinson,[100] and B. Hughes,[101] the Board of Managers.

In the course of inquiries respecting the condition and progress of the "Demosthenian Institute," I have been furnished by the President, Mr. Z. J. Purnell, and the Secretary, Mr. T. S. Crouch,[102] with a brief written history, containing particulars, and from it make the following extract:-

"Here [at the house of Mr. Burr] the meetings were held for nearly a year, during which time several addresses were delivered and numerous questions discussed;—but in the presence of the members only, owing to a general wish that the Institute should be made a preparatory school, until the members had gained sufficient confidence and experience, to fit them for an appearance before a public auditory. As the institute emerged for its obscurity, the number of its members rapidly augmented, till it became necessary to secure a more commodious place of meeting. Accordingly, *Salter's Hall* was engaged; and the first meeting of the institute there, took place December 18th, 1839."

From the period here mentioned, to the present, the "Demosthenian Institute" has continued its meetings at "Salters' Hall"; where, though but of recent origin, it has, in the words of its President, "made a great deal of noise"; though not, it is believed, without much good reason. The addresses and course of lectures during the past season (1840–41,) show great energy and enterprise on the part of its members, and also forcibly exhibit the abiding interest which actuates them for its continued prosperity and usefulness. It should also be borne in mind, that these lectures, are the work, chiefly, of the members of the Institute; and it is very doubtful whether many of them ever ventured before the public, for such purposes, previous to becoming connected therewith.

The debating department has likewise been a source of great improvement to the young men of the "Demosthenian Institute." In this respect they have not remained in the rear of their predecessors. They are still improving, and will, ere long, be undoubtedly enabled to cope with the oldest of those in existence before them.

The members of the Institute number, at the present time, forty-two, with a gradual increase. Its Library contains over one hundred volumes, comprising many valuable historical and scientific works.‡‡[103]

Having now endeavored in a few words, to point out the condition and chief sources of improvement afforded by the literary associations among the gentlemen, I shall proceed briefly to glance at those in existence among the ladies.[111] The first of these that comes under notice is—

"THE MINERVA LITERARY ASSOCIATION"[105]

This association was formed in "October, 1834." There were present at the formation thirty ladies, all of whom constituted themselves members.

---

‡‡Shortly after this notice of the "Demosthenian Institute" was written, I was shown the first number of a very neat little paper, entitled the "DEMOSTHENIAN SHIELD," which has been established by the enterprise of the young men who compose the Institute, and intended to be published weekly, from the time of its first appearance (June 29, 1841). Its subscription list numbered "over one thousand subscribers" before the first number was issued—and success, therefore, seems certain. Its typographical appearance is very neat; and, judging from No. 1, it promises dignity—which is very important—and ability in the editorial department. The whole is calculated to reflect great credit upon the *"Demosthenian Institute,"* and is a far better evidence of its onward march, in general improvement, than the brief notice we had taken of it, previous to the appearance of the "Shield." It is pleasing, therefore, to see what was said hereby so promptly corroborated.

With this good beginning, the daughters of the goddess whose name they bear, went into immediate active operation; and were soon permanently organized into a school for the encouragement and promotion of polite literature. The order of their exercises were [sic] readings and recitations of original and selected pieces, together with other appropriate matters. Many of the essays and other original productions, both in prose and poetry, have been deemed highly meritorious, and at different periods have appeared in the "poets' corner" or other department of some of the friendly publications.

"The Minerva Literary Association" is composed of a large number of members at the present. It still holds its meetings once each week as heretofore, to the improvement and edification of all who are connected with it.

There is also among the ladies—

"THE EDGEWORTH LITERARY ASSOCIATION," whose object and exercises are so identically the same as those of the "Minerva," that a repetition thereof seems unnecessary.[113] It is sufficient to say that the ladies consider them both worthy of being cherished, which is a sufficient guaranty [sic] that they are not wanting in importance and usefulness.§§

The last of the literary institutions which I shall here notice, is the nondescript—

"GILBERT LYCEUM."[107]

This institution is composed, as will be seen by the names of its founders, of individuals of both sexes, and is the first, and only one established by the colored classes of Philadelphia, for both literary and scientific pursuits. The name "Gilbert" is prefixed in honor to the gentleman of that name, who recommended its formation. It is of but recent origin,—instituted (as I am informed by Mr. R. Douglass, junr.) January 31, 1841. The persons who composed the meeting, that gave it a "local habitation and a name,"[108] were eleven in number— as follows:—Messrs. Robert Douglass, senr.,[109] Joseph Cassey,[110] Jacob C. White,[111] John C. Bowers,[112] Robert Purvis;[113] and Mrs. Amy M. Cassey,[114] Miss Sarah M. Douglass,[115] Mrs. Hetty Burr,[116] Mrs. Grace Douglass,[117] Mrs. Harriet Purvis,[118] and Miss Amelia Bogle.[119]

§§It may be due to the ladies, and therefore proper to state, that I should have very cheerfully taken a more extended notice of the "Minerva," and the "Edgeworth," had I not failed in attempts to procure such authentic information, in regard to them, as was requisite to a correct detailed understanding of their condition, &c. &c.

In consequence of the late period of its formation, the "Lyceum" has not been able to do much towards effecting the objects of its formation. It has, however, already had a course of scientific and other lectures delivered before it, which generally have been well attended. It is understood, also, that the "Lyceum" proposes the collection of a cabinet of minerals, curiosities, &c., as soon as its permanent organization will admit of so doing.

The number of members at the present time are about forty—exhibiting a great increase in a short period. If governed by a proper spirit, the "Gilbert Lyceum" may no doubt be made a source of improvement to its members, not to be surpassed by any literary institution previously in existence.

In addition to those already established, and in active operation, it is in contemplation with a number of young men, to form a new literary association, the object of which will be to encourage and promote among the colored classes, literature, science and the arts; and to embody all the good features of those now in existence, while it will be the aim to avoid such as have proved disadvantageous. The plan of this contemplated institution, as drawn up and exhibited to me by Mr. *James Needham*,[120] is of the most liberal and enlightened character; and seems well calculated to become universally popular, with all the lovers and seekers of knowledge in the colored community. It proposes that "not only the learned, but the unlearned—the old and the young—male and female—without any other qualification than a good character, should become members"; and that frequent meetings should be held, and have such a varied detail of exercises presented at each, as might be found best calculated to call into exercise the degree of education and ability of each member. It is further proposed to have "lectures delivered, by competent persons, at stated periods;—to encourage men of color to become professors in particular branches of science;—to establish a library, collect a cabinet of minerals, and procure philosophical apparatus," as soon as its permanent organization might allow of so doing. This seems to be in every way plausible and practicable; and if carried out in the spirit of the outline here given, could not possibly fail to be of great advantage, to such as might connect themselves therewith.

There are some errors that have become matters of course with the older associations, which it would be well for the one now in contemplation, studiously to guard against. The ease and facility with which persons applying have succeeded in getting themselves voted to the membership, has had the effect to incorporate a large number of young men who take little, or no interest whatever, in the prosperity and success of the institution, after they have once got their names enrolled as members. They seldom appear at the stated meetings for any purpose; and many of them never appear for the purpose of complying with the periodical assessment!

This class of self-constituted *honorary members* should, if possible, be kept out; for no society can for any length of time withstand the evil influence that is generated by their conduct. A heavy, immoveable weight, they totally destroy the usefulness of the association whose constitution they have subscribed to support, and dishearten those who are sensible of the obligation, and earnestly desire to acquit themselves accordingly. All such, be it repeated, should be steadily shunned.

These short notices of the principal literary institutions, though not so full and comprehensive as was originally contemplated, will be sufficient to show that the colored classes are not at all behind the age, in their efforts to raise the standard of education and polite literature, to a much greater height among themselves than they have yet been enabled to do. Heretofore they have had to encounter innumerable discouragements, in almost every ennobling undertaking; but these there is every reason to believe, will be withdrawn, in proportion as the former shall demonstrate by their acts, the gross injustice of their infliction. This, it is contended, they have long ago done—in fact they *never deserved* the tyrannical prejudices they are constantly exposed to—but the great community have closed their eyes to this view of the case, and seem resolved that nothing short of a "miraculous working of their own salvation"[121] shall ever secure to them those equitable and just considerations which are enjoyed by all others of a different descent. And even this the people of color are equal to, if they will only give a right direction to the elements which they have among themselves. It becomes them, of all others, to be *united* in all efforts for their general improvement; and whether they will hereafter seek to banish the unworthy causes upon which their present disunion is founded,—a disunion which renders them, as a body, powerless for good in any common cause, and so furnishes rich food for prejudice,—time will make known. There is, unquestionably, much to be done, and *the sooner it is done*, the sooner will they secure that estimation, from those who now oppress them, which is undoubtedly the aim of all, and without which they can never hope for entire enfranchisement, or live in quiet, undisturbed possession of their civil liberty. Let them, then, take a lesson from the past; and let the future be devoted to amendment.

NOTES

1. Willson obviously had in mind such works as Harriet Martineau's *Society in America* (1837) and *Retrospect of Western Travel* (1838), Frederick Marryat's *A Diary in America* (1839), and Frances Trollope's infamous but immensely readable *Domestic Manners of the Americans* (1832). Travelers to the United States, particularly those from Britain, had established a tradition of writing very unflattering accounts of conditions in the "new republic." Ironically, their works often sold well in America, either because of their literary merit or because of Americans' curiosity to see what foreigners thought of them. The year after *Sketches of the Higher Classes* appeared, Charles Dickens contributed to the genre with his highly critical *American Notes*.

2. Othello speaks these words in the final act of Shakespeare's *Othello, The Moor of Venice* (act 5, scene 2, lines 342–43):
   Speak of me as I am. Nothing extenuate,
   Nor set aught down in malice.

3. Proverbs 30:8: "Remove far from me vanity and lies; give me neither poverty nor riches; feed me with food convenient for me."

4. The Philadelphia community did have at least one enthusiastic amateur scientist. Robert Bridges Forten (1813–1864), the son of wealthy sailmaker James Forten, was an avid astronomer. He made a nine-foot-long telescope, and ground and set the lenses himself. The telescope was put on display at the Franklin Institute, and Forten used it to give astronomy classes at the school run by his friend, AME cleric Daniel Alexander Payne, who was himself a keen naturalist. Payne, *Recollections of Seventy Years* (Nashville: AME Sunday School Union, 1888; reprint, New York: Arno Press, 1968), 51. *CA,* April 3, 1841.

5. Led by such divines as William Ellery Channing and Hosea Ballou, the Universalists diverged from the Congregationalists in the early nineteenth century. They preached that good would ultimately triumph over evil, that Christ's death had brought salvation to all, and that no one would face eternal damnation.

6. In 1838 the community had sixteen churches: one Episcopal, one Lutheran, eight Methodist, two Presbyterian, and four Baptist. Many of the churches were clustered in the South Street corridor. The two oldest were St. Thomas's African Episcopal, on Fifth and Adelphi, and "Mother" Bethel AME, on South Sixth between Lombard and Pine. Both had been founded in the 1790s. Union Baptist and Union Methodist were neighbors, on Little Pine between Sixth and Seventh. Nearby were AME Wesley (on Hurst, between Fifth and Sixth), Wesley Methodist (on Lombard between Fifth and Sixth), and Second African Presbyterian (on St. Mary's Street between Sixth and Seventh). First African Presbyterian was on South Seventh, near Shippen, in Southwark, and two more, Union AME and Zoar Methodist Episcopal, were in the Northern Liberties. First African Baptist was relatively isolated on Pearl and Eleventh. The churches enjoyed varying degrees of autonomy. Only the AME congregations belonged to an African-American parent body. Some African-American churchgoers chose not affiliate with any of the black congregations. They attended predominantly white churches. As Willson notes, there was no black Catholic congregation. However, in 1838 some 3 percent of the black population was Catholic.

Charters of Incorporation, Book 2, 180, 245; Book 3, 442; Book 4, 78, 228; Book 6, 171; Book 7, 89, 116; Book 8, 259, PSA. *JM* 3 (July 1813), 21–22. Pennsylvania Abolition Society, *The Present State and Condition of the Free People of Color in the City of Philadelphia, and Adjoining Districts* (Philadelphia: Merrihew and Gunn, 1838), 32; William W. Catto, *A Semi-Centenary Discourse Delivered in the First African Presbyterian Church, Philadelphia, on the Fourth Sabbath of May, 1857* (Philadelphia: Joseph M. Wilson, 1857), 105–11; Emma J. Lapsanksy, " 'Since They Got Those Separate Churches': Afro-Americans and Racism in Jacksonian Philadelphia," *AQ* 32 (Spring 1980), 54–78.

7. The earliest black benevolent society in Philadelphia of which there is any record was the all-male Free African Society, established in 1787. It was soon joined by the African Friendly Society of St. Thomas (1795) and the Female Benevolent Society of St. Thomas (1796). Over the years the number of mutual relief societies grew steadily. Most churches had at least two, one for women and another for men. Some, like St. Thomas's, had several, divided not just according to gender but also by age. Various occupations had their own organizations. African-American coachmen, for instance, established a relief society, as did porters. In 1831 the community had forty-four beneficial societies. By 1838 the number had risen to eighty. All the societies were run in essentially the same way. Each week or each month members paid a set amount into a common fund. In the event of misfortune—the loss of employment, an illness that prevented a member from working, a death in the household—the officers of the society would visit the member's family and determine first whether there was a valid claim on the common fund, and second, how much money should be appropriated. By 1841 more than fifty societies had gone to the effort and expense of seeking incorporation—an assertion that their members were "citizens of the Commonwealth." Their charters are preserved in the Pennsylvania State Archives. *HR*, March 12, 1831. PAS, *Present State and Condition;* "Notes on Beneficial Societies, 1828–1838," PAS Manuscripts, HSP. William Douglass, *Annals of the First African Church in the United States of America, Now Styled the African Episcopal Church of St. Thomas* (Philadelphia: King and Baird, 1862), 15–47. *JM* 3 (July 1813), 22.

8. The women had a Dorcas Society to supply clothing to the needy. Founded in 1830, it had seventy-two members by 1838. Its president was Elizabeth Butler, wife of affluent barber Thomas Butler (see below), and its secretary was Amelia Bogle (note 119). Although not admitted as members, the women also played an important role in promoting the work of the all-male Association for Moral and Mental Improvement (note 13). One goal of that organization was to provide poor black children with clothing and shoes so they could attend school. Willson wisely did not refer to another kind of "out-doors benevolence" sponsored by the women in the community, the collecting of money and clothing for fugitive slaves. "Notes on Beneficial Societies, 1828–1838," PAS MSS, HSP. *NASS,* May 4, 1843. *NECAUL,* September 7, 1837. *PF,* July 5, 1838; March 12, 1840; November 5, 1840.

9. When the Pennsylvania Abolition Society surveyed Philadelphia's black community in 1838 its officers counted ten schools being operated by African-American teachers, eight by women and two by men. Several might have closed by the time Willson was writing, but at least two more had opened, one run by Amelia Bogle (note 119) and another by Daniel Alexander Payne. Some African-American parents expressed dissatisfaction with the treatment their children received in the segregated

public schools and preferred, if they could afford it, to send them to a private school. *JM* 3 (July 1813), 2–3, 18–19. PAS, *Present State and Condition,* 29. *Minutes of Proceedings at the Council of the Philadelphia Association for the Moral and Mental Improvement of the People of Color, June 5th–9th, 1837* (Philadelphia: Merrihew and Gunn, 1837), 9–10. *CA,* April 3, 1841; Harry C. Silcox, "Delay and Neglect: Negro Education in Antebellum Philadelphia, 1800–1860," *PMHB* 97 (Oct. 1973), 444–64.

10. For the full report, see *Minutes and Proceedings of the First Annual Meeting of the American Moral Reform Society, Held at Philadelphia from the 14th to the 19th of August, 1837* (Philadelphia: Merrihew and Gunn, 1837), in Dorothy Porter, ed., *Early Negro Writing, 1760–1837* (Boston: Beacon Press, 1971), 212–13. In fact, the AMRS was following in the footsteps of the national conventions, which had called for the compiling of statistics on the various free black communities in the North, the Midwest, and the Upper South. See *Minutes and Proceedings of the Third Annual Convention, for the Improvement of the Free People of Colour in these United States, Held by Adjournments in the City of Philadelphia, from the 3d to the 13th of June Inclusive, 1833* (New York: By Order of the Convention, 1833), 23–24, 25; *Minutes of the Fourth Annual Convention, for the Improvement of the Free People of Colour, in the United States, Held by Adjournments in the Asbury Church, New York, from the 2d to the 13th of June Inclusive, 1834* (New York: By Order of the Convention, 1834), 25; *Minutes of the Fifth Annual Convention for the Improvement of the Free People of Color in the United States, Held by Adjournments, in the Wesley Church, Philadelphia, from the First to the Fifth of June, Inclusive, 1835* (Philadelphia: William P. Gibbons, 1835), 5.

11. Reputed to be the son of Aaron Burr and his Haitian-born governess, New Jersey native John P. Burr (b. 1792) was one of the most active individuals in the Philadelphia community. In business as a hairdresser by 1818, he did moderately well but never achieved the status of a homeowner. However, that seemed in no way to diminish his standing. His activities ranged from promoting emigration to Haiti to serving as agent for the *Liberator,* protesting disfranchisement, sheltering fugitive slaves, and aiding those charged with treason in the infamous Christiana Riot of 1851. A stalwart of the American Moral Reform Society, he helped publish its journal, the *National Reformer.* He was involved in the national convention movement of the early 1830s and in the organization of the Pennsylvania Anti-Slavery Society. Burr was also an officer of two community institutions, the Mechanics' Enterprise Hall and the Moral Reform Retreat, a refuge for black alcoholics. His commitment to the antislavery struggle was shared by his wife, Hetty, his daughter, J. Matilda, and his sons, John E. and David. *CA,* June 3, 1837; August 5, 1837; March 22, 1838; September 8, 1838; September 15, 1838; September 22, 1838; February 2, 1839; November 2, 1839; June 13, 1840; July 25, 1840; August 24, 1841; July 3, 1841. *FDP,* November 13, 1851. *Lib,* February 6, 1836; July 2, 1836. *NECAUL,* October 29, 1836. *PF,* August 10, 1837; September 6, 1838; April 16, 1840; February 1, 1844; August 14, 1845. *NR,* September 1838; October 1838; January 1839; February 1839; March 1839; April 1839; September 1839; November 1839. *NS,* November 10, 1848; September 7, 1849. *VF,* January 15, 1852. Haytien Emigration Society of Philadelphia, *Information for the Free People of Colour, Who Are Inclined to Emigrate to Hayti* (Philadelphia: J. H. Cunningham, 1825). Robert Purvis, *Appeal of Forty Thousand Citizens, Threatened with Disfranchisement, To the People of Pennsylvania* (Philadelphia: Merrihew and Gunn, 1838), 2. *AMRS Convention . . . 1837,* in Porter, ed., *Early Negro Writing,*

224. Pennsylvania Abolition Society, *Register of the Trades of the Colored People in the City of Philadelphia and Districts* (Philadelphia: Merrihew and Gunn, 1838). PAS census (1838); Friends' census (1847). U.S. census, Philadelphia (1830), Dock Ward, 132; (1840), Dock Ward, 52; (1850), Moyamensing, Ward 2, 243; (1860), Philadelphia, Ward 7, 259. Philadelphia directories, 1818–22, 1825, 1828–48. C. Peter Ripley et al., *Black Abolitionist Papers* (Chapel Hill: University of North Carolina Press, 1991), vol. 3, 196n.

12. From Epistle IV of Alexander Pope's "An Essay on Man":
Order is Heav'n's first law; and this confest,
Some are, and must be, greater than the rest,
More rich, more wise; but who infers from thence
That such are happier, shocks all common sense.

13. Various organizations existed within the African-American community dedicated to ensuring that children received a good education. In 1818, for instance, a group of well-to-do black men founded the Pennsylvania Augustine Society to establish "a Seminary, in which children of colour shall be taught all the useful and scientific branches of education." There were a number of other societies. Some, like the Rush Education Society, sought to promote education generally. Others, like the society organized at Mother Bethel, targeted a specific group. The Bethel Education Society offered assistance to young men contemplating a career in the ministry. The ministers and prominent laymen who founded the Philadelphia Association for Moral and Mental Improvement in 1837 proposed a twofold approach to the issue of education. They would visit parents to emphasize the importance of school attendance, and they would try to provide shoes and clothing for children whose families wanted to send them to school but were too poor to outfit them properly. *Constitution of the Augustine Society,* Black Abolitionist Papers microfilm (New York: Microfilm Corporation of America, 1981–83). *Rush Education Society Constitution* (n.p., n.d.). *Philadelphia Association for Moral and Mental Improvement.* Committee to Improve the Condition of the African Race, PAS MSS, HSP. *FJ,* September 28, 1827; October 5, 1827. *PF,* November 17, 1841.

14. From "The Pleasures of Imagination" (book 1, line 481) by the English poet Mark Akenside (1721–1770).

15. It is not clear whether Willson was advocating women appearing in public as speakers (one of the most controversial issues of his day) or whether he believed they should debate only within their own societies.

16. In addition to Robert Douglass Jr., whose career is discussed below, the community boasted several talented artists. Sarah Mapps Douglass, Robert's sister (note 115), was an accomplished painter. The artistic career of their brother, William Penn Douglass, was cut short by his death at age twenty-five in 1839. A cousin, David Bustill Bowser, distinguished himself as a portrait painter. Alfred Cassey, the son of Joseph and Amy Cassey (see below), did ornamental work as a gilder, carver, and painter. A neighbor, James Forten Jr., earned his living as a sailmaker, but the numerous examples of his work in the albums in the Stevens-Cogdell, Saunders-Venning Papers at the Library Company of Philadelphia indicate that he too was a gifted artist.

17. As Willson would have been the first to admit, ability cut across denominational lines. Over the years Philadelphia, with one of the largest free black communities and a network of churches, attracted some of the most talented and best educated

black ministers in the United States. There was Joseph M. Corr, a gifted AME minister who died tragically young in 1835. Then there were the members of the Gloucester dynasty. Ex-slave John Sr. (ca. 1776–1822) was the pastor of the first black Presbyterian congregation in the city. His eldest son, Jeremiah (1798–1828), a graduate of the school of the Presbyterian Synod of New York and New Jersey, served as pastor of the Second African Presbyterian Church until his untimely death from tuberculosis. Jeremiah's brother, John Jr. (1794–1831), was also noted for his piety and his eloquence. The author of *Sketches of the Higher Classes* would not have known John Sr. and his two eldest sons, who died before the Willsons relocated to Philadelphia, but he probably met another Gloucester, Stephen (1802–1850), who occupied the pulpit at Second Presbyterian, and possibly Stephen's brother, James, minister of a Presbyterian church in New York.

Willson would have heard about another young churchman who had fallen victim to consumption. Russell Parrott (1791–1824) had been a candidate for holy orders at St. Thomas's, the church Willson attended. A printer by trade like Willson, he was exceptionally well read and a forceful preacher, as his surviving sermons indicate. Willson may have met Andrew Harris, a graduate of the University of Vermont. Harris came to Philadelphia in 1839 to be a licentiate at the Second African Presbyterian Church. Ordained by the white Presbytery in the spring of 1841, he died later that same year. Then there was South Carolina emigré Daniel Alexander Payne, a man of very considerable scholarly attainments and a future bishop of the AME Church—and someone whose physical health was rather better than that of so many of his colleagues. In short, the pulpits of many of Philadelphia's black churches were graced by men of considerable learning and great personal piety. Edward Dorr Griffin, *A Plea for Africa: A Sermon Preached October 26, 1817, In the First Presbyterian Church in the City of New York, Before the Synod of New York and New Jersey, at the Request of the Board of Directors of the African School Established by the Synod* (New York: Gould, 1817), 68–69; Catto, *Semi-Centenary Discourse;* Jeremiah Gloucester, *An Oration, Delivered on January 1, 1823. In Bethel Church: On the Abolition of the Slave Trade* (Philadelphia: John Young, 1823); John Gloucester Jr., *A Sermon, Delivered in the First African Presbyterian Church in Philadelphia, on the 1st of January, 1830, Before the Different Coloured Societies of Philadelphia* (Philadelphia, 1830); Russell Parrott, *An Oration on the Abolition of the Slave Trade, Delivered on the First of January, 1812, at the African Church of St. Thomas, Philadelphia* (Philadelphia: James Maxwell for the Different Societies, 1812); *An Oration on the Abolition of the Slave Trade, Delivered on the First of January, 1814* (Philadelphia: Thomas T. Stiles, 1814), in Porter, ed., *Early Negro Writing; An Address on the Abolition of the Slave Trade, Delivered Before the Different African Benevolent Societies, on the 1st of January, 1816* (Philadelphia: T. S. Manning, 1816); *CA,* May 8, 1841; *Lib,* December 21, 1841.

18. Baltimore native William Douglass (1805–1862) was, as Willson indicates, a man of considerable education. Tutored by the black emigrationist Daniel Coker, he was proficient in Latin, Greek and Hebrew. Initially ordained an AME minister, he pastored a church in Baltimore for several years. He became a prominent member of that city's African-American community, speaking out with other leaders like William Watkins on such issues as slavery and African colonization. In the early 1830s he left the AME Church and moved to Philadelphia in response to a call from the vestry to become the minister of St. Thomas's African Episcopal Church. He was

ordained to the priesthood on February 14, 1836 by the venerable Bishop Henry Onderdonk. In Philadelphia he published a volume of his sermons and a carefully researched history of his church. Historians have reason to be grateful to Douglass. In his *Annals of St. Thomas* he preserved many documents that were subsequently lost or destroyed. An accomplished public speaker, Douglass was much in demand to address community gatherings. Somewhat conservative in his attitudes, and alive to the damage that had been caused to other churches by anti-abolition mobs, he refused to allow antislavery advocates to hold meetings at St. Thomas's. For this he was attacked by Frederick Douglass, who used the *North Star* to condemn the minister as a tool of pro-slavery forces. In an able defense of his actions, Reverend Douglass succeeded in refuting the editor's charges. In 1852 William Douglass traveled to England on the mission circuit and was apparently well received.

The death of his first wife, Elizabeth, daughter of Baltimore businessman Hezekiah Grice, in 1853 left him to raise twelve children, ranging in age from twenty-one-year-old Martha Ann to newborn Joseph, on his own. He promptly proposed marriage to teacher Sarah Mapps Douglass (note 115). She was persuaded to accept him by her friend, white abolitionist Sarah Grimké. The marriage proved an unhappy one, at least for Sarah. As for Reverend Douglass, the fact that he had secured a stepmother for his children left him free to continue serving his congregation and working to advance the interests of the African-American community. William Douglass, *A Discourse Commemorative of the Rt. Rev. William White, Delivered in St. Thomas's Church, Philadelphia, August 18, 1836* (Philadelphia: William Stavely, 1836); *Sermons Preached in the African Protestant Episcopal Church of St. Thomas, Philadelphia* (Philadelphia: King and Baird, 1854); *Annals of St. Thomas. AAM*, July 23, 1859. *CA*, December 2, 1837; December 9, 1837; August 18, 1838; September 15, 1838; September 4, 1841. *CR*, February 16, 1861; March 2, 1861; January 11, 1862. *FDP*, April 7, 1854; December 1, 1854. *NECAUL*, October 15, 1836. *NR*, October 1838. *NS*, January 21, 1848; March 17, 1848; October 19, 1848; October 27, 1848; November 10, 1848; November 24, 1848; December 8, 1848; December 29, 1848; June 8, 1849; June 15, 1849. *PA*, June 28, 1862. *PF*, February 15, 1838; October 10, 1839. *ProvF*, August 22, 1855. *Third Annual Convention of the Free People of Colour*, 4. *Proceedings of the Colored National Convention, Held in Franklin Hall, Sixth Street Below Arch, Philadelphia, October 16th, 17th and 18th, 1855* (Salem, N.J.: By Order of the Convention, 1856), 7. William Wells Brown, *The Black Man, His Antecedents, His Genius, and His Achievements*, 2nd ed. (New York: Thomas Hamilton, 1863), 271–72. *Proceedings of the 51st Convention of the Protestant Episcopal Church in the State of Pennsylvania* (Philadelphia: By Order of the Convention, 1835), 19. *Proceedings of the 52nd Convention of the Protestant Episcopal Church in the State of Pennsylvania* (Philadelphia: By Order of the Convention, 1836), 20. George Combe, *Notes on the United States of North America, during a Phrenological Visit in 1838-9-40* (Philadelphia: Carey and Hart, 1841), vol. 1, 63. Philadelphia Board of Health Records. PAS census (1838); Friends' census (1847). U.S. census (1830) Baltimore, 319; (1840), Philadelphia, Pine Ward, 300; (1850), South Mulberry Ward, 252; (1860), Ward 5, 563. Philadelphia directories, 1837–41.

19. As the career of New Yorker James McCune Smith demonstrates, it was no easy matter for a man of color to secure a formal medical training in the United States. Smith was eventually obliged to go to Scotland to earn his medical degree. It was one of the goals of delegates to the national convention of 1835 to promote

medical instruction. A committee was appointed "to inquire into the expediency of devising ways and means by which colored students of medicine may obtain a regular and legal diploma." Philadelphia's African-American community did not secure the services of a university-trained medical doctor until the arrival of David J. Peck in 1847—and he soon moved on. However, as Willson notes, the community had many healers of different sorts, from bleeders to dentists, from midwives to phrenologists, from "cancer doctors" to practitioners of various forms of traditional medicine. As for their patients, they were drawn from many of Philadelphia's different ethnic groups.

James J. G. Bias, a former slave, was a cupper, a bleeder, and a dentist. His wife, Eliza, was his medical assistant. Bias also practiced phrenology and wrote a treatise on the subject. Friend and neighbor Peter Gardiner (note 60) was a "Thompsonian Practitioner" or "botanic" physician. Belfast Burton (note 47), another former slave, was accorded the title "Doctor" in the city directories. Samuel Wilson, a West African brought to Philadelphia as a slave, supported himself as a free man by his skill as a "cancer doctor." Barber Thomas Butler was a bleeder, as were cabinetmaker Charles Nash and shoemaker John Purdy. His account books in the Leon Gardiner Collection at the Historical Society of Pennsylvania show that barber, bleeder, and dentist Jacob C. White Sr. (note 111) had a clientele that included not only African Americans but many German and Irish immigrants. *Minutes of the Fifth Annual Convention for the Improvement of the Free People of Color* (1835), 5, 9. PAS, *Register of Trades*. PAS census (1838). Jacob C. White Sr. Account Books, Leon Gardiner Collection, Box 12B, and AMS 361, HSP. Philadelphia directory, 1811. David W. Blight, "In Search of Learning, Liberty, and Self-Definition: James McCune Smith and the Ordeal of the Antebellum Black Intellectual," AANYLH 9 (July 1985), 7–25.

20. Willson is referring to Robert Douglass Jr. (1809–1887), a gifted painter who studied art in the United States and in England and who traveled extensively in Europe and the Caribbean. Douglass's career illustrates clearly the trials and tribulations of an African American who sought to distinguish himself in the artistic and intellectual realms.

The son of affluent barber Robert Douglass Sr. (note 109) and Grace Bustill Douglass (note 117), Robert Douglass Jr. received his early education in Philadelphia at a school established by his mother and another wealthy member of the African-American community, sailmaker James Forten. In the early 1830s he set up in business as a sign-painter and graphic artist, receiving commissions from, among others, tavern-owners who wanted ornate painted signs for their establishments. Douglass could tackle just about any subject, but it was in portraits, like the fine painting of Napoleon for the tavern just across the street from his studio on Front and Arch, that he excelled.

The majority of white Philadelphians were not receptive to the idea of a black man trying to gain recognition as an artist. Douglass was turned away from a viewing at Independence Hall and informed that he would only be admitted to another exhibition when it was closed to white visitors. In 1837, in a bid to escape such proscription, he traveled to Haiti with two white abolitionists. He spent eighteen months there, touring the country, painting, and becoming proficient in Spanish and French. His glowing reports to friends and family on life in the independent black republic were reprinted in the Philadelphia press and in abolitionist newspapers.

One white Philadelphian who did befriend Douglass, tutor him and help him to further his career was artist Thomas Sully. In 1839, when Douglass decided to travel to England to study, Sully gave him a letter of introduction to his professional colleagues there. Douglass received other letters from friends in the antislavery movement, among them Sarah and Angelina Grimké and Lucretia Mott. Grateful though he was for their help, he was angry that he could not travel abroad as an American citizen. He was refused a passport on the grounds of his race.

Douglass found London very much to his liking. No one objected to his presence at lectures or exhibitions. He was admitted without hindrance to the British Museum, Saville House and the National Gallery, and enjoyed the companionship of fellow artists. In fact, so frank was he in contrasting his treatment in England to that he received in his native Philadelphia that neither the *United States Gazette* nor the *Pennsylvanian* would print his letters.

Douglass returned to Philadelphia early in 1841. To his skill as a painter he had added other accomplishments. He had mastered daguerreotyping and he also offered his services as a teacher of languages and music. Deeply committed to the antislavery cause, like his parents and his sister, Sarah (note 115), he put his artistic talents to the service of that cause, taking daguerreotypes of prominent abolitionists, like Abby Kelley Foster and the Motts, and lending examples of his work for display at antislavery events. He also resumed his involvement in the intellectual life of Philadelphia's African-American community.

However, Philadelphia was no more hospitable to a black artist in the 1840s than it had been a decade earlier. In 1848 Douglass eagerly accepted a commission to paint views of mission stations in Jamaica. He spent several months traveling about the island before reluctantly concluding that it was "economically inexpedient to stay long." He was back in Philadelphia by 1850, but growing disenchantment with prospects for men and women of color in the United States prompted him to consider emigration. In 1858 he volunteered to join African-American explorer Martin R. Delany's Niger Valley expedition as official artist. However, the venture ran into financial problems and Douglass was dropped from the team. The rest of his life was spent in Philadelphia where he struggled to make a living as an artist. Bustill-Mossell Family Papers, Box 1, folder 41, University of Pennsylvania Archives. *CA*, March 3, 1838; June 16, 1838; July 27, 1839. *GUE*, February 1833. *Morning Journal* (Kingston, Jamaica), December 20, 1847; October 28, 1848. *NASS*, January 29, 1846; April 20, 1848. *NS*, June 2, 1848; July 6, 1849; August 24, 1849. *PF*, June 11, 1840; March 31, 1841; March 14, 1844. American Anti-Slavery Society, *Fourth Annual Report* (1837), 18. *Proceedings of the Colored National Convention . . . 1855*, 7. Sarah Grimké to Elizabeth Pease, August 25, 1839, in Gilbert H. Barnes and Dwight L. Dumond, eds., *Letters of Theodore Dwight Weld, Angelina Grimké Weld, and Sarah Grimké, 1822–1844* (New York: D. Appleton-Century, 1934), 792. PAS, *Register of Trades*. Martin R. Delany, *The Condition, Elevation, Emigration, and Destiny of the Colored People of the United States* (Philadelphia: The Author, 1852; reprint, New York: Arno Press, 1968), 117. Ripley et al., *Black Abolitionist Papers*, vol. 1, 77n. Frederick B. Tolles, ed., *Slavery and the "Woman Question"—Lucretia Mott's Diary of Her Visit to Great Britain to Attend the World's Anti-Slavery Convention of 1840* (Haverford, Pa.: Friends' Historical Association, 1952), 26, 34, 49. James de T. Abajian, comp., *Blacks in Selected Newspapers, Censuses and Other Sources: An Index to Names and Subjects. A Supplement* (Boston: G. K. Hall, 1985), vol. 1, 312. Cyril E. Griffith, *The African Dream: Martin R. Delany and the Emergence of Pan-African Thought*

(University Park: Penn State University Press, 1975), 35, 36. U.S. census, Philadelphia (1830), Chestnut Ward, 485; (1850) High Street Ward, 176; (1870) Ward 4, dist. 14, 314. Philadelphia directories, 1833, 1835–37, 1842.

21. This is from a poem entitled "Prejudice Reproved" by Lydia Sigourney (1791–1865), a prolific and immensely popular writer of sentimental verse. The poem was set to music and sung at antislavery meetings. Willson was not the only member of his circle struck by its sentiments. Mary Virginia Wood, an acquaintance of the Willson family, copied it into her album. The poem reads, in part:

>God gave to Afric's sons
>A brow of sable dye,
>And spread the country of their birth
>Beneath a burning sky . . .
>. . . To me, He gave a form
>Of fairer, whiter clay,
>But am I therefore, in His sight,
>Respected more than they? . . .
>. . . Not by the tinted cheek
>That fades away so fast,
>But by the color of the soul
>We shall be judged at last.

Vicki L. Eaklor, comp., *American Anti-Slavery Songs: A Collection and Analysis* (Westport, Conn. : Greenwood, 1988), 26–27. Album of Mary Virginia Wood, Francis J. Grimké Papers, Moorland-Spingarn Research Center, Howard University.

22. This is a variation on line 203, Epistle IV, of Alexander Pope's "An Essay on Man," which reads: "Worth makes the man, and the want of it, the fellow."

23. I have been unable to find the source of this quotation.

24. Criticism or censure.

25. I have been unable to identify this quotation.

26. Former, erstwhile (French).

27. This is a garbled version of Katherine's final speech from Shakespeare's *The Taming of the Shrew* (act 5, scene 2, lines 142–46):

>. . . dart not scornful glances from those eyes
>To wound thy lord, thy king, thy governor.
>It blots thy beauty as frosts do bite the meads,
>Confounds thy fame as whirlwinds shake fair buds,
>And in no sense is meet or amiable.

28. Proverbs 27:5–6: "Open rebuke is better than secret love. Faithful are the wounds of a friend; but the kisses of an enemy are deceitful."

29. A type of heavy leather work shoe that reached to the ankle.

30. Joshua 9:21: "And the princes said unto them, 'Let them live; but let them be hewers of wood and drawers of water unto all the congregation; as the princes had promised them.' "

31. These words are spoken by Lear in Shakespeare's *King Lear*, act 3, scene 2, lines 59–60.

32. On the antebellum parlor, its function and its furnishings, see Jack Larkin, *The Reshaping of Everyday Life, 1790–1840* (New York: Harper and Row, 1988), 125–26; John F. Kasson, *Rudeness and Civility: Manners in Nineteenth-Century Urban America* (New York: Hill and Wang, 1990), 174–80; and Kenneth L. Ames,

Death in the Dining Room, and Other Tales of Victorian Culture (Philadelphia: Temple University Press, 1992), 190–95.

33. Informally (French).

34. If not quite as rigid as that which pertained in England, an increasingly complex code of "calling" had developed in American cities among the upper and middle classes by the time Willson was writing. Who waited upon whom, whether or when a call was returned, and where a caller was received (in the hall in the case of social inferiors, or in the parlor in the case of persons of equal or superior rank) were all important considerations. On the etiquette of calling, see Ames, *Death in the Dining Room*, 35–42, and Daniel Pool, *What Jane Austen Ate and Charles Dickens Knew: From Fox Hunting to Whist—The Facts of Daily Life in 19th-Century England* (New York: Simon and Schuster, 1993), 66–69.

35. Venturing outside their homes, on business, to make social calls, or to participate in the many diversions a city like Philadelphia had to offer could be risky for members of the "higher classes of colored society." As Sarah Louisa Forten, one of the daughters of wealthy sailmaker James Forten, explained to abolitionist Angelina Grimké: "(W)e never travel far from home and seldom go into public places unless quite sure that admission is free to all; therefore, we meet with none of those mortifications which might otherwise ensue." She could have added that it was not just a wish to avoid "mortifications" that kept her and her family close to home. During the 1830s and 1840s Philadelphia's black community experienced five major race riots, and numerous acts of casual violence. In 1834 Sarah's younger brother was attacked in the street. On another occasion the Forten home was threatened. Sarah L. Forten to Angelina Grimké, April 15, 1837, in *Weld-Grimké Letters*, 381. Julie Winch, *Philadelphia's Black Elite: Activism, Accommodation, and the Struggle for Autonomy, 1787–1848* (Philadelphia: Temple University Press, 1988), 142–51. Edward S. Abdy, *Journal of a Residence and Tour in the United States of North America, from April 1833, to October 1834* (London: John Murray, 1835; reprint, New York: Negro Universities Press, 1969), vol. 3, 320. Lapsanksy, " 'Since They Got Those Separate Churches,' " 54–78.

36. Willson is referring to the custom of presenting dinner guests with a first and second service. The first service consisted of soup, fish, meat, vegetables, and possibly a fowl. After a brief respite, there would be a second service—a different kind of meat and vegetables, followed by puddings and various desserts. There might even be a third service, consisting of fruits and nuts. On fashionable dining in the antebellum era, see Kasson, *Rudeness and Civility*, 204–6.

37. Several of those in Willson's "higher classes" ran boardinghouses. In the advertisements they placed in such journals as the *Liberator* they emphasized that they catered only to "genteel" persons, lest it be thought they were maintaining houses of ill repute. Peter and Serena Gardiner (note 60) operated a boardinghouse on Powell Street, and later on Elizabeth Street, for "respectable persons of COLOR." Mrs. E. Johnson was the proprietor of a boardinghouse at 150 Spruce. An ex-slave who did well in Philadelphia as a carpenter and house-builder, James Gibbons, took in boarders at 163 Pine. In 1835 Amelia Shadd described her boardinghouse at 178 Pine as very convenient for gentlemen coming to the city to attend the national convention. After all, regardless of their wealth and degree of refinement, African-American travelers could not be sure of getting a room in any of Philadelphia's hotels. *Lib*, July 23, 1831; July 6, 1833; August 16, 1834; April 25, 1835; May 23, 1835.

38. I have been unable to discover what the "secrets papers" were and what kind of mottoes they contained. Judging by the context, reading and exchanging mottoes was a decorous form of entertainment and one considered appropriate for mixed company.

39. On the strict observance of temperance by black Philadelphians, see Donald Yacovone, "The Transformation of the Black Temperance Movement, 1827–1854: An Interpretation," *JER* 8 (Fall 1988), 281–97; Winch, *Philadelphia's Black Elite*, 101, 106, 117, 148–50; Jane H. Pease and William H. Pease, *They Who Would Be Free: Blacks' Search for Freedom, 1830–1861* (New York: Atheneum, 1974), 56–57, 121, 124–26. Delegates to the national conventions regularly condemned the consumption of alcohol and advocated total abstinence. In Philadelphia the black churches were at the forefront of the temperance movement. Bethel had its own temperance society, while ministers and prominent laymen at the other churches endeavored to convince their congregations of the wisdom of avoiding alcohol. Mutual benefit societies invariably excluded drunkards and investigated claims for relief to determine whether alcohol had contributed to an individual's illness or incapacity. Ironically, a year after the publication of Willson's book, when Yacovone estimates (296) there were ten active black temperance societies in Philadelphia, the success of the African-American community's temperance crusade precipitated a race riot. The crusade, which was aimed at black and white Philadelphians alike, was so effective it cut into the profits of rum-sellers and bar-owners. They banded together and incited a mob to attack black temperance marchers. In the aftermath of the riot a black temperance hall in Moyamensing was ordered to be demolished as a "public nuisance" on the grounds that it might be attacked and that would endanger nearby white-owned property!

40. I have been unable to identify this quotation.

41. The Roman god of wine.

42. Leon Litwack estimates that on the eve of the Civil War only 6 percent of Northern free blacks lived in states where they could vote on the same basis as whites. Some states, like New York, imposed property qualifications on black voters but not on whites. In other states, like Pennsylvania, black men could not vote at all by the time Willson was writing. In fact, the situation in Pennsylvania was a complicated one. The constitution of 1790 gave the right to vote to "freemen" of age twenty-one or older who had lived in the state for at least two years and been assessed for a county tax. The term "freeman" was vague. In some counties it was held to mean any man who was not a slave. In those areas black men could and did vote. Elsewhere, most notably in Philadelphia, officials insisted that only whites could be "freemen," and black men who tried to vote were turned away from polling places. The confusion ended with the revision of the constitution in 1838, when delegates to the so-called Reform Convention (note 68) specifically disfranchised all men of color, regardless of wealth or status. Things did not change until the passage of the Fifteenth Amendment. Leon Litwack, *North of Slavery: The Negro in the Free States, 1790–1860* (Chicago: University of Chicago Press, 1961), 91. Winch, *Philadelphia's Black Elite*, 134–42.

43. As Willson notes, the main item of business at the convention was the establishment of a manual labor college, but there were other items on the agenda. Delegates endorsed several antislavery newspapers, foremost among them the *Liberator*. They praised various European powers for taking steps to abolish slavery and de-

plored the failure of the United States to act. They condemned the passage of racially restrictive laws by a number of states, and they advocated temperance and moral reform. The one question that divided them was Canadian emigration. Some favored it, while others argued there was little difference between emigrating to Canada and accepting the arguments advanced by the American Colonization Society about the merits of Liberia. A compromise was eventually reached. Delegates welcomed the progress black exiles had made in Canada, but they were careful to spell out that they did not approve of the schemes of the ACS. "If we must be sacrificed to their philanthropy, we would rather die at home." There is nothing in the published minutes to substantiate Willson's theory about a day having been set aside for each of the states represented at the convention. *Minutes and Proceedings of the First Annual Convention of the People of Colour, Held by Adjournments in the City of Philadelphia, From the Sixth to the Eleventh of June, Inclusive, 1831* (Philadelphia: By Order of the Convention, 1831). Winch, *Philadelphia's Black Elite*, 94–96. *Lib*, May 28, 1831.

44. The plan for a manual labor college was first put forward at the convention of 1831 by three white abolitionists, William Lloyd Garrison, Arthur Tappan, and Simeon S. Jocelyn. New Haven was chosen because it was already home to Yale University and, according to Jocelyn, a New Haven native, its residents were "friendly, pious, generous and humane." Jocelyn also pointed out that New Haven carried on "an extensive West India trade," and if a college were established, "many of the wealthy colored residents of the Islands, would . . . send their sons there."

The convention approved the plan and committees were formed in various cities, including Philadelphia, to raise funds. As the members of the Philadelphia committee explained in their appeal to the public, the projected college had much to commend it. They acknowledged "the difficult admission of our youths into seminaries of learning and establishments of mechanism." There was the moral argument. Education had an "efficient influence . . . in cultivating the heart and restraining the passions and improving the manners." An additional advantage was that the manual labor plan would enable students to work their way through college because they would combine classroom instruction with labor on the college's farm and in its workshops, and what they produced could be sold at a profit.

The reaction in New Haven was swift and predictable. At a public meeting organized by the mayor and aldermen a pledge was made to "resist the establishment of the proposed College . . . by every lawful means." Jocelyn tried every argument he could think of, from civic pride to profit, but to no avail.

The proposal to found a college was approved again at the conventions of 1832 and 1833, but delegates expressed doubt about whether New Haven would be the ideal site. The manual labor plan continued to be popular with both black and white reformers throughout the antebellum era, and a number of interracial schools were begun on manual labor principles. African-American reformers helped fund them and sent their children to them. For instance, wealthy sailmaker James Forten was a member of the Philadelphia Provisional Committee to raise funds for the New Haven college. In the 1830s he enrolled his youngest son at Oneida Institute, a manual labor school in upstate New York; he also helped establish a scholarship fund there for poor but deserving black students; and in the 1850s three of his grandsons attended nearby Central College, another manual labor institution. *Minutes of the First Annual Convention of the People of Colour*, 6–7; *Minutes and Proceedings of the Second*

Annual Convention, for the Improvement of the Free People of Color in these United States, Held by Adjournments in the City of Philadelphia, from the 4th to the 13th of June Inclusive, 1832 (Philadelphia: By Order of the Convention, 1832), 22–23, 27; *Third Annual Convention of the Free People of Colour,* 5, 10, 13, 14. *College for Colored Youth. An Account of the New-Haven City Meeting and Resolutions, With Recommendations of the College, and Strictures Upon the Doings of New-Haven* (New York: By the Committee, 1831).

45. Willson tactfully avoided mentioning the controversy that derailed the convention movement in the mid-1830s. Conventions met regularly every year from 1830 until 1835. The first four were held in Philadelphia, to the chagrin of the New Yorkers, who wanted to advance the claims of their own city. A compromise was reached, and it was agreed that New York would host the convention one year and Philadelphia the next. Accordingly, the 1834 convention met in New York, and the 1835 convention met in Philadelphia. The convention of 1836, which the New Yorkers were to have hosted, never met. A new organization, dominated by the Philadelphians, had emerged at the 1834 convention. The American Moral Reform Society was represented as being an auxiliary to the convention movement to put into effect the delegates' agenda of promoting education, temperance, abolition, and a host of other reforms. It gained more adherents at the convention of 1835, and in 1836 its annual meeting superseded the convention. There was soon bitter wrangling over the policies of the AMRS. Its officers, the vast majority of whom were drawn from Philadelphia's "higher classes," rejected terms of racial identification, resolved to direct their efforts to whites as well as blacks, and adopted a sweeping program of reform that critics condemned as "visionary in the extreme." They eventually alienated not only the resentful New Yorkers, but many Philadelphians. The dissidents repeatedly called for a revival of the convention movement. As for the American Moral Reform Society, it held its last meeting in 1841. Winch, *Philadelphia's Black Elite,* 91–129.

46. John Bowers (1773–1844) was a freeborn migrant from Boston who probably arrived in Philadelphia as a sailor. By 1809 he had made the city his home. After a number of voyages, including one to China, he left the sea and became a secondhand clothing dealer. Keenly interested in education, he was a trustee of the school sponsored by St. Thomas's African Episcopal Church (he was also a member of the vestry) and president of the Rush Education Society. An admirer of Prudence Crandall, the Connecticut teacher persecuted for opening her school to "young ladies and little misses of color," Bowers contributed the substantial sum of $25 to have her portrait painted. In addition to presiding at the national convention of 1831, he was a delegate to the conventions of 1830 and 1832. He subscribed to the *Liberator* and supported the *Emancipator.* He was instrumental in establishing the Pennsylvania Anti-Slavery Society and was active in the Association for Moral and Mental Improvement. Seamen's Protection Certificates for the Port of Philadelphia (1809), RG 36, NA. Philadelphia Crew Lists (1809), HSP. Joseph Cassey to William Lloyd Garrison, February 12, 1833; John Bowers to Garrison, May 14, 1834; BPL. *CA,* September 8, 1838. *Eman,* July 13, 1833. *FJ,* May 11, 1827; September 28, 1827. *HR,* March 12, 1831. *Lib,* July 2, 1836. *NECAUL,* October 29, 1836. *NR, September* 1838. *PF,* September 6, 1838; September 12, 1839; November 3, 1841. *Constitution of the American Society of Free Persons of Colour, For Improving Their Condition in the United States; For Purchasing Lands; and For the Establishment of a Settlement in Canada, Also the*

Proceedings of the Convention, With Their Address To The Free People of Colour in The United States (Philadelphia: J. W. Allen, 1831), 4. *Minutes of the Second Annual Convention of the Free People of Color,* 3. Douglass, *Annals of St. Thomas,* 111, 137. "Register of Confirmations by Bishop White 1787 to 1836 Inclusive," HSP. Charters of incorporation, Book 2, 28, PSA. U.S. census (1810), Philadelphia, Cedar Ward, 259; (1820), Cedar Ward, 233; (1830), Pine Ward, 336; (1840), Pine Ward, 311. Will of John Bowers, PCA.

47. Belfast Burton (ca. 1772–1849) told PAS members gathering data for their 1838 census that he was freeborn. In fact, he had been born a slave. In 1796 his master, Woolsey Burton, of Sussex County, Delaware, undertook to free him after sixteen more years of service. Legal freedom may have come sooner than this; in 1810 Burton headed his own household in Philadelphia. He initially supported his family by working as a laborer, but his skill as a healer was quickly recognized. In the city directories he was listed as a physician and accorded the title "Dr.," an unusual distinction for a man of color. He emigrated to Haiti in 1825, where he apparently did well, but he eventually returned to Philadelphia. He was a delegate to the conventions of 1830 and 1831, having been admitted to the 1830 meeting only after an acrimonious exchange with Bishop Allen, who apparently saw the redoubtable Burton as a rival in the struggle for influence within the African-American community. For three decades Belfast Burton was a highly respected member of St. Thomas's African Episcopal Church, but toward the end of his life he converted to Methodism and joined the congregation of Mother Bethel. Manumission Book D, 317, PAS MSS, HSP. *AAM,* October 1859. *GUE,* June 1825. *Lib,* October 22, 1831. *Poulson,* March 2, 1822. *Constitution of the American Society of Free Persons of Colour,* 3. Philadelphia Board of Health Records. PAS census (1838). U.S. census, (1810), Philadelphia, West Southwark, 117; (1820) Cedar Ward, 219; (1830) New Market Ward, 243; (1840) Thornborough Township, Delaware County, Pa.., 59. Philadelphia directories, 1811, 1814, 1819–22, 1829–30, 1840, 1845, 1848.

48. The younger brother of minister and editor Samuel E. Cornish (1795–1858), sailmaker James Cornish (ca. 1803–1869) was one of the most active members of the Philadelphia community. Born free in Delaware, he had moved to Philadelphia by the time he was in his mid-twenties. The range of his activities is impressive, as is his material success. He defended free people of color from attacks in the press and protested disfranchisement. He endorsed newspapers published by African Americans and by white abolitionists. He was one of the founders of the Colored Free Produce Society of Pennsylvania and a member of the Philadelphia Young Men's Anti-Slavery Society. He attended four of the six conventions held between 1830 and 1835. A member of the Sons of St. Thomas and the Humane Mechanics' Association, he helped author a report on black benevolent organizations. He was an officer and founding member of the Association for Moral and Mental Improvement. An accomplished orator, he took a keen interest in intellectual pursuits, joining in founding both the Library Company of Colored Persons and the Young Men's Philadelphia Library Association. As for his rise to prosperity, in 1838 he and his wife Mary, a laundress, were renters. Nine years later, when the Friends compiled their census of Philadelphia's African-American population, James and Mary Cornish owned a home on Hubbell Street valued at $600, all their children were in school, and the family was judged to be "doing well." *CA,* June 10, 1837; March 22, 1838; August 4, 1838; September 8, 1838; October 13, 1838; October 5, 1839; May 8, 1841. *Eman,*

July 13, 1833. *FJ*, July 18, 1828; July 25, 1828. *GUE*, May 1831. *HR*, March 12, 1831. *Lib*, March 12, 1831. *NECAUL*, August 17, 1836. *NR*, October 1839. *PF*, July 26, 1838; August 9, 1838; January 17, 1839; September 26, 1839; October 10, 1839. *RA*, October 9, 1829. *Constitution of the American Society of Free Persons of Colour*, 4. *Minutes of the Fifth Annual Convention for the Improvement of the Free People of Color*, 20. *Register of Trades. Appeal of Forty Thousand*, 2. *Minutes of the First Annual Convention of the American Moral Reform Society*, in Porter, ed., *Early Negro Writing*, 225. *Philadelphia Association for Moral and Mental Improvement*, 3. Records of the Philadelphia Young Men's Anti-Slavery Society, in PAS MSS, HSP. Charters of incorporation, Book 4, 352; Book 5, 317; Book 6, 54, PSA. PAS census (1838); Friends' census (1847). U.S. census (1840), Philadelphia, Cedar Ward, 249; (1860), Ward 3, 381. Philadelphia directories, 1841, 1843–44, 1848, 1860. Benjamin Quarles, *Black Abolitionists* (New York: Oxford University Press, 1969), 74. James de T. Abajian, comp., *Blacks in Selected Newspapers, Censuses, and Other Sources: An Index to Names and Subjects* (Boston: G. K. Hall, 1977), vol. 1, 119.

49. Junius C. Morel (ca. 1801–1874) was born in North Carolina, the son of a slaveowner and "his chattel personal." He probably came to Philadelphia in his early teens, for he recalled working on the city's defenses in 1814. He traveled extensively in the United States and abroad as a sailor before settling down.

Morel took an early interest in the African-American and antislavery press, raising funds for Samuel Cornish's *Rights of All* and Garrison's *Liberator*. He had plans to edit his own newspaper. In 1831 he and John P. Thompson entered into a partnership to publish a paper in Philadelphia, *The American*. The project never got off the ground.

Morel strenuously opposed African colonization, describing Liberia as "a kind of Botany Bay for the United States." However, in 1830 he helped organize a meeting to endorse resettlement in Canada. It was that interest that led him to attend the national convention of 1830, since the main item on the agenda was how best to coordinate aid to the people of color forced out of Ohio by hostile legislation and obliged to seek refuge north of the border. Morel continued to play a leading role in the convention movement. He was a delegate to five out of the six conventions that met between 1830 and 1835.

The militant Morel grew increasingly frustrated at the "criminal apathy and idiot coldness" of many of Philadelphia's black leaders. He initially endorsed the American Moral Reform Society (note 45), but was vociferous in condemning what he saw as its weak-kneed approach to racial proscription and its lack of racial pride. He urged black Philadelphians to fight for their rights if they did not wish to lose them. In an effort to prevent disfranchisement, he formed the "Political Association" and took legal advice about the best way to proceed. He was furious when community leaders refused to cooperate.

Perhaps because of his growing alienation from the city's "higher classes of colored society," Morel left Philadelphia for Harrisburg in 1837. Tragically, his wife, Caroline, herself an active reformer, died shortly after the move. Morel relocated several more times over the next few years. In 1841 he was in Newark, New Jersey. By 1850 he had moved to Brooklyn, where he found work as a teacher. He eventually became the principal of a black public school. A steadfast supporter of integration, he petitioned for white students to be allowed to attend classes. The success of this experiment greatly aided the effort to desegregate Brooklyn's public schools.

Morel had long been active in the antislavery movement. In Philadelphia he had been a member of the Young Men's Anti-Slavery Society. His commitment to the cause continued after he left Philadelphia. He called for more vigilance committees to be formed to aid fugitives. He pleaded for unity among abolitionists, especially in the aftermath of the Garrison-Tappan split. He raised money to help send the *Amistad* captives back to their homeland. He kept in touch with developments in the United States and overseas and forwarded information about the progress of emancipation to the antislavery press. He was a supporter of liberty in all its forms. In New York City in 1852 he joined other black leaders in welcoming Hungarian patriot Louis Kossuth, comparing his struggle to the struggle of African Americans.

The Compromise of 1850, especially the Fugitive Slave Law, drew bitter denunciations from Morel. He urged African Americans to defend themselves with force if force were used against them. He helped establish the National Council of the Colored People and represented Brooklyn blacks at the 1855 convention. Interested though he was in voluntary emigration and the prospects for black men and women abroad, he fought Lincoln's efforts to resettle people of color in the Caribbean and Central America. They must, he insisted, have the right to decide where their future lay.

Some years after the death of his first wife, Morel married again. In 1870 he was living in Brooklyn with his second wife, Sarah, a New York native, and their daughter, Alice. All three were categorized as "Indians" by the census-taker. Morel owned real estate worth $15,000, and $800 worth of personal property. Philadelphia Crew Lists (1824), HSP. *Constitution of the American Society of Free Persons of Colour*, 3, 9–12; *Minutes of the Second Annual Convention of the Free People of Color*, 3; *Minutes of the Fourth Annual Convention of the Free People of Colour*, 3. *Minutes of the Fifth Annual Convention for the Improvement of the Free People of Color*, 20. *ASB,* January 3, 1852. *CA,* November 11, 1837; December 9, 1837; May 3, 1838; August 11, 1838; September 22, 1838; December 22, 1838; December 29, 1838; February 9, 1839; July 13, 1839; May 30, 1840; June 13, 1840; July 25, 1840; January 30, 1841; July 17, 1841; September 25, 1841; December 4, 1841. *CR,* March 1, 1862. *FDP,* January 15, 1852; February 26, 1852; December 18, 1852; May 20, 1853; January 20, 1854; January 27, 1854; February 3, 1854; July 28, 1854. *GUE,* October 1837. *HR,* February 27, 1830. *Lib,* March 12, 1831; June 11, 1831; July 16, 1831; April 21, 1832; April 20, 1833; February 8, 1850. *NASS,* January 30, 1840; October 31, 1850. *NECAUL,* August 17, 1836; August 24, 1836; August 31, 1836; March 11, 1837; November 2, 1837. *NR,* September 1838; October 1838; February 1839; September 1839; October 1839; November 1839. *NS,* January 25, 1850; April 17, 1851. *RA,* October 9, 1829. *WAA,* December 24, 1859. Arnold Buffum to William Lloyd Garrison, January 29, 1834, BPL. Austin Steward, *Twenty-Two Years a Slave, and Forty Years a Freeman: Embracing a Correspondence of Several Years, While President of Wilberforce Colony, London, Canada West* (Rochester, N.Y.: William Alling, 1857), 208–9. Carleton Mabee, *Black Education in New York State from Colonial to Modern Times* (Syracuse: Syracuse University Press, 1979), 86, 123, 126–27. Ripley et al., *Black Abolitionist Papers,* vol. 4, 218–19. Winch, *Philadelphia's Black Elite,* 66–67, 70, 81, 85, 90, 92–100, 104–7, 110, 123, 140. U.S. census (1870), Brooklyn, New York, Ward 9, 123.

50. William Whipper was born in Little Britain Township, Lancaster County, Pennsylvania, on February 22, 1804. Not much is known about his parentage. One account of his life says he was the child of a black domestic and her wealthy white

employer, but there were two black families named "Whipper" in New Britain in the 1820 census, and William might have been a member of either. One fact about his upbringing is abundantly clear though. Whether formally educated or largely self-taught, he developed a deep love of learning at an early age and read extensively. The breadth of his knowledge was impressive. Perhaps it was the lure of Philadelphia's network of black schools and educational societies that prompted William Whipper to move there as a young man. By 1828 he was working in the city as a steam scourer.

Whipper quickly established himself as a forceful and effective advocate for the African-American community. One of his earliest appearances on the speaker's platform was in March 1828 when he gave an address on behalf of the newly formed Colored Reading Room Society. Whipper lacked the eloquence of men like Robert Purvis and Junius C. Morel, but he more than made up for that with his energy and his skill as a writer and organizer. He was much in demand when it came to drawing up petitions and drafting resolutions. He was soon hard at work leading the charge against the ACS, defending the black community from attacks in the press, and promoting such publications as the *Rights of All* and the *Liberator*. In 1832 he joined Robert Purvis and James Forten in petitioning the state legislature to reject a proposed law that would deprive black Pennsylvanians of many of their fundamental rights. In 1833 he became one of the charter members of the Library Company of Colored Persons. That same year he was chosen by a committee of black citizens to give a memorial oration on the death of British abolitionist William Wilberforce.

Meanwhile, he was devoting more and more of his time and money to the twin causes of temperance and free labor. He gave a number of speeches on the evils of alcohol, equating the power of strong drink over an individual with the control of the master over the slave. In 1834 he opened a temperance and free labor store near Mother Bethel at 161 South Sixth. The store also stocked antislavery publications. Whipper's wedding in 1836 to Harriet L. L. Smith in Columbia, Pennsylvania, was a temperance and free labor affair, with no alcohol served and no slave-produced sugar used in the wedding cake.

Whipper was present at each of the national conventions that met between 1830 and 1835, seizing every opportunity to pursue his agenda of sweeping reforms—which, he confidently believed, would bring about not only the total abolition of slavery and the eradication of prejudice, but a moral regeneration of the United States. At the 1834 convention he took the lead in establishing the American Moral Reform Society. Although not initially intended to replace the conventions, it effectively did so after 1835. Whipper wanted the AMRS to be interracial in its goals and membership. Any individual or group committed to the concept of social and moral reform was eligible to join. The society's figure-head was seventy-year-old James Forten, but it was Whipper who dominated it. In 1838 he became the editor of its short-lived journal, the *National Reformer,* and this offered him a forum for a wide range of "reformist" ideas. The AMRS was soon mired in controversy over Whipper's rejection of terms of racial designation and his insistence that the society must direct its efforts to aiding all Americans without regard to race. He was attacked by the likes of Samuel Cornish, editor of the *Colored American,* Frederick A. Hinton, and Junius C. Morel for lacking in racial pride (a charge he vehemently denied) and for being unrealistic and hopelessly visionary. He was also vilified for sowing seeds of dissension within the African-American community.

In time, Whipper came to question many of his earlier views. In the 1830s he insisted that free people of color must remain in the United States and not be lured away to Liberia, Canada, or the West Indies. By the 1850s he was no longer so sure that emigration was wrong. A brother, a sister and a much-loved nephew had settled in Canada. He visited them, was impressed by what he saw, bought real estate in Canada, and was preparing to emigrate when the Civil War intervened and demanded his attention closer to home. With characteristic energy, Whipper joined in the task of enlisting young black men into the Union forces.

In the 1830s Whipper had shunned racial terms and insisted that the moral reform of the black community was the key to civil and social equality. In 1848, at the Pennsylvania state convention called to petition for the restoration of the franchise, he publicly renounced that position. Race, and race alone, he now believed, was the basis on which whites denied blacks fundamental rights. No amount of self-improvement on the part of African Americans could counter that basic prejudice.

Although Whipper was closely involved with the doings of the "higher classes of colored society" in Philadelphia, his home for many years was actually Columbia, Pennsylvania. He moved there in 1835 and entered into a business partnership with Stephen Smith, an African-American lumber and coal merchant. Whipper lived in Columbia for more than twenty-five years, managing Smith's business affairs there when the older man moved to Philadelphia. Smith and Whipper regularly shipped many hundreds of tons of lumber in their freight cars. They also owned a merchant ship on Lake Erie. After the war Whipper confessed that the firm of Smith & Whipper had often transported fugitive slaves as well as lumber in their cars and then ferried them to Canada across Lake Erie.

After the war William Whipper became cashier of the ill-fated Freedman's Savings Bank. He was also active in the Pennsylvania State Equal Rights League. He died in Philadelphia on March 9, 1876. William Whipper, *An Address Delivered in Wesley Church on the Evening of June 12, Before the Colored Reading Society of Philadelphia* (Philadelphia: John B. Roberts, n.d.); *Eulogy on William Wilberforce, Esq., Delivered at the Request of the People of Colour of the City of Philadelphia, in the Second African Presbyterian Church on the Sixth Day of December, 1833* (Philadelphia: W. P. Gibbons, 1833). *CA*, March 4, 1837; July 15, 1837; August 19, 1837; August 26, 1837; September 9, 1837; September 16, 1837; September 23, 1837; September 30, 1837; February 3, 1838; March 3, 1838; March 29, 1838; July 26, 1838; August 25, 1838; September 15, 1838; September 22, 1838; January 12, 1839; July 13, 1839; July 18, 1840. *CR*, February 16, 1861. *Eman*, May 18, 1833; July 13, 1833. *FDP* May 13, 1852. *FJ*, June 6, 1828; June 20, 1828; July 18, 1828; July 25, 1828; December 26, 1828. *Lib*, March 12, 1831; May 28, 1831; March 22, 1834; June 21, 1834; July 5, 1834; April 30, 1836. *NASS*, September 10, 1840; October 1, 1840; August 21, 1845. *NR* (editor), September 1838–December 1839. *NS*, September 1, 1848; September 29, 1848; December 1, 1848; December 8, 1848; December 15, 1848; March 9, 1849; November 23, 1849; December 14, 1849. *PF*, September 12, 1839; September 11, 1845. *Prov. Free*, July 2, 1854; April 14, 1855; October 6, 1855; March 22, 1856; March 29, 1856; August 22, 1857. *RA*, October 16, 1829. *WA*, January 7, 1837. *Constitution of the American Society of Free Persons of Colour*, 4; *Minutes of the Second Annual Convention of the Free People of Color*, 3. *Third Annual Convention of the Free People of Colour*, 3. *Minutes of the Fourth Annual Convention of the Free People of Colour*, 9. *Minutes of the Fifth Annual Convention for the Improvement of the Free People of Color*, 21. *Proceedings of the National Convention, Held in Rochester, July 6th, 7th and 8th,*

1853 (Rochester: At the Office of Frederick Douglass' Paper, 1853), 6. *Proceedings of the Colored National Convention . . . 1855,* 7. *Minutes of the State Convention of the Colored Citizens of Pennsylvania, Convened at Harrisburg, December 13th and 14th, 1848,* in Philip S. Foner and George E. Walker, eds., *Proceedings of the Black State Conventions, 1840–1865* (Philadelphia: Temple University Press, 1979–81), vol. 1, pp. 2, 4, 5, 6, 8–12, 13–22. *Proceedings of the Pennsylvania Convention, Assembled to Organize a State Anti-Slavery Society, at Harrisburg, on the 31st of January and 1st, 2d and 3d of February, 1837* (Philadelphia: Merrihew and Gunn, 1837), 52–54. *AMRS Convention . . . 1837,* in Porter, ed., *Early Negro Writing,* 224. U.S. census (1820), Little Britain Township, Lancaster County, Pa.., 308 (Benjamin Whip(p)er) and 311 (John Whipper); (1830), High Street Ward, Philadelphia, 24; (1840), Columbia, Lancaster County, Pa., 176; (1860), Columbia, 159. Winch, *Philadelphia's Black Elite,* 64–65, 92–98, 109–10, 114–16, 118, 120, 121, 126, 163–64. Henry W. Minton, *The Early History of the Negro in Business in Philadelphia, Read Before the American Negro Historical Society, March, 1913* (Nashville, Tenn.: AMESS Union, 1913), 17. Ripley et al., *Black Abolitionist Papers,* vol. 3, 129–30. William Still, *The Underground Railroad* (Philadelphia: People's Publishing Co., 1879; reprint, New York: Arno, 1968), 735–40. Delany, *Destiny of the Colored People,* 95–96, 107. Richard P. McCormick, "William Whipper: Moral Reformer," *Pa. Hist* 43 (January 1976), 23–46. Louis C. Jones, "A Leader Ahead of His Times," *AH* 14 (June 1963), 58–59, 63.

51. John C. Peck (1802–1875) was born in Hagerstown, Maryland, and grew up in Virginia. When he was nineteen he moved to Pennsylvania, settling first in Carlisle and then in Pittsburgh. He prospered, having learned early in his career the wisdom of diversifying his interests. He was a barber, wigmaker, and perfumer, as well as the owner of a clothing store and an oyster house.

Although raised a Catholic, Peck converted to Methodism when he was still a child. As an adult he joined the AME denomination, became a preacher, and eventually helped found the Wylie Street AME Church in Pittsburgh. A zealous advocate of abolition, Peck acted as an agent for a number of antislavery journals, among them the *Liberator,* the *Emancipator,* and his friend Martin R. Delany's *Pittsburgh Mystery.* He was president of Pittsburgh's Philanthropic Society, an organization that assisted runaway slaves. In January 1837 he traveled to Harrisburg for the inaugural meeting of the Pennsylvania Anti-Slavery Society and eventually emerged as a leading member of its western wing.

Peck owed his early education to a sympathetic white Presbyterian minister in Virginia who had taught him to read and write. As an adult he determined to promote educational opportunities for African Americans. In 1849 philanthropist Charles Avery donated money to establish a college in Pennsylvania to train young black men as teachers and ministers. Peck praised Avery's generosity and served as one of the trustees of what became known as Avery College.

In addition to promoting education, Peck devoted his energies to securing civil and political rights for African Americans. A veteran of the national conventions of the early 1830s (he attended every convention from 1831 to 1835), Peck turned again to the idea of a convention in the late 1830s when black Pennsylvanians lost the right to vote. In 1841 he was one of the organizers of the State Convention of the Colored Freemen of Pennsylvania. The goal of the convention was to mobilize the free black population to petition for the restoration of the franchise. The failure of the statewide initiative disappointed Peck but did not dishearten him. He attended the 1853 national convention in Rochester, New York, and was one of the founders of the short-lived National Council of the Colored People, an organization that sought to achieve at the national level the reforms he had tried to effect in Pennsylvania.

In the years immediately before the Civil War, Peck became pessimistic about prospects in the United States. He spoke out in favor of emigration to Canada (his son, David, had lived for some time in Toronto) and he announced his own intention of leaving the United States. In fact, though, he did not emigrate. He remained in Pittsburgh for the rest of his life. *Minutes of the Second Annual Convention of the Free People of Color*, 3. *Third Annual Convention of the Free People of Colour*, 3. *Minutes of the Fourth Annual Convention of the Free People of Colour*, 9. *CA*, March 4, 1837; April 12, 1838; December 1, 1838; July 18, 1840; July 25, 1840; May 29, 1841; July 24, 1841. *CR*, February 22, 1862; April 26, 1862. *NEW*, July 28, 1853. *NR*, September 1839; November 1839. *NS*, August 25, 1848; September 29, 1848; August 31, 1849. *ProvF*, April 25, 1857. Ripley et al., *Black Abolitionist Papers*, vol. 4, 161–62n. U.S. census (1830), Carlisle Township, Chester County, Pa., 10; (1840), Pittsburgh, North Ward, 328; (1850), Ward 6, 370; (1860), Ward 8, 441. Abajian, comp., *Blacks in Selected Newspapers*, vol. 3, 28–29. Quarles, *Black Abolitionists*, 20, 26, 33, 231.

52. In the words of the Baltimore Conference of the AME Church, Abner Coker was "a useful and zealous local deacon." He died in Baltimore in the fall of 1833, "in the full assurance of faith, and full of years," leaving a widow, Sarah, "and a large number of bereaved children." Sarah Coker was still living in Baltimore in 1840. Abner Coker was probably a relative of Daniel Coker, the AME minister, teacher and emigrationist who left Baltimore for Liberia in the early 1820s. *Nineteenth Baltimore Annual Conference of the African Methodist Episcopal Church, Convened in Washington City, D.C., April 19, 1834*, in Porter, ed., *Early Negro Writing*, 186. U.S. census (1810), Baltimore, 158; (1820), Ward 3, 139; (1830), Ward 3, 147; (1840), Ward 3, 117.

53. Robert Cowley, a teacher at the Bethel AME church school in Baltimore, also attended the conventions of 1832 and 1833. *Minutes of the Second Annual Convention of the Free People of Color*, 4. *Third Annual Convention of the Free People of Colour*, 3. *CA*, September 23, 1837. U.S. census (1840), Baltimore, Ward 8, 85. Leroy Graham, *Baltimore: The Nineteenth-Century Black Capital* (Washington, D.C.: University Press of America, 1981), 119.

54. William Miller was born free in Queen Annes County, Maryland, in 1775. By 1796 he had moved to New York City and established himself as a cabinetmaker. Raised a Methodist, he joined a group of black Methodists who worshiped at the predominantly white Methodist church on John Street. Initially granted permission by Bishop Francis Asbury to meet separately in the "interval of the regular preaching hours of our white brethren," the black Methodists, led by Peter Williams Sr., James Varrick, and William Miller, eventually requested leave to establish a separate church. In 1800 Zion Church was organized within the Methodist Episcopal Conference. For two decades the relationship between the black congregation and the Methodist Episcopal denomination was a harmonious one. Such tensions as there were surfaced *within* Zion. Before they had a church building of their own, the members of Zion met at Miller's home and workshop at 36 Mulberry Street, in New York City's Sixth Ward. Miller was ordained a Methodist deacon in 1808. Six years later, in a move attributed by his critics to his "unstayable ambition," he led a group of disaffected

members out of Zion to form the African Asbury Church. However, in 1820–21 New York's black Methodists united to separate from the white denomination, and Miller was recruited to assist in drawing up church discipline for what would emerge as the African Methodist Episcopal Zion Church.

William Miller's religious odyssey was not over. He left the AMEZ Church in the early 1820s to affiliate with the Philadelphia-based AME denomination headed by Richard Allen. He was ordained an AME elder in 1823 and assigned to a church in Washington, D.C. After a few years he returned to the AMEZ fold and was given the pastorate of First Wesley (or Big Wesley) in Philadelphia. In 1840 he was appointed bishop of the AMEZ's New York conference, but he remained at Big Wesley and died in Philadelphia toward the end of 1845.

Miller's activities extended beyond the church. He was a key figure in New York City's African Masonic Lodge. A man of considerable education, he devoted much of his energy to teaching others in the community. For many years he ran a school in his Mulberry Street home. He was director of the New York African Bible Society, which endeavored to put Bibles in the hands of African Americans and ensure they could read them. He was on the advisory board of the African Dorcas Society, a group of black women who had as their goal supplying poor black children with clothing and shoes so they could attend school. Miller was also active in the abolitionist cause, delivering the annual sermon on the abolition of the slave trade in 1810 and joining in planning the observances in 1827 to mark the end of slavery in New York.

In the late 1820s Miller married Harriet Judah (1785–1869), a free woman of color from South Carolina. For many years Judah had been the "beloved friend" of an English merchant, William Purvis. On Purvis's death in 1826 she had inherited $10,000. When she married Miller he became the stepfather to her three sons, William Jr., Robert (note 113), and Joseph. William Miller, *A Sermon on the Abolition of the Slave Trade: Delivered in the African Church, New-York on the First of January, 1810. By the Rev. William Miller, Minister of the African Methodist Episcopal Church* (New York: John C. Totten, 1810). *CA*, October 21, 1837; June 8, 1839; June 29, 1839; July 27, 1839; September 14, 1839; May 2, 1840; May 30, 1840; May 8, 1841; May 15, 1841. *FJ*, March 16, 1827; May 4, 1827; June 29, 1827; January 11, 1828; February 1, 1828; March 21, 1829; March 28, 1829. *Lib*, July 7, 1832. Ripley et al., *Black Abolitionist Papers*, vol. 2, 80–81. U.S. census, New York (1800) Ward 6, 246; (1810) Ward 6, 145; (1820) Ward 6, 32; (1830) Ward 6, 451. Will of Reverend William Miller, PCA. William J. Walls, *The African Methodist Episcopal Zion Church* (Charlotte, N.C.: AME Zion Publishing House, 1974), 47, 50, 68, 90–91, 124, 129, 172–73, 567. Leonard P. Curry, *The Free Black in Urban America, 1800–1850: The Shadow of the Dream* (Chicago: University of Chicago Press, 1981), 179–81. Edward D. Smith, *Climbing Jacob's Ladder: The Rise of Black Churches in Eastern American Cities, 1740–1877* (Washington, D.C.: Smithsonian Institution Press, 1988), 39–40.

55. Henry Sipkins (1788–1838), who also attended the conventions of 1832 and 1834, was a well-known abolitionist, reformer, and community activist. In 1808, when he gave the introductory address to Reverend Peter Williams's January 1 oration on the ending of the foreign slave trade, Sipkins was already a prominent member of New York's free black community. The following year Sipkins himself gave the January 1 oration. His determination to eradicate slavery went hand in hand with a resolve to improve the lot of all African Americans, free and slave. For many years

he served as an officer of the New York African Society for Mutual Relief. In the early 1830s he became one of the directors of the Phoenixonian Society, the organization that replaced it. Realizing that his community's influence was limited without equal access to the franchise, Sipkins was in the vanguard of an effort in 1837 to petition the state legislature to grant black men the same access to the polls that white men enjoyed. The campaign was unsuccessful. In order to vote in the state of New York, a free man of color had to own real estate worth $250. No such qualification was imposed upon white men. Peter Williams, *Oration on the Abolition of the Slave Trade* (New York: Samuel Wood, 1808). Henry Sipkins, *An Oration on the Abolition of the Slave Trade, in The City of New-York, January 2, 1809. By Henry Sipkins, A Descendant of Africa* (New York: John C. Totten, 1809). *Minutes of the Second Annual Convention of the Free People of Color*, 3. *Third Annual Convention of the Free People of Colour*, 4. *Minutes of the Fourth Annual Convention of the Free People of Colour*, 8. *CA*, March 18, 1837; August 12, 1837; August 19, 1837; September 23, 1837; November 4, 1837; December 30, 1837; January 13, 1838; January 20, 1838; March 15, 1838; June 16, 1838; September 8, 1838; October 6, 1838; October 27, 1838; November 17, 1838; November 24, 1838; February 16, 1839; January 16, 1841. *FJ*, May 4, 1827; January 11, 1828; March 21, 1829; March 28, 1829. U.S. census (1820), New York City, Ward 8, 21; (1830), Ward 6, 385. Quarles, *Black Abolitionists*, 101–2, 171.

56. New York City abolitionist and community activist Thomas L. Jennings (ca. 1790–1859) was a tailor by trade. After serving an apprenticeship, he went into business on his own and invented a "method of renovating garments" which he patented. According to Frederick Douglass, the framed certificate signed by President John Quincy Adams was one of his most cherished possessions, not merely because it testified to his scientific ability but also because it described him as a citizen of the United States.

For more than four decades Jennings was a leading member of New York City's African-American community. His career is chronicled in *Freedom's Journal* and the *Colored American*, both of which were published in New York. Scarcely an issue appeared in which Jennings (his name was sometimes spelled "Jinnings") was not mentioned in connection with one worthy cause or another. He was one of the founders of the Phoenixonian Society and of the Wilberforce Society. He was also a trustee of New York's Abyssinian Baptist Church. In addition to serving as a delegate to the convention of 1831, Jennings was one of the New York representatives at the conventions of 1833 and 1835.

In the 1820s Jennings was at the forefront of the struggle to abolish slavery in New York, and when his native state finally outlawed slavery in 1827 he helped organize a day of thanksgiving. With the battle in New York won, he directed his energies to the national and international crusade against slavery. Eleven years after the New York victory, he coordinated his city's celebration of emancipation in the British West Indies.

Hand in hand with the abolition of slavery went the securing of full civil rights, and Jennings insisted that those rights must be secured to people of color *in* the United States. He spoke out repeatedly against the American Colonization Society and readily assisted Garrison in publishing and distributing his *Thoughts on African Colonization*. In 1837 Jennings was one of the organizers of what proved to be an unsuccessful campaign to petition the New York state legislature to equalize the requirements for the franchise. Another of his targets was discrimination on public conveyances. Throughout the 1840s Jennings made it a point to refuse to relinquish his seat on trains and move to the "colored" car. Then, in 1854, his twenty-four-year-old daughter, Elizabeth, was violently ejected from a New York City streetcar while on her way to church. She and her father successfully brought suit again the company. Greatly encouraged, Jennings and other African-American leaders formed the New York Legal Rights Association to challenge discriminatory practices by other companies throughout the city and state. Jennings was the president of the Association at the time of his death. *AAM*, April 1859. *CA*, March 18, 1837; April 8, 1837; August 5, 1837; August 12, 1837; October 7, 1837; November 4, 1837; November 11, 1837; November 25, 1837; December 2, 1837; December 16, 1837; December 30, 1837; January 13, 1838; January 28, 1838; June 16, 1838; July 14, 1838; October 20, 1838; October 27, 1838; November 17, 1838; November 24, 1838; July 13, 1839; November 23, 1839; September 5, 1840. *FDP,* July 20, 1855. *FJ,* March 30, 1827; April 20, 1827; April 27, 1827; May 4, 1827; June 29, 1827; October 12, 1827; January 11, 1828; April 4, 1828; January 9, 1829. *Lib,* June 29, 1833. *Minutes of the First Annual Convention of the People of Colour,* 3; *Minutes of the Second Annual Convention of the Free People of Color,* 3. *Third Annual Convention of the Free People of Colour,* 4; *Minutes of the Fifth Annual Convention for the Improvement of the Free People of Color,* 20. U.S. census, New York City (1830), Ward 14, 461; (1850), Ward 5, 22. Ripley et al., *Black Abolitionist Papers,* vol. 3, 48, 262n, 343n. Quarles, *Black Abolitionists,* 102, 123, 170–71. Pease and Pease, *They Who Would Be Free,* 107–8, 167.

57. There was gossip that New York City carpenter and community activist William Hamilton (1773–1836) was the illegitimate son of Alexander Hamilton. William Hamilton was involved in a number of causes, ranging from abolition to the provision of education for African-American children. He was an officer of the African Society for Mutual Relief, the Phoenixonian Society (which was renamed the Hamilton Institution in his memory in 1841), and the Philomathean Society. He attended five of the six national conventions held between 1830 and 1835, spearheaded the opposition of black New Yorkers to the American Colonization Society, and played an important role in the struggle for abolition at the local and national levels. An eloquent speaker, he was often called upon to voice the concerns of his community. A number of his speeches have survived. William Hamilton, *An Address to the New York African Society, for Mutual Relief, Delivered in the Universalist Church, January 2, 1809* (New York, 1809); *An Oration, on the Abolition of the Slave Trade. Delivered in The Episcopal Asbury African Church, in Elizabeth St. New-York, January 2, 1815* (New York: C. W. Bunce, for the N.Y. African Society, 1815); *An Oration Delivered in the African Zion Church, on the Fourth of July, 1827, in Commemoration of the Abolition of Domestic Slavery in this State* (New York: Gray and Bunce, 1827); *Address to the Fourth Annual Convention of Free People of Colour in the United States. Delivered at the Opening of Their Session in the City of New-York, June 2, 1834* (New York: S. W. Benedict and Co., 1834). *Minutes of the Second Annual Convention of Free People of Color,* 3. *Third Annual Convention of Free People of Colour,* 4. *Minutes of the Fourth Annual Convention of the Free People of Colour,* 8. *CA*, October 28, 1837; July 13, 1839; December 4, 1841. *FJ,* April 27, 1827; October 12, 1827; January 11, 1828. Ripley et al., *Black Abolitionist Papers,* vol. 3, 359–60n. U.S. census (1830), New York, Ward 5, 383.

58. James W. C. Pennington (1807–1870) was born James Pembroke, a slave on a

farm on Maryland's eastern shore. Trained as a blacksmith and, as he admitted, more privileged than many of his peers, he still endured whippings and was forced to watch as family members suffered. Pembroke escaped from slavery in 1827, headed North, and changed his name to Pennington to avoid detection. Not until 1851 were friends able to negotiate to buy his freedom.

By 1829 Pennington had settled in Brooklyn, New York, where he worked as a coachman. As a slave he had struggled to become literate. When he crossed from Maryland into Pennsylvania he was sheltered for some months by a Quaker farmer, who taught him reading, writing, ciphering and astronomy. In Brooklyn he pressed ahead with his quest for an education, even dipping into his modest earnings to pay tutors to teach him Latin and Greek. He soon acquired sufficient education to get an appointment as a teacher in a school for black children in Long Island.

Pennington rapidly established himself as a community leader. In 1831, when a branch of the American Colonization Society was organized in Brooklyn, black residents met to denounce it. Pennington gave an especially forceful speech and, as a result, was elected to represent the community at the national convention in Philadelphia. (His employer was the president of the Brooklyn branch of the ACS, but Pennington managed to win him over and he disbanded the newly formed society!) Pennington represented Long Island at the conventions of 1831, 1832, 1833, and 1834. He also emerged as an effective antislavery lecturer.

In 1835 Pennington moved to Connecticut, where he continued to be active in the abolitionist cause and in the promoting of temperance within the African-American community. Determined to become an ordained minister, he applied to Yale Divinity School. He was rejected on the basis of race, but he was able to attend lectures informally and was ordained in 1838. In 1840 he moved to Hartford to become the minister of the Talcott Street Congregational Church. He stayed until 1848, when he moved to New York City.

In many respects Pennington was a radical. He admired white abolitionists, but he called for independent action. Black people, he insisted, must campaign for their own improvement and not let others do it for them. In that spirit he called for a revival of the convention movement. The American Moral Reform Society, he maintained, had led African Americans astray with its rejection of terms of racial identification and its insistence that members should work for the reform of the entire community, black and white. He angered many African-American community leaders by calling for the formation of a black educational society and the establishing of black schools. They were urging integration, but he insisted black children learned better in their own schools. Pennington's sense of the glorious past of the black peoples of the world, and his deep sense of racial pride, can perhaps best be seen in his *Text Book of the Origin and History of the Colored People*, published in 1841.

Pennington's growing fame as a preacher, educator, and reformer prompted the American Peace Society to select him as a delegate to the first Peace Conference in London (1843). He also represented the Connecticut State Anti-Slavery Society at the second World's Anti-Slavery Convention in London that same year. Pennington was favorably impressed with the treatment he received in Britain and seldom passed up a chance to compare it with the restrictions he faced in the United States. He traveled freely, received many invitations to preach to white congregations, and was welcomed as a guest in the homes of reformers.

He returned to the United States to start a newspaper, which he called the *Clark-*

sonian, in honor of abolitionist Thomas Clarkson, whom he had met in England. The paper failed. Undeterred, Pennington embarked on another project, traveling to Jamaica to promote missionary work there and foster closer ties between African Americans and Jamaicans. Then it was back to Connecticut to become involved in what turned out to be an unsuccessful attempt to secure the franchise for African-American men.

In 1848 Pennington moved to New York to become pastor of the First Colored Presbyterian Church (later Shiloh). The following year he left for Europe. He attended another Peace Congress in Paris and met many of the leading intellectuals of the day. He returned to England to lecture, and during his stay published his autobiography, *The Fugitive Blacksmith; or, Events in the History of James W. C. Pennington, Pastor of a Presbyterian Church, New York, Formerly a Slave in the State of Maryland, United States.* It proved an immense success. He then made a trip to Germany, where he received an honorary doctorate from the University of Heidelberg.

A renowned author, preacher, and reformer, enjoying celebrity status on both sides of the Atlantic, Pennington was at the height of his powers in the 1840s. His descent into poverty and obscurity over the next decade was swift and tragic. There were difficulties over his growing involvement with the hierarchy of the Presbyterian Church. Critics assailed him for seeming to endorse a church that counted among its members and its ministers slaveholders and defenders of slavery. He was attacked for his alleged mishandling of funds collected in Jamaica years before. His wife fell ill. He was forced to leave his New York congregation and return to Hartford's Talcott Church. Desperately short of money, he had to beg from friends in the abolitionist movement. Then the erstwhile temperance crusader found himself battling alcoholism. A trip to Britain in the fall of 1861 was hardly the triumph his earlier visits had been. He was arrested and convicted of stealing a book from a bookseller in Liverpool. He blamed absentmindedness. His detractors blamed alcohol.

Pennington returned to the United States without a church. In 1864, angered at the failure of the Presbyterian Church to take a stand on issues of race and slavery, he left to join the Missouri Conference of the AME Church. He worked in Mississippi as a preacher and teacher. After the war there was a rapprochement with the Presbyterians and their allies. Pennington moved to Portland, Maine, to take charge of a Congregational church. Then he received an appointment in Jacksonville, Florida, to work for a Presbyterian mission to the freedmen. In failing health for some time, he died in Jacksonville on October 22, 1870. His passing went almost unnoticed. *Minutes of the Second Annual Convention of the Free People of Color,* 3. *Third Annual Convention of the Free People of Colour,* 4. *Minutes of the Fourth Annual Convention of the Free People of Colour,* 8. Ripley et al., *Black Abolitionist Papers,* vol. 3, 477–78n. Delany, *Destiny of the Colored People,* 113. U.S. census (1870) Jacksonville, Duval County, Florida, 503. R. J. M. Blackett, *Beating Against the Barriers: Biographical Essays in Nineteenth-Century Afro-American History* (Baton Rouge: Louisiana State University Press, 1986), 1–84. David E. Swift, *Black Prophets of Justice: Activist Clergy Before the Civil War* (Baton Rouge: Louisiana State University Press, 1989), 204–43.

59. Abraham Doras Shadd (1801–1882) was born in Delaware, the grandson of Hans Schad, a Hessian mercenary who came to North America with the British forces during the French and Indian War, and Elizabeth Jackson, the free woman of color he married. Abraham's father and grandfather were butchers, but he became a

shoemaker, and he met with a modest degree of success in his native Wilmington. He married a free woman of color from North Carolina, Harriet Parnell. In 1833, possibly in search of better educational opportunities for their children, the Shadds moved to West Chester, Pennsylvania. For some years Abraham continued to work as a shoemaker, but eventually he purchased a small farm.

Staunch abolitionists, the Shadds sheltered fugitives in their homes in Pennsylvania and in the slave state of Delaware. Abraham took an active role in the work of the American Anti-Slavery Society and acted as an agent for various antislavery newspapers, including the *Liberator,* the *Emancipator,* the *National Reformer,* and the *Colored American.* Before he left Delaware, Shadd had made his mark as a vocal abolitionist and an opponent of African colonization. He had represented Delaware's African-American population at the conventions of 1830, 1831, and 1832. In 1833, attending as a delegate from West Chester, he was chosen president of the convention. He represented Chester County at the Pennsylvania State Convention in Harrisburg in 1841 called to protest the disfranchisement of black citizens. Shadd also attended the state convention of 1848 in Pittsburgh. He helped draft addresses to the white electorate and to the legislature, and was appointed an officer of the newly created Citizens' Union of the Commonwealth of Pennsylvania.

Eventually, disenchanted with the pace of reform in the United States, Abraham Shadd decided to investigate conditions in Canada. If satisfied, he declared that he, his family, and "many others" would forsake the United States for "the Queen's Free Soil." In 1852 the Shadds did indeed move to Ontario, where they prospered. Abraham and Harriet's daughter, Mary Ann, who had already embarked on a career as a writer and activist in the United States, became co-editor of the *Provincial Freeman.* There were return visits to West Chester, but, unlike Mary Ann and several of their other children, Abraham and Harriet Shadd were never inclined to resettle permanently in the United States, even after the Civil War. In 1859 Abraham Shadd became the first black elected officeholder in Canada, when he was elected to the town council in Raleigh, Ontario. In the 1871 Canadian census Abraham and Harriet Shadd were recorded as living peacefully on their farm in Raleigh with several other members of their extended family. American Anti-Slavery Society, *Third Annual Report* (1836), 25. *Constitution of the American Society of Free Persons of Colour,* 4. *Minutes of the Second Annual Convention of the Free People of Color,* 3. *Third Annual Convention of Free People of Colour,* 3. *Minutes of the Fourth Annual Convention of Free People of Colour,* 9. *Minutes of the State Convention of the Colored Citizens of Pennsylvania . . . 1848,* in Foner and Walker, eds., *Proceedings of the Black State Conventions,* vol. 1, 2–4, 8–12, 13–22. *CA,* March 4, 1837; July 27, 1839; July 25, 1840; August 15, 1840. *NR,* September 1838; February 1839; September 1839; October 1839; November 1839. *PF,* February 26, 1852. *ProvF,* November 3, 1855; March 29, 1856. Abajian, *Blacks in Selected Newspapers,* vol. 3, 298. Ripley et al., *Black Abolitionist Papers,* vol. 3, 106–7n. U.S. census (1830), Wilmington, Del., 212; (1840), West Chester, Chester County, Pa., 138; (1850), West Chester, 321. Canadian census (1871), Raleigh, Kent County, Ontario, film C-9891, 20. Jane Rhodes, *Mary Ann Shadd Cary: The Black Press and Protest in the Nineteenth Century* (Bloomington: University of Indiana Press, 1998), 2–4, 8–20, 23–24, 72, 78–79, 101, 236.

60. Peter Gardiner (b. 1800) was a Rhode Island native. He and his older sister, Elizabeth, moved to Philadelphia in the 1810s. Peter Gardiner eventually became a prominent member of that city's African-American community, supporting schemes

for emigration to Haiti and to Canada, endorsing the pioneering black newspaper *Rights of All*, helping found the Benezet Philanthropic Association, and joining in the antislavery crusade. In the national conventions he served as a delegate from Delaware in 1830, 1831, and 1832; in 1833 he represented Carlisle, Pennsylvania, and in 1834 he was listed as a Philadelphia delegate. He and his wife, Serena, ran a boardinghouse for "respectable persons of COLOR" on fashionable Powell Street. Gardiner also worked as a traveling AME preacher (he was one of the founding members of the African Methodist Episcopal Church of the City of Philadelphia in 1816) and a "Thompsonian practitioner" or botanic physician.

Peter and Serena Gardiner eventually moved in with his sister and her husband, prosperous North Carolina–born oysterman Richard Howell. In a roundabout way Joseph Willson was connected with the Gardiners and the Howells. Eliza Ann Howell, the daughter of Richard and Elizabeth Gardiner Howell, was the first wife of Frederick A. Hinton. Little more than a year after Eliza's death, Hinton married Willson's sister. Charters of incorporation, Book 1, 487; Book 2, 245; Book 3, 425, PSA. Haytien Emigration Society of Philadelphia, *Information for the Free People of Colour*. *CA*, October 13, 1838. *CR*, January 16, 1861; March 23, 1861; March 30, 1861; June 29, 1861; November 23, 1861; April 12, 1862. *FDP*, September 4, 1851. *HR*, February 27, 1830. *Lib*, July 23, 1831; April 25, 1835. *NS*, September 1, 1848. *RA*, October 9, 1829. *Constitution of the American Society of Free Persons of Colour*, 4; *Minutes of the First Annual Convention of the People of Colour*, 4; *Minutes of the Second Annual Convention of the Free People of Color*, 3; *Third Annual Convention of the People of Colour*, 3, 5; *Minutes of the Fifth Annual Convention for the Improvement of the Free People of Color*, 9–10, 13–14. Philadelphia Association for Moral and Mental Improvement. Will of Richard Howell, PCA. Friends' census (1847). U.S. census, (1830), Philadelphia, Pine Ward, 333; (1850) Dock Ward, 503; (1860), Ward 5, 88. Philadelphia directories, 1833, 1835–36, 1837, 1839, 1840.

61. William Duncan, of Henrico County, Virginia, attended the convention of 1830, as well as that of 1831. *Constitution of the American Society of Free Persons of Colour*, 4. U.S. census (1830), Henrico County, Virginia, 327.

62. Charles W. Gardner (1782–1863) was a native of New Jersey. Although trained as a shoemaker, he forsook that trade in his mid-twenties to become an itinerant Methodist preacher. He traveled extensively in the Upper South until his vigorous denunciations of slavery prompted the white Methodist hierarchy to try to silence him. As for his attacks on African colonization, they almost cost him his liberty. On a visit to Baltimore he fell ill and was obliged to stay longer than the ten days free people of color from outside Maryland were permitted to stay. At the instigation of the local agent of the ACS he was arrested. Several individuals intervened to get him released. Understandably, though, the episode intensified his opposition.

In the early 1830s Gardner settled in Philadelphia. In 1836 he was invited to become the pastor of the city's First African Presbyterian Church. He accepted, and served the congregation for more than a decade. Gardner and his family were not among the wealthy of the community. In 1848 their personal property amounted to only $50. Nevertheless, Gardner's piety, eloquence, and organizational ability won him a place in the "higher classes." He was an officer of both the American Moral Reform Society and the Association for Moral and Mental Improvement. He was also very active in the work of the Demosthenian Institute. He officiated as chaplain at several of the national conventions, and in 1837 he was chosen, with Frederick A.

Hinton, to go to Harrisburg to present to the Reform Convention a petition against disfranchisement.

Gardner took a keen interest over the years in compiling facts and figures on Philadelphia's African Americans. In 1838 he assisted Benjamin Bacon of the Pennsylvania Abolition Society in conducting a census of the black population. He was a tireless antislavery crusader. He worked with the Vigilance Association to help the hundreds of fugitive slaves who flocked to Philadelphia every year. He regularly attended conventions of the Pennsylvania Anti-Slavery Society and the American Anti-Slavery Society. His 1837 speech to the national body was ordered published. At the divisive convention of 1839, though, he voted in favor of restricting the role of women within the antislavery movement, and eventually left the Garrisonian camp for the American and Foreign Anti-Slavery Society.

Evidently Gardner was contemplating a move in the late 1840s. This led to an unexpected attack from Frederick Douglass. Douglass alleged that Gardner had accepted a call to minister to slaveholders in Tennessee, and implied that the "Janus-faced divine" had made his peace with the upholders of the "peculiar institution." Gardner was outraged, as were the members of his congregation who sprang to his defense. Gardner did not go to Tennessee. Instead, he took a series of appointments at African-American churches in Northern cities—Hartford, Connecticut; Princeton, New Jersey; Newport, Rhode Island; and finally Harrisburg, Pennsylvania. To the end of his life he continued to press for full civil rights and for the abolition of slavery. *Speech of the Rev. Charles W. Gardner (A Presbyterian Clergyman of Philadelphia) on the Fourth Anniversary of the American Anti-Slavery Society, May 9th, 1837* (Philadelphia: Merrihew and Gunn, 1837). AMRS Convention . . . 1837, in Porter, ed., *Early Negro Writing*, 224. Catto, *Semi-Centenary Discourse*, 84–86, 88–93, 95. AR, May 1835. CA, June 10, 1837; August 19, 1837; September 9, 1837; October 21, 1837; February 3, 1838; March 15, 1838; March 22, 1838; June 9, 1838; September 8, 1838; September 15, 1838; May 23, 1840; August 25, 1840; November 7, 1840; November 14, 1840; January 24, 1841; April 3, 1841; May 8, 1841; June 23, 1841; July 10, 1841; August 28, 1841; September 4, 1841; December 26, 1841. *Eman*, May 18, 1833. FDP, August 12, 1853. Lib, August 18, 1832; October 22, 1836. NASS, September 2, 1847. NECAUL, February 11, 1837. NEW, January 27, 1848. NR, September 1838; January 1839; September 1839; October 1839. NS, September 1, 1848; November 24, 1848; April 7, 1849. PA. June 6, 1863. PF, September 6, 1838; February 27, 1840; May 14, 1840; November 5, 1840; December 29, 1841. *Constitution of the American Society of Free Persons of Colour*, 8. *Minutes of the Second Annual Convention of the Free People of Color*, 6. *Minutes of the Fourth Annual Convention of Free People of Colour*, 9. *Appeal of Forty Thousand*, 2. American Anti-Slavery Society, *Fourth Annual Report* (1837), 11–15, 18; *Sixth Annual Report* (1839), 33, 38, 46; *Seventh Annual Report* (1840), 10, 31. Ripley et al., *Black Abolitionist Papers*, vol. 3, 212–13n. U.S. census, Philadelphia (1830), New Market Ward, 240; (1860), Dauphin County, Harrisburg, Ward 4, 1061.

63. Samuel Todd was an AME cleric from Dorchester County, Maryland. He was an honorary member of the 1830 convention at which he represented Maryland. In the early 1830s he moved to Philadelphia. FJ, August 17, 1827; February 1, 1828. *Nineteenth Baltimore Annual Conference of the AME Church*, in Porter, *Early Negro Writing*, 186. *Constitution of the American Society of Free Persons of Colour*, 4. Philadelphia directory, 1833.

64. The words are from Katherine's final speech in Shakespeare's *The Taming of the Shrew* (act 5, scene 2, lines 166–69):
I am ashamed that women are so simple
To offer war where they should kneel for peace,
Or seek for rule, supremacy, and sway,
When they are bound to serve, love, and obey.

65. Ecclesiastes 7:7: "Surely oppression maketh a wise man mad; and a gift destroyeth the heart."

66. In act 1, scene 1, of Shakespeare's *The Merchant of Venice* (lines 88–94) Gratiano describes
. . . a sort of men whose visages
Do cream and mantle like a standing pond,
And do a willful stillness entertain
With purpose to be dressed in an opinion
Of wisdom, gravity, profound conceit—
As who should say, "I am Sir Oracle,
And when I ope my lips, let no dog bark!"

67. Sometimes the publication of proceedings was delayed because of sheer inefficiency. Philadelphia community leader James Forten, in a letter to abolitionist William Lloyd Garrison, wrote that he believed this to be the reason for the tardiness in getting the minutes of the 1831 convention to the printer. (Forten to Garrison, August 9, 1831, BPL.) The following year he hinted at a more serious problem. The convention of 1832 had not been noted for its harmony. In fact, there had been a heated exchange on the question of Canadian emigration. The dispute apparently continued after the formal sessions. Forten learned that publication of the proceedings was being held up "owing to some disagreement . . . between the publishing committee." (Forten to Garrison, July 28, 1832; BPL.) On allegations of duplicity on procedural issues and the manipulation of the rules of order during conventions, see Winch, *Philadelphia's Black Elite*, 113–14.

68. Pennsylvania's Reform Convention met in 1837 to revise the state's constitution. The new constitution, presented to voters the following year, increased the number of white males eligible to vote by doing away with property qualifications, but it also disfranchised all black Pennsylvanians, regardless of wealth.

69. This is from the last stanza of Thomas Gray's "Ode on a Distant Prospect of Eton College":
Yet ah! why should they know their fate?
Since sorrow never comes too late,
And happiness too swiftly flies.
Thought would destroy their paradise.
No more; where ignorance is bliss,
'Tis folly to be wise.

70. From Shakespeare's *Othello, The Moor of Venice*, act 3, scene 3, lines 342–43:
He that is robbed, not wanting what is stol'n,
Let him not know't, and he's not robbed at all.

71. The founders of the Library Company emphasized that theirs was no "sectarian" effort. Their aim was to promote "among our rising youth, a proper cultivation of literary pursuits and the improvement of the faculties and powers of their minds" and "to add something to the general char(ac)ter of our people for the improvement

of our intellectual faculties." Incidentally, Willson seems to have been unaware that other individuals besides the nine he named took an early interest in the organization. Those who signed the Library Company's charter included Pennsylvania-born cleaner and dyer Ebenezer Black; Thomas Butler, a barber and a bleeder, and a prominent member of the African-American elite; clothier Clayton Miller; and James Forten Jr., the eldest son of one of the wealthiest and most articulate black leaders in the North. Daniel B. Brownhill (an affluent barber), William S. Gordon (also a barber), Daniel Colly (a Philadelphia-born bootmaker active in the American Moral Reform Society, the Association for Moral and Mental Improvement, and a stalwart of the Vigilance Committee), Robert Purvis (note 113), Junius C. Morel (note 49), and Morris Brown Jr. (a migrant from South Carolina, a bootmaker by trade, an accomplished amateur musician, and the son of AME bishop Morris Brown Sr.) were all included on the list of those authorized to receive donations of books and money. In 1838 the Library Company had 150 members and a library containing 600 volumes. In addition to serving as a circulating library and debating society, the organization sponsored a program of lectures by "distinguished Citizens, and members of the Bar" and occasional concerts. The Company's relations with St. Thomas's Church, which hosted its meetings, were not always harmonious. In 1839, for instance, the church authorities denied the Library Company the use of a room for its anniversary celebration. Committee to Improve the Condition of the African Race, Minute Book, 1837–53, PAS MSS, HSP. *Present State and Condition*, 30. CA, December 2, 1837; December 23, 1837; October 5, 1839; December 26, 1840. CR, February 16, 1861; March 16, 1861; May 11, 1861; April 5, 1862. HR, November 1833. NECAUL, June 24, 1837. NR, January 1839. NS, February 1, 1850. Mifflin Wistar Gibbs, *Shadow and Light: An Autobiography* (Washington, D.C., 1902; reprint, New York: Arno Press, 1968), 11. Dorothy Sterling, *Speak Out in Thunder Tones: Letters and Other Writings by Black Northerners, 1787–1865* (Garden City, N.Y.: Doubleday, 1973), 222.

72. Raleigh, North Carolina, native Frederick Augustus Hinton (1804–1849) was Joseph Willson's friend and brother-in-law. In 1827, when he opened his "Gentleman's Dressing Room," a hairdressing salon and barber shop at 51 South Fourth Street, he was a newcomer to Philadelphia. He quickly established himself as a member of the city's "higher classes of colored society." In 1828 he married Eliza Ann Howell, the sixteen-year-old daughter of prosperous oysterman Richard Howell. (Like Hinton, Howell was an emigré from North Carolina.) Hinton proudly announced his marriage to his new acquaintances in Philadelphia and to friends and family back in North Carolina. The following year he joined the Howells' church, St. Thomas's, was confirmed along with Eliza, and became a member of one of its benevolent societies, the Sons of St. Thomas. Eventually he was elected to the vestry. In 1837 he represented St. Thomas's in the Association for Moral and Mental Improvement. A strict sabbatarian, Hinton earned high praise for refusing to open his shop on Sunday.

In the two decades from his arrival in Philadelphia to his death in the cholera epidemic of 1849 Hinton was involved in almost every cause supported by Philadelphia's free community of color. He soon emerged as an advocate of an independent black press, serving on committees to promote the *Rights of All* and the *Colored American*. He also endorsed abolitionist journals like the *Liberator* and the *Emanci-*

pator, and he took over as Philadelphia agent for the *Liberator* when Joseph Cassey gave it up.

A tireless crusader for abolition, Hinton helped establish the Colored Free Produce Society of Pennsylvania. He joined in the call in 1836 for the formation of an immediatist antislavery organization in Pennsylvania. The result was the establishment of the Pennsylvania Anti-Slavery Society. Hinton attended a number of its conventions as a delegate from the interracial Philadelphia Anti-Slavery Society. A decade later, however, the splits within the ranks of the white abolitionists, the lack of progress on civil and political rights, and his own deep misgivings about the nature of the Garrisonian platform prompted Hinton to denounce William Lloyd Garrison. He alleged that the editor of the *Liberator* "*advocated the abominable doctrine of men taking women for wives, and when tired of them, casting them off, as they did their old shoes.*"

Hinton was a delegate to five out of six of the national conventions that met between 1830 and 1835. For two years he was an active member of the organization that superseded the convention movement, the American Moral Reform Society. In 1836 he even helped draft the organization's "Address to the Colored Churches." He attended the AMRS convention the following year, but the policies being pursued by the society's officers troubled him. He interpreted their rejection of terms of racial designation as a lack of pride and denounced the methods used to get their agenda approved by the AMRS membership. His very public break with the AMRS temporarily estranged him from old friends like Robert Purvis and William Whipper.

Hinton consistently opposed infringements of the rights of black Pennsylvanians. In 1837, when the issue of disfranchisement was first raised by the Reform Convention, Hinton and Presbyterian minister Charles W. Gardner were chosen to take to Harrisburg a petition from the free people of color of Philadelphia. When the Reform Convention *did* propose making black citizens ineligible to vote, Hinton sank his differences with the officers of the American Moral Reform Society and joined with them in drafting the *Appeal of Forty Thousand,* an address to white voters calling on them to reject the proposed constitution and allow black Pennsylvanians to retain the right of suffrage.

In the late 1830s, in a radical departure from his community's long-established policy of rejecting emigration and colonization, Hinton called on Philadelphia's black citizens to reconsider the wisdom of remaining in a state that denied them their basic rights. His first move was to advocate an exodus to Trinidad. Promoting this scheme with his usual energy and enthusiasm, he accepted an appointment as recruiting agent for the British government. When the Trinidad scheme foundered for lack of recruits, Hinton and his brother-in-law briefly considered relocating to Liberia as commission merchants. Apparently, though, both men had second thoughts.

Hinton continued to prosper in Philadelphia. In 1847 he was earning $800 a year, he owned real estate and personal property worth $4,500, and his wife was able to devote herself to "domestic duties." Despite his material success, though, over the years Hinton endured a series of personal tragedies. In 1829 he and his first wife lost an infant daughter to cholera. Six years later, in the space of a week, Eliza Hinton and her young son died of scarlatina. Hinton was left to raise a son and a daughter on his own. In 1837 he married again. His new wife was Joseph Willson's sister, Elizabeth. Of their children, a baby daughter died in 1841, and a five-year-old son died in 1847. Two years later, on July 16, 1849, Hinton himself succumbed to cholera.

He was forty-five years old. Philadelphia Board of Health Records. Charters of incorporation, Book 4, 352; Book 6, 54; Book 7, 247, PSA. Arnold Buffum to William Lloyd Garrison, February 4, 1834, BPL. Benjamin Coates to Samuel Wilkeson, July 17, 1840, ACS micro., reel. 34. "Register of Confirmations," HSP. Douglass, *Annals of St. Thomas,* 137. *CA,* June 10, 1837; August 5, 1837; August 19, 1837; September 2, 1837; September 9, 1837; September 16, 1837; December 2, 1837; December 9, 1837; December 23, 1837; February 3, 1838; March 3, 1838; March 15, 1838; March 22, 1838; July 14, 1838; September 8, 1838; November 11, 1839; April 11, 1840; September 25, 1841; November 13, 1841. *Eman,* May 18, 1833; July 16, 1833. *FJ,* October 12, 1837. *GUE,* May 1831. *Lib,* March 12, 1831; April 18, 1845. *NECAUL,* October 29, 1836; November 2, 1837. *NR,* September 1838; October 1838; October 1839. *NS,* January 21, 1848. *PF,* October 10, 1839; October 31, 1839; December 12, 1839; May 7, 1840; May 14, 1840; November 12, 1840; November 3, 1841. *Poulson,* June 12, 1828; December 4, 1835. *Raleigh Register,* June 20, 1828. *RA,* August 14, 1829. *Constitution of the American Society of Free Persons of Colour,* 4. *Minutes of the Second Annual Convention of the Free People of Color,* 3. *Third Annual Convention of the Free People of Colour,* 3. *Minutes of the Fourth Annual Convention of the Free People of Colour,* 9. *Minutes of the Fifth Annual Convention for the Improvement of the Free People of Color,* 21. *Appeal of Forty Thousand,* 2. *Philadelphia Association for Moral and Mental Improvement,* 3. PAS census (1838). Friends' census (1847). U.S. census (1830), Philadelphia, Walnut Ward, 477; (1840), Pine Ward, 300. McBride, "Black Protest Against Racial Politics," 149–62.

73. James Needham was born in Philadelphia on January 31, 1807, the son of James Needham Sr., a native of Delaware, and his wife, Elizabeth. A hairdresser by trade, the younger James worked at various hotels in the city. In 1831 he married Philadelphian Martha Matthews. The couple made their home at 25 Elizabeth Street. Over the years Needham was a prominent member of the congregation of St. Thomas's African Episcopal Church. He served as a vestryman, he represented the church in the Association for Moral and Mental Improvement, he was secretary of one of its benevolent societies, the Sons of St. Thomas, and he directed its Juvenile Singing School. Needham took an active role in the work of abolition, joining the Philadelphia Young Men's Anti-Slavery Society, helping found the Pennsylvania Anti-Slavery Society, and aiding runaways as an officer of the Vigilance Committee. Twice, in 1834 and 1835, he was elected to serve as corresponding secretary of the Pennsylvania Committee of the National Convention Board. He was a vociferous opponent of disfranchisement and the program of the American Colonization Society. His activism continued through the 1850s and 1860s. He was an officer of the Pennsylvania Grand Lodge of Prince Hall Masons. He attended the national convention of 1855 in Philadelphia and the 1864 convention in New York, and in 1865 he was a delegate to the Pennsylvania State Equal Rights League. In addition to his work with the Library Company of Colored Persons, he was a member of the Young Men's Philadelphia Library Association. Seamen's Protection Certificates for the Port of Philadelphia (1807), RG 36, NA. *CA,* June 10, 1837; December 9, 1837; December 23, 1837; September 8, 1838; October 5, 1839; January 30, 1841; May 8, 1841; September 25, 1841; October 16, 1841. *CR,* January 11, 1862. *FDP,* April 29, 1852. *HR,* November 1833. *Lib,* July 2, 1836. *NECAUL,* October 29, 1836; September 28, 1837; October 12, 1837. *NS,* June 13, 1850. *PF,* January 17, 1839; June 20, 1839; September 26, 1839; May 14, 1840; December 29, 1841; August 20, 1846. "Notes on Beneficial Societies,

1828-1838," PAS MSS, HSP. Charters of incorporation, Book 4, 352, PSA. Philadelphia Young Men's Anti-Slavery Society Records, in PAS MSS, HSP. Douglass, *Annals of St. Thomas*, 137, 171. *Philadelphia Association for Moral and Mental Improvement. Appeal of Forty Thousand*, 2. *Proceedings of the Colored National Convention . . . 1855*, 7. *Proceedings of the National Convention of Colored Men, Held in the City of Syracuse, N.Y., October 4, 5, 6, and 7, 1864; With the Bill of Wrongs and Rights, and the Address to the American People* (Boston: J. S. Rock and George L. Ruffin, 1864), 5. *Register of Trades*. Philadelphia directories, 1830–31, 1833–37, 1839, 1840–42. St. Thomas's Parish Registers. PAS census (1838); Friends' census (1847). U.S. census (1840), Philadelphia, Pine Ward, 308; (1850), Pine Ward, 326; (1860), Ward 5, 550; (1870), Ward 4, dist. 14, 261.

74. See above, note 48.

75. Robert C. Gordon Jr. (b. 1800) was the son of fruit-seller Robert Gordon, a resident of Philadelphia since the early 1790s and his Barbadian-born wife, Sarah Ann. The younger Gordon was a shoemaker and bootmaker by trade. Like his father, he was an active member of St. Thomas's African Episcopal Church. He and his first wife were confirmed by Bishop William White on October 25, 1829. He served as a vestryman and as secretary of one of the church's beneficial societies, the Sons of St. Thomas. He also represented St. Thomas's at the convention of the Association for Moral and Mental Improvement in 1837. Gordon was a zealous promoter of Samuel Cornish's *Colored American*. He also took part in the campaign to secure the restoration of the franchise, and he was a member of the Philadelphia Young Men's Anti-Slavery Society. Gordon's life was marred by personal tragedy. His first wife, Sarah, died in 1833. He remarried, and it was his second wife, Mary, who raised his sons, Robert and Walter. Both died of tuberculosis within months of each other, Robert in 1847, at age twenty-two, and Walter in 1848, at age twenty-one. Philadelphia Board of Health Records. St. Thomas's Parish Registers. Register of Confirmations. Douglass, *Annals of St. Thomas*, 137. Charters of incorporation, Book 4, 352, PSA. *CA*, December 9, 1837; September 8, 1838; January 30, 1841; May 8, 1841; September 25, 1841. *HR*, November 1833. *Lib*, July 2, 1836. Records of the Young Men's Anti-Slavery Society of Philadelphia, PAS MSS, HSP. U.S. census (1840), Philadelphia, Pine Ward, 290; (1850), Pine Ward, 279.

76. John Dupee (also Depee, D'Pee, or Dupuy) was a staunch opponent of the American Colonization Society and was described by an ACS supporter as one of the "gentlemen of Philadelphia, who have assumed the right of ruling over all the colored people of this country" on the merits of colonization. Dupee was also active in the antislavery cause and in defending the rights of Pennsylvania's people of color. In 1833 he joined three other community leaders in petitioning the state legislature to reject a bill that would curtail their freedom. That same year he was a delegate to the national convention and served as clerk of the convention. *AR*, September 1833; *Lib*, October 19, 1833. *Memorial to the Honourable the Senate and House of Representatives of the Commonwealth of Pennsylvania, in General Assembly Met, the Memorial of the Subscribers, Free People of Colour, Residing in the City of Philadelphia* (Philadelphia, 1833). *Third Annual Convention of the Free People of Colour*, 5. U.S. census (1820), Philadelphia, Passyunk, 142; (1840), North Ward, 182.

77. See above, note 50.

78. John C. Bowers (1810–1873) was the son of community leader John Bowers (note 46) and his wife, Henrietta. A tailor by trade, he was also an accomplished

musician and was for some time the organist at St. Thomas's Church. Bowers, a fervent abolitionist and outspoken opponent of colonization, was much in demand as a public speaker. A member of the Young Men's Anti-Slavery Society of Philadelphia, he joined in the call that led to the formation of the Pennsylvania Anti-Slavery Society, and he traveled to Harrisburg for its first convention. Returning home after the meeting, he was refused a meal at a hotel in Lancaster. His outrage was tempered by his gratitude to his white colleagues, who rose from the table and accompanied him to another hotel. On several occasions Bowers was a delegate to the American Anti-Slavery Society's conventions. He was active in both the American Moral Reform Society—he gave a speech on temperance at its 1837 meeting—and in the Association for Moral and Mental Improvement. He was an agent for the *Weekly Advocate* and its successor, the *Colored American*. In the 1840s he helped sell subscriptions to Martin R. Delany's newspaper, the *Mystery*. A champion of civil and political rights, in 1838 he was on the committee that wrote the *Appeal of Forty Thousand*. He also joined in fund-raising efforts to pay for publishing it and distributing copies to white voters. A decade later, as a delegate to a black state convention in Harrisburg, he agitated for a restoration of the voting rights of Pennsylvania's African-American citizens. His activism continued through the 1850s and 1860s. He attended the national convention of 1855, which met in Philadelphia, and in 1865 he joined the Pennsylvania State Equal Rights League, an organization that worked to achieve many of the goals he had championed for so long.

Bowers's personal life was marked by tragedy. His marriage in 1835 to Mary Collins, daughter of a fellow vestryman at St. Thomas's, ended with her death little more than a year later. Bowers was devastated, and it was many years before he married again. For a long time he made his home with his sister, Henrietta, and her husband, cabinetmaker Francis Duterte. *AAM,* February 18, 1860; December 22, 1860. *CA,* March 4, 1837; December 9, 1837; January 27, 1838; February 3, 1838; March 28, 1838; November 14, 1840. *FDP,* April 7, 1852; April 29, 1852; December 1, 1854; May 25, 1855; February 17, 1860. *Lib,* August 30, 1834; July 2, 1836. *NECAUL,* August 31, 1836; October 29, 1836; February 11, 1837. *NR,* September 1838; September 1839. *NS,* June 15, 1849. *PF,* June 24, 1837; September 14, 1838; April 2, 1840; August 20, 1846; February 19, 1852. *WA,* January 7, 1837; February 25, 1837. Douglass, *Annals of St. Thomas,* 71. William J. Simmons, *Men of Mark: Eminent, Progressive and Rising* (Cleveland: George M. Rewell and Co., 1887; reprint, New York: Arno, 1968), 202. American Anti-Slavery Society, *Fourth Annual Report* (1837), 18; *Fifth Annual Report* (1838), 5; *Seventh Annual Report* (1840), 31. *Proceedings of the Colored National Convention . . . 1855,* 7. *Minutes of the First Annual Meeting of the American Moral Reform Society,* in Porter, ed., *Early Negro Writing,* 225. *Minutes of the Pennsylvania State Convention . . . 1848,* in Foner and Walker, eds., *Black State Conventions,* vol. 1, 2–4. *Appeal of Forty Thousand,* 2. U.S. census (1840), Philadelphia, Walnut Ward, 37; (1850), Spruce Ward, 351; (1860), Ward 20, dist. 1, 194; (1870), Ward 7, dist. 18, 288. Abajian, *Blacks in Selected Newspapers,* vol. 1, 212. Delany, *Destiny of the Colored People,* 99. Will of John C. Bowers, PCA.

79. I could learn little about Trulier, other than that he was a resident of Philadelphia in 1834 and that he subscribed to the *Liberator*. Joseph Cassey to William Lloyd Garrison, February 15, 1834, BPL.

80. See above, note 20.

81. James C. Mathews was a freeborn Pennsylvanian. A hairdresser and hair-

worker (maker of hair-pieces) by trade, he was in business in the 1830s in Barley Alley. He and his family rented a home at 63 South Fourth Street. He was a vestryman at St. Thomas's Church and a member of the Sons of St. Thomas. In addition to his involvement with the Library Company of Colored Persons, he was an energetic supporter of the African-American and antislavery press. In 1832 he was elected to serve on the national convention board to consult with other community leaders and arrange the following year's convention. His wife, Henrietta, a seamstress, was the president of the Female Minervian Literary Society. *Register of Trades. CA,* September 8, 1838; May 8, 1841. *Lib,* July 2, 1836. *PF,* April 28, 1841. Charters of incorporation, Book 4, 352, PSA. PAS census (1838).

82. William White (1748–1836) was the first Protestant Episcopal bishop of the Diocese of Pennsylvania. A generous man, he gave his support to many benevolent and charitable organizations. He endorsed, among other things, the plan to build a black manual labor college in New Haven, Connecticut (note 44). On his support of black literary societies, see William Douglass, *A Discourse Commemorative of William White,* 9–10.

83. Incorporated as the Rush Librarian Debating Society, this organization was named for white abolitionist and humanitarian Dr. Benjamin Rush (1745–1813). In addition to the half-dozen men Willson names, a dozen more helped found it, among them bootmaker Daniel Colly, clothing dealer Garretson Sylvan, and shoemaker-turned-grocer John B. Roberts. Membership was restricted to men over the age of twenty-one. As was the case with the other societies, there were weekly meetings at which members read their own compositions. There was also a program of lectures and debates. The society was still flourishing in December 1843, by which time it had thirty members and a library of some one hundred volumes. The members had forsaken Salter's Hall for Union Hall, on the corner of Seventh Street and Bradford Alley, in the heart of the South Street corridor. Charters of incorporation, Book 6, 66, PSA. "Committee to Improve the Condition of the African Race," Minute Book, PAS MSS, HSP. *Present State and Condition.*

84. Born into slavery in Delaware, John L. Hart (1796–1854) secured his freedom and moved to Philadelphia when he was in his twenties. Unlike many of the people Willson writes about in *Sketches of the Higher Classes,* Hart lacked a skilled trade. He was a porter. He and his wife, Elizabeth, a washerwoman and seamstress, never earned sufficient money to buy a home. However, they struggled to send their children to school and secure apprenticeships for them. Hart's relatively humble status did not bar him from becoming a respected member of the community. In addition to his involvement with the Rush Library Company, he was a vestryman at St. Thomas's African Episcopal Church (he had defected from First Colored Wesley Methodist, of which he was a founding member), joined the temperance crusade, and subscribed to Garrison's *Liberator.* He served as secretary of no less than five benevolent societies—the United Daughters of Wilberforce, the Union Sons of Industry, the Male Harrison Benevolent, the Friendly Daughters of Nehemiah, and the Female Simeon—and was a member of three more, the United Sons of Wilberforce, the Wilberforce Benevolent, and the Rush Benevolent. *CA,* February 3, 1838; September 25, 1841. *PF,* December 8, 1841. *RA,* October 9, 1829. "Notes on Beneficial Societies, 1828–1838," in PAS MSS, HSP. Charters of incorporation, Book 3, 208; Book 4, 78, 343; Book 6, 66, 382; Book 7, 156, PSA. PAS census (1838); Friends'

census (1847). U.S. census (1830), Philadelphia, Locust Ward, 77; (1840), Walnut Ward, 44; (1850), New Market Ward, 362. Philadelphia Board of Health Records.

85. William D. Banton was a bootblack. In 1838 the value of his personal property was $150. Within a decade he had $500 in personal property, and real estate in New Jersey worth $100. His children attended private schools. It is unclear from the 1838 Pennsylvania Abolition Society census whether he was the member of the Banton household who had been born into slavery and manumitted. In addition to his involvement with the Rush Education Society, his membership of at least one benevolent society, the Citizen Sons of Philadelphia (he served as its secretary), and his affiliation with Brick Wesley, one of the city's black Methodist churches, Banton subscribed to the *Liberator* and took a keen interest in the antislavery cause. Joseph Cassey to William Lloyd Garrison, February 15, 1834, BPL. "Notes on Beneficial Societies, 1828–1838," in PAS MSS, HSP. PAS Census (1838); Friends' Census (1847); Philadelphia directory, 1850. Charters of incorporation, Book 6, 66, 359, PSA.

86. Littleton Hubert (b. 1805) was a well-to-do grocer from Delaware who moved to Philadelphia some time before 1837 with $150. By 1847 he had $3,800 in real estate and $2,000 in personal property. It is not clear from the Friends' Census whether it was Hubert or his wife, Ann, who had been born a slave and manumitted. In 1837 Hubert was a delegate to the American Moral Reform Society from the Rush Library Company. In 1841 he joined other Philadelphians in calling for a revival of the national convention movement. Charters of incorporation, Book 6, 66, PSA. *Minutes of the First Annual Meeting of the American Moral Reform Society*, in Porter, ed., *Early Negro Writing*, 225. *CA*, September 25, 1841. *FDP*, April 29, 1852. *PF*, December 8, 1841. PAS census (1838); Friends' census (1847). U.S. census (1850), Philadelphia, Spruce Ward, 364; (1860), Ward 5, 353; (1870), Ward 4, dist. 14, 274.

87. Harrison R. Sylva was a clothing dealer of modest means. His place of birth is not known, but he had been born free and had settled in Philadelphia before 1837, when he attended the American Moral Reform Society convention as a delegate from the Rush Education Society. *Minutes of the First Annual Meeting of the American Moral Reform Society*, in Porter, ed., *Early Negro Writing*, 225. PAS census (1838).

88. James Bird (d. 1848) settled in Philadelphia some time before 1829 and took an active role in a number of community enterprises. He was a steadfast opponent of the American Colonization Society. He championed newspapers published by free people of color and their white abolitionist allies. He was involved in the convention movement from its inception to 1835. He served as a delegate to the American Moral Reform Society conventions of 1837 and 1839. He was vice-president of the Mechanics' Enterprise Hall Company and president of a benevolent society, the Citizen Sons of Philadelphia. In 1838 he helped raise money to publish the *Appeal of Forty Thousand*. Bird was a bootmaker by trade. Although not as wealthy as some of those in Willson's "higher classes," he prospered in Philadelphia. By 1838 he had accumulated real estate and personal property valued at $2,000. *Register of Trades. CA*, April 22, 1837; September 8, 1838; September 25, 1841. *Eman*, July 20, 1833. *NR*, September 1838; September 1839. *PF*, August 10, 1837; September 6, 1838. *RA*, October 9, 1829; October 16, 1829. *Minutes of the First Annual Meeting of the American Moral Reform Society*, in Porter, ed., *Early Negro Writing*, 225. Joseph Cassey to William Lloyd Garrison, February 12, 1833, BPL. "Notes on Beneficial Societies, 1828–1838," PAS MSS, HSP. Charters of incorporation, Book 6, 66, 359, PSA. *Constitution of the American Society of Free Persons of Color . . . 1830*, 8. *Third Annual Conven-*

tion of the Free People of Colour, 3, 5; *Minutes of the Fourth Annual Convention of the Free People of Colour*, 9–10, 13–14. PAS census (1838). Friends' census (1847). U.S. census, Philadelphia (1830), Walnut Ward, 474.

89. Charles Brister or Bristol (b. 1798) lived for many years in Portland Lane, in Philadelphia's Pine Ward. He was a laborer in a sugar refinery and in 1847 earned $30 a month. A respected member of the community, he was president of the African Porters' Benevolent Society. Brister had been born in Pennsylvania after passage of that state's Gradual Emancipation Law, but two members of his household had been born into slavery and had purchased their freedom. Unlike many of his contemporaries, Brister had had several years of formal education. From 1809 to 1813 he attended a school operated by Arthur Donaldson, a white teacher. *JM*, July 1813. "Notes on Beneficial Societies, 1828–1838," in PAS MSS, HSP. Charters of incorporation, Book 6, 66, 359, PSA. PAS census (1838); Friends' census (1847). U.S. census, (1830), Philadelphia, Pine Ward, 334; (1840), Pine Ward, 306; (1850), Pine Ward, 324.

90. Paris Salter (1789–1849) was a bricklayer, plasterer, slater, and stonemason who lived at 2 Elizabeth Street. Willson probably knew him fairly well, since both were members of the congregation of St. Thomas's. Salter was a delegate to the American Moral Reform Society's convention in 1837 from the Mechanics' Association of Philadelphia. He died in the cholera epidemic of 1849. The "hall" Willson refers to was the Mechanics' Enterprise Hall. Its construction was apparently sponsored by members of the Humane Mechanics' Association, one of the most venerable intellectual and mutual relief organizations in the Philadelphia community. It cost $10,000 to build, and the money was raised by selling stock in the African-American community. The organizers of the Mechanics' Enterprise Hall Company were members of the "higher classes" who wanted to reach out to "persons occupying the humblest stations in life." As a builder, Paris Salter probably oversaw the construction of the hall. It was located on Elizabeth Street, close to his home. *NECAUL, August* 17, 1836; August 31, 1836. *NR, September* 1839. *PF,* August 10, 1837; July 26, 1838. *Register of Trades. Minutes of the First Annual Meeting of the American Moral Reform Society*, in Porter, ed., *Early Negro Writing*, 225. U.S. census (1840), Philadelphia, Pine Ward, 306. Philadelphia Board of Health Records. Philadelphia directories, 1825, 1841.

91. The Demosthenian Institute was initially known as the Young Men's Union Literary Association. It was subsequently renamed for the celebrated Greek orator Demosthenes (ca. 383–322 b.c.). The young men who founded the Demosthenian Institute expressed their belief that their endeavors would benefit the entire African-American community by countering assertions that people of color were incapable of intellectual improvement. Membership in the Institute was restricted to men "of strict moral character." between the ages of eighteen and forty. The Demosthenian Institute celebrated its second anniversary on January 11, 1841, at Philadelphia's First African Presbyterian Church. An ode was composed for the occasion, and some of the most able African-American musicians and singers in the city were recruited for a concert. George Washington Goines, visiting from New York, was much impressed and sent an account of the celebration to the *Colored American.* "Remus," another correspondent to the *Colored American,* made note of the series of public lectures the members of the Institute had organized, and singled out for praise Isaac J. White's discussion of the rise and fall of the Moorish empire in Spain. At the time he was writing, the Demosthenian Institute had about forty members and maintained a small

library of "very choice books." *CA,* February 2, 1839; December 12, 1840; January 23, 1841; April 24, 1841.

92. John Emery Burr (b. 1818) was the son of Hetty (note 116) and John P. Burr (note 11). He was a barber by trade, like his father and one of his brothers, David. (Two more brothers, Edward and Martin, were carpenters.) He was active in the antislavery cause, helping collect subscriptions for Garrison's *Liberator* and joining in the call for the formation of the Pennsylvania Anti-Slavery Society. Arnold Buffum to Isaac Knapp, February 2, 1836; BPL. *NECAUL,* November 19, 1836. *NS,* October 5, 1849; October 12, 1849. U.S. census (1850), Philadelphia, Moyamensing, Ward 2, 243; (1860), Philadelphia, Ward 7, 259; (1870), Ward 7, dist. 18, 274.

93. South Carolina native David Gordon (b. 1819/20) worked as a barber at the city's fashionable Washington House hotel. In addition to his membership of the Demosthenian Institute, he was active in the American Moral Reform Society during the 1830s. He eventually married a woman from Philadelphia, Mary. By 1870 the couple had six children: Alice (age 25), a schoolteacher; Walter (23), a barber like his father; Eliza (19), a dressmaker; Mary (13); David (11); and Ella (7). Eliza and her younger siblings had been born in Connecticut. David Gordon and two of his children, Walter and Eliza, were described as black, and the rest of the family as mulattoes. Gordon owned real estate worth $2,000 and personal property to the value of $1,000. *CA,* February 2, 1839; April 24, 1841. *NR,* September 1839; November 1839. *PF,* January 7, 1841. U.S. census (1860), Philadelphia, Ward 15, 447; (1870), Ward 15, dist. 44, 512. Philadelphia directory, 1841.

94. Benjamin Stanley or Stanly (b. 1822) was originally from North Carolina and was reputed to be related to Congressman Edward Stanly. He may also have been a member of the family of wealthy African-American barber-turned-planter John Carruthers Stanly. Benjamin Stanly was a hairdresser. In 1841, when *Sketches of the Higher Classes* was written, he was working with Alexander F. Hutchinson (note 100) in an establishment at 44 North Fourth and living in Moyamensing, one of the city's unincorporated "liberties." In addition to his involvement in the Demosthenian Institute, he was active in the antislavery campaign and in the work of moral reform. In 1839 he was a member of the Association for Moral and Mental Improvement, and the following year he was a delegate to the Pennsylvania Anti-Slavery Society. In 1841 he helped organize a meeting to protest the disfranchisement of the state's black citizens. At the second-anniversary celebrations of the Demosthenian Institute Benjamin Stanly delivered an address on the character of Demosthenes.

By the mid-1840s Stanly had moved to New York City. As he had done in Philadelphia, he insisted on equal voting rights. He also called for an end to discrimination in the churches and, with the passage of the Fugitive Slave Act, he urged resistance—armed if necessary—to slave catchers. *Register of Trades. CA,* June 29, 1839; January 30, 1841; April 24, 1841; May 8, 1841; September 25, 1841. *NR,* September 1839; October 1839. *NS,* October 24, 1850. *PF,* January 24, 1839; June 20, 1839; October 10, 1839; May 14, 1840. PAS census (1838). U.S. census (1840), Philadelphia County, Moyamensing, 26; (1850), New York City, Dist. 1, Ward 16, 76. Ripley et al., *Black Abolitionist Papers,* vol. 3, 473; Loren Schweninger, "John Carruthers Stanly and the Anomaly of Black Slaveholding," *N.C.HR* 68 (April 1990), 159–92.

95. At the time the Demosthenian Institute was established, nineteen-year-old William M. Jennings was working at Philadelphia's Third Street Hall as a barber. He died of consumption on June 13, 1848, at age twenty-eight, and was buried in the

cemetery of St. Thomas's Church. *Register of Trades. CA,* February 2, 1839. Philadelphia Board of Health Records.

96. The account of the founding of the Young Men's Union Literary Society (later known as the Demosthenian Institute) in the *Colored American* gives Gibbons's full name as George Washington Gibbons. He was probably the son of well-to-do carpenter and house-builder James Gibbons. George Washington Gibbons left Philadelphia for New York City around the time *Sketches of the Higher Classes* was published. He served as New York agent for the *Demosthenian Shield* and became as deeply involved in community reform efforts in New York as he had been in Philadelphia. He also did well in business. Moving into a home at 108 West Broadway, in the city's Fifth Ward, he quickly established himself as a carpenter and builder, and "the only colored coffin-maker in this city." On November 8, 1841, in a ceremony at Zion Baptist Church, he married New Yorker Anne B. Poole. *CA,* February 2, 1839; July 24, 1841; September 4, 1841; October 2, 1841; November 20, 1840; December 4, 1841. U.S. census (1840), Philadelphia, Spring Garden, Dist. 2, 1.

97. Lewis Mead Jr. (1818–1839) was the son of Lewis and Mary Mead. Lewis Sr. (1780–1848) was a native of Virginia who prospered in Philadelphia as a hairdresser. Lewis Jr. had several brothers who joined their father in business, and he too became a barber when he completed his formal education at the Pennsylvania Abolition Society's Clarkson School. The Meads lived at 473 Market Street and belonged to the First African Presbyterian Church. Both Lewis Sr. and Mary were active in the community. He was involved in a number of reform efforts, and she was an officer of the Female Vigilance Committee, a group of women who coordinated aid to fugitive slaves. Lewis Jr.'s career was cut short by his death from an inflammation of the lungs on August 25, 1839. He was twenty-one years old. Clarkson School, Statement of Tuition (1835), PAS MSS, HSP. Joseph Cassey to William Lloyd Garrison, March 23, 1834, BPL. *CA,* February 2, 1839; April 24, 1841. *NR, November* 1838. *PF,* July 5, 1838; October 10, 1839. *Register of Trades.* PAS census (1838); Friends' census (1847). U.S. census, Philadelphia (1830), Middle Ward, 183; (1840), North Ward, 195. Philadelphia Board of Health Records. Philadelphia directories, 1830, 1840.

98. An account of the founding of the Demosthenian Institute identifies "E. Parkinson" as "Eben Parkenson." He is not listed in any of the city directories of the 1830s, nor does his name appear in the federal censuses of 1840 and 1850, the PAS census of 1838, or the Friends' census of 1847. *CA,* February 2, 1839.

99. Zedekiah Johnson Purnell (born 1813) was a member of one of the most socially active families in Philadelphia's black community. He began his working life as a sailor, but he soon gave up the sea for a more stable life ashore. In 1839, when he helped found the organization that would become the Demosthenian Institute, Purnell ran a successful hairdressing business at the corner of Carpenter and Decatur Streets, and owned real estate. He and his wife, Ann Sammons, were members of the congregation of the church of the black elite, St. Thomas's. In the 1840s Purnell emerged as a champion of the black press, supporting Samuel Cornish and Charles B. Ray's *Colored American* and Martin R. Delany's *Mystery.* He also served as editor of the *Demosthenian Shield* (note 103). He joined in the call for a revival of the convention movement at both the state and the national levels. In 1841 he traveled to Pittsburgh to attend the Pennsylvania state convention of "Colored Freemen," and in 1847 he was the only delegate from Pennsylvania at the national convention in Troy, New York. He eventually moved to California, where he continued to be active

in the cause of civil rights. He also turned to the sea once more to earn a living. In 1880 Purnell, listed as a steward on a steamship, was living in Oakland, California, with his wife, their son, and their two married daughters. Seamen's Protection Certificates for the Port of Philadelphia (1833), RG 36, NA. *Register of Trades. CA,* October 13, 1838; February 2, 1839; December 5, 1840; May 8, 1841. *NR,* September 1839. *PF,* January 7, 1841; April 28, 1841; December 8, 1841; August 20, 1846. *Proceedings of the State Convention of the Colored Freemen of Pennsylvania, Held in Pittsburgh, on the 23d, 24th and 25th of August, 1841, for the Purpose of Considering Their Condition, and the Means of Its Improvement,* in Foner and Walker, eds., *Proceedings of the Black State Conventions,* vol. 2, 116. *Proceedings of the National Convention of Colored People, and Their Friends, Held in Troy, New York, on the 6th, 7th, 8th and 9th of October, 1847* (Troy: J. C. Kneeland, 1847), 3. Abajian, *Blacks in Selected Newspapers,* vol. 3, 119–20; Abajian, *Supplement,* vol. 2, 262. St. Thomas's Parish Registers. PAS census (1838). U.S. census, Philadelphia (1860), Ward 2, 272; (1880), Oakland, Alameda County, California, e.d. 10, 18. Philadelphia directory, 1845.

100. Alexander F. Hutchinson received his formal education at the Pennsylvania Abolition Society's Clarkson School. He became a barber and worked with fellow Demosthenian Institute member Benjamin Stanly at 44 North Fourth. He died of consumption on November 26, 1844, at the age of twenty-four. Clarkson School, Statement of Tuition (1835), PAS MSS, HSP. *Register of Trades. CA,* February 2, 1839. Philadelphia Board of Health Records.

101. B. Hughes was Benjamin Hughes. His full name is given in the account of the founding of the Demosthenian Institute published in the *Colored American.* However, no one of that name appears in the directories or the censuses. He was probably not the same Benjamin F. Hughes, a member of the Philadelphia Presbytery, who taught school in New York City in the late 1820s. That individual seems to have been an older man. As Willson notes, the members of the Demosthenian Institute were all under the age of twenty-one. *CA,* February 2, 1839.

102. Thomas Smith Crouch (b. 1821) was a barber from Virginia who was working in a barbershop at 16 Arcade when he helped organize the Demosthenian Institute. He gave a speech at the Institute's second-anniversary observances on "morality and religion" entitled "3 Hours Ramble." Crouch eventually moved to San Bernardino County, California. He was living there in the 1870s. *CA,* January 23, 1841. Philadelphia directory, 1840. Abajian, *Supplement,* vol. 1, 266.

103. The young editors of the *Demosthenian Shield* received generous praise from two men who were their potential rivals, Charles B. Ray and Samuel Cornish, of the New York–based *Colored American.* (There was also some fairly good-natured bantering over the *Shield*'s Latin motto.) The new paper's "literary contents evince creditable talent; the editorials are respectable; the selections are amusing and well arranged." The *"feature* of the paper" consisted of "Sketches of Eminent Colored Men in Philadelphia." The "venerable patriot, James Forten" was the subject of the first, and Robert Douglass Sr. was the subject of the second. The *Demosthenian Shield* was to be published every Tuesday, and subscriptions cost $1 a year. Apparently no copies have survived. According to William Carl Bolivar, the community historian who signed himself "Pencil Pusher," the paper foundered when Benjamin Stanly moved to New York. *CA,* July 17, 1841; July 24, 1841; July 31, 1841; September

25, 1841; October 16, 1841. *Tribune,* June 7, 1913. Delany, *Destiny of the Colored People,* 127.

104. Willson omitted the oldest of the female organizations, the Female Literary Association of Philadelphia, founded in September 1831. The women in the Association developed an agenda for their meetings that their sister organizations would follow. Time was set aside for reading aloud and discussing works of literature and items from the antislavery press, but the women were also keen to encourage original literary composition. Each week members would bring along their work—unsigned or identified only by a *nom de plume*—and place it in a box. One of the officers would then read it, and the other members would offer comments. In this way views could be expressed, and stylistic and grammatical corrections made, without embarrassment or personal affront. Poetry and prose by members appeared regularly in the *Liberator* and the *Pennsylvania Freeman. Lib,* December 3, 1831; October 13, 1832; January 28, 1832; July 7, 1832; July 21, 1832; March 1, 1834. Sarah M. Douglass to William Lloyd Garrison, December 6, 1832; Garrison to Douglass, March 5, 1832, BPL. Julie Winch, " 'You Have Talents—Only Cultivate Them': Philadelphia's Black Female Literary Societies and the Abolitionist Crusade," in Jean Fagan Yellin and John C. Van Horne, eds., *The Abolitionist Sisterhood: Women's Political Culture in Antebellum America* (Ithaca: Cornell University Press, 1994), 101–18.

105. The organization's official title was the Female Minervian Literary Society, and it was several months older than Willson gave it credit for being. It was established toward the end of 1833 and named for Minerva, the Roman goddess of wisdom. Its first president was seamstress Henrietta Mathews, the wife of James C. Mathews, one of the founding members of the Library Company of Colored Persons (note 81). In 1838 it had twenty members and a modest fifty-volume library. Membership was limited to African-American women, but others were welcome to attend meetings. Among those who did were community leaders John C. Bowers and Henry B. Miller, and white abolitionist Lucretia Mott. Mott described a typical weekly gathering in the meeting-room in the basement of St. Thomas's Church. The women "pass the evening in intellectual study—frequently employing their hands in sewing or knitting, while one is reading for the benefit of the whole." The society survived until at least 1861. *CR,* August 10, 1861. *Lib,* March 1, 1834; August 30, 1834. *PF,* February 27, 1840. *Present State and Condition.* Winch, " 'You Have Talents,' " 101–18.

106. The Edgeworth Literary Association, founded in 1836, was named in honor of Irish novelist Maria Edgeworth (1767–1849), the author of such works as *Castle Rackrent* and an advocate of women's education. In 1838 the society had thirty members. *Present State and Condition. NECAUL,* September 7, 1837. Winch, " 'You Have Talents,' " 101–18.

107. The Gilbert Lyceum did indeed flourish. Weekly meetings for "diffusing scientific and literary knowledge" were still being held at Sarah M. Douglass's school more than two years after the publication of Willson's book. The Lyceum owned "a collection of objects of natural history, and some chemical apparatus, with the use of which some . . . members are very conversant." Each winter the Lyceum organized a series of lectures on subjects ranging from Jerusalem and "the character and exploits of Hannibal" to "Physiology, Anatomy, Chemistry & Natural Philosophy." Some of the lectures were given by members , others by invited guests. The only clue to the identity of the "gentleman . . . who recommended (the) formation" of the Ly-

ceum comes from a stray item in the *Colored American.* Around the time the Lyceum was organized, Sarah M. Douglass forwarded to a friend a poem on the death of abolitionist Benjamin Lundy by one Howard W. Gilbert of Philadelphia. Committee to Improve the Condition of the African Race, Minute Book, 1837–53, PAS MSS, HSP; Leon Gardiner Collection, HSP. *CA,* April 3, 1841.

108. Willson is quoting act 5, scene 1, line 17, of Shakespeare's *A Midsummer Night's Dream.*

109. Robert Douglass Sr. (1777–1849) came to Philadelphia from St. Kitts in the British West Indies when he was in his early twenties. By 1801 he had established himself at 54 Mulberry (later Arch) Street as a hairdresser and perfumer. He married Grace Bustill, daughter of community leader Cyrus Bustill, on November 17, 1803, at St. Thomas's African Episcopal Church. Although initially affiliated with St. Thomas's, Douglass eventually left to join the First African Presbyterian Church, of which he became a highly respected elder. Deeply interested in education and intellectual improvement, he served as treasurer of the Pennsylvania Augustine Society, president of the Library Company of Colored Persons, and one of the trustees of St. Thomas's school, in addition to his involvement in the Gilbert Lyceum. He was the president of one of the community's beneficial organizations, the Benezet Philanthropic Society. A Garrisonian, he opposed colonization, endorsed the *Liberator,* and raised funds for the manual labor college Garrison and his supporters hoped to establish in New Haven (note 44). Douglass prospered as a businessman. By 1838 he owned real estate worth $7,000 and had personal property valued at $1,000.

Robert Douglass had his share of personal tragedies. He lost his eldest daughter, Elizabeth, to a "diseased hip joint," and two sons, William and Charles, to tuberculosis. In 1842 his wife died. His daughter, Sarah (note 115), kept house for him, as well as running a private school. She survived her father, as did two of his sons, James, who succeeded him in business, and Robert Jr. (note 20), who achieved considerable distinction as an artist. Bustill-Mossell Family Papers, UPA. *Resolutions and Remonstrances of the People of Colour against Colonization on the Coast of Africa* (Philadelphia, 1817), 3. *CA,* March 28, 1840; December 26, 1840; July 24, 1841. *Lib,* March 12, 1831; April 13, 1833. *NR,* September 1839; November 1839. *NS,* February 16, 1849. *Poulson,* March 2, 1822. *PF,* April 2, 1840. *True American Commercial Advertiser,* November 22, 1803. *Constitution of the Augustine Society.* "Notes on Beneficial Societies, 1828–1838," PAS MSS, HSP. Anna Davis Hallowell, ed., *James and Lucretia Mott, Life and Letters* (Boston: Houghton Mifflin, 1884), 130. Douglass, *Annals of St. Thomas,* 111. Charters of incorporation, Book 2, 28; Book 3, 425, PSA. PAS census (1838). Friends' census (1847). U.S. census (1800), Philadelphia, 103; (1810), High Street Ward, 24; (1830), High Street Ward, 46; (1840), High Street Ward, 244. Marie Lindhorst, "Politics in a Box: Sarah Mapps Douglass and the Female Literary Association, 1831–1833," *PA Hist* 65 (Summer 1998), 272.

110. One of the few men of color to be designated a "gentleman" in the city directories, Joseph Cassey (1789–1848) moved to Philadelphia from the French West Indies sometime before 1808. A hairdresser and perfumer, he was also a moneylender and amassed substantial real estate holdings in Philadelphia, nearby Bucks County, and New Jersey's Burlington County. Cassey was active in a number of community endeavors. In 1824 he was keenly interested in a scheme to recruit free people of color to emigrate to Haiti, and he agreed to serve as treasurer of the Haytien Emigration Society of Philadelphia. He was a zealous promoter of education

within the black community. In 1818 he was an officer of the Pennsylvania Augustine Society—a post that brought him into contact with one of the proponents of Haitian resettlement, Prince Saunders—and in the early 1830s he helped raise money for the ill-fated manual labor college in New Haven (note 44). Some years later, in 1839, he joined with other African-American entrepreneurs—business partner Robert Purvis, lumber merchant Stephen Smith, and sailmaker James Forten—to purchase a ten-year scholarship at Oneida Institute, a manual labor college in upstate New York that pursued a race-blind policy on admissions. Cassey also supported newspapers published by African Americans and by white abolitionists. As his correspondence with William Lloyd Garrison shows, he was a tireless and very able agent for the *Liberator*. He was also a generous supporter of the American Anti-Slavery Society, serving on its Board of Managers from 1834 to 1836 and helping to fund its work. A moral suasionist, he was treasurer of the American Moral Reform Society from its birth in 1835 to its demise six years later. A member of the congregation of St. Thomas's Church for many years, he was an officer of one of its benevolent societies, the Sons of St. Thomas, and of the nondenominational Benezet Philanthropic Society. In 1840, worth an estimated $75,000, Cassey retired, moved away from his hairdressing establishment on South Fourth Street and purchased an elegant home on Lombard Street. When the census-takers from the Society of Friends called upon him in 1847, he informed them that his personal property was worth $2,000, but he declined to disclose any details about his real estate holdings. On his death in 1848 he left a substantial estate to be divided among his six surviving children and his wife, Amy Williams Cassey. Joseph Cassey to Isaac Knapp, October 16, 1832; Cassey to William Lloyd Garrison, February 12, 1833; Cassey to Garrison, March 23, 1833; Cassey to Garrison, February 15, 1834, BPL. *ASR*, February 1836. *CA*, September 9, 1837; September 23, 1837; February 9, 1839. *Eman*, May 18, 1833. *Lib*, March 9, 1833; April 13, 1833; October 19, 1833; August 9, 1839. *NASS*, January 20, 1848. *NR*, September 1838; September 1839. *NS*, January 21, 1848; February 18, 1848. *PF*, January 18, 1844. *Poulson*, September 28, 1826. *RA*, October 9, 1829. Charters of incorporation, Book 1, 487; Book 4, 352, PSA. Haytien Emigration Society of Philadelphia, *Information for the People of Colour*. American Anti-Slavery Society, *First Annual Report* (1834), 32, 35, 36, 38; *Second Annual Report*, 27; *Third Annual Report*, 25. *Constitution of the American Society of Free Persons of Colour*, 8; *Minutes of the First Annual Convention of the People of Colour*, 7; *Minutes of the Fifth Annual Convention for the Improvement of the Free People of Color*, 32. *College for Colored Youth* (1831), 3. *Constitution of the Augustine Society* (1818). *Minutes of the First Annual Convention of the American Moral Reform Society*, in Porter, ed., *Early Negro Writing*, 224. Philadelphia Board of Health Records. Burial Records, Board of Health, 1807–1814, PCA. Philadelphia County Deeds, Bucks County Deeds, Burlington County, N.J., Deeds. Philadelphia directories, 1808–36, 1840–48. Friends' Census (1847). U.S. census, (1810), Philadelphia, Middle Ward, 203, and Moyamensing, 127; (1820), Chestnut Ward, 11; (1830), Chestnut Ward, 497; (1840), New Market Ward, 167. Will of Joseph Cassey, PCA. Delany, *Destiny of the Colored People*, 95. Minton, *The Negro in Business in Philadelphia*, 17.

111. Pennsylvania-born Jacob C. White (1806–1872) was one of the wealthiest individuals in Philadelphia's African-American community. He began in business as a barber, bleeder, and dentist, but his account books indicate that he saw the wisdom of diversifying his investments. Soon he was the proprietor of a small retail store.

Then, in 1847, he bought a piece of land at Ninth and Lombard and opened a cemetery. Lebanon Cemetery was one of the few black-owned burial grounds in the city and the only one not attached to a church.

Aside from his business interests, White took the lead in a number of organizations and enterprises. In 1833 he petitioned the state legislature on behalf of the people of color of Philadelphia County when measures were being debated that would deprive them of many of their basic liberties. He subscribed to the *Liberator* and supported the *Colored American*. He was a member of both the American Moral Reform Society and the Association for Moral and Mental Improvement. He and his wife, seamstress Elizabeth Miller White, worked as a highly effective team in aiding runaways. He was secretary and agent of the Vigilance Committee, and she was an officer of the female auxiliary. White was also treasurer of the interracial Agricultural and Mechanical Association of Pennsylvania and New Jersey and an officer of the Humane Mechanics' Association, a black benevolent and educational organization. In addition to his involvement with the Gilbert Lyceum, in the 1850s White emerged as a leading light in the Banneker Institute, an all-male educational and mutual improvement society that attracted many of the younger men in the community. Widely read and articulate, White was much in demand as a speaker. His addresses to the Banneker Institute dealt with such issues as the evils of intemperance, the virtues of industry and thrift, and the moral duty of free people of color to abstain from the use of slave-produced goods. White was also a highly respected and very active member of the Second African Presbyterian Church. The White family lived for many years at 100 Old York Road. Jacob C. White was survived by his wife and six of their ten children. Jacob C. White to the Humane Mechanics' Association, ca. 1839; Leon Gardiner Collection, HSP. Jacob C. White Sr. Account Book of China Store, Leon Gardiner Collection, HSP. Dentist Accounts, 1845–53, and Rent Accounts, 1845–58, AMS 361, HSP. White Family Letters, Leon Gardiner Collection, Box 2G, HSP. Charters of incorporation, Book 4, 228, PSA. *CA,* August 19, 1837; September 9, 1837; December 2, 1837; February 3, 1838; June 30, 1838; September 8, 1838; July 25, 1840. *CR,* March 22, 1862. *NECAUL,* September 28, 1837; October 10, 1837. *NR,* September 1838; January 1839; September 1839; October 1839. *PF,* July 26, 1838; June 20, 1839; October 10, 1839; March 15, 1840. *ProvF,* July 8, 1854; November 11, 1854. *Minutes of the First Annual Convention of the American Moral Reform Society,* in Porter, ed., *Early Negro Writing,* 224. *Proceedings of the Colored National Convention . . . 1855,* 7. *Proceedings of the National Convention of Colored Men . . . 1864,* 5. Joseph Cassey to William Lloyd Garrison, February 15, 1834, BPL. Catto, *Semi-Centenary Discourse,* 91–92, 99, 102. U.S. census, (1830), Philadelphia, Northern Liberties, Ward 2, 36; (1840), Northern Liberties, Ward 4, 90; (1850), Northern Liberties, 214; (1860), Philadelphia, Ward 12, 125; (1870), Ward 11, dist. 34, 115. Quarles, *Black Abolitionists,* 76, 93, 177.

112. See above, note 78.

113. Robert Purvis (1810–1898) was born in Charleston, South Carolina, the son of Anglo-Scottish merchant William Purvis and his "beloved friend," Harriet Judah, a free woman of North African and German-Jewish ancestry. William Purvis moved his family to Philadelphia in 1819 with the intention of settling his business affairs in the United States and relocating with Harriet and their children in England. Robert and his brothers, Joseph and William, were educated at the Pennsylvania Abolition Society's Clarkson School. He was then sent to a school in Pittsfield, Massachusetts,

where his father's brother, John, had settled. William Purvis eventually enrolled his son at Amherst Academy, a preparatory school affiliated with nearby Amherst College. He left after a brush with school authorities over a July Fourth prank.

Had Robert Purvis chosen to do so, he could have lived his life as a white man. He was light-skinned enough to "pass." He told abolitionist Samuel J. May he "had traveled much in stage-coaches, and stopped days and weeks at Saratoga and other fashionable summer resorts, and mingled, without question, among the beaux and belles." He was also wealthy enough to arouse few suspicions. William Purvis died in 1826 leaving a fortune of more than $200,000. Harriet Judah inherited $10,000, and the rest was divided among their sons. The death of William Jr. two years later, unmarried and without issue, left Robert and Joseph to divide his share between themselves. Robert Purvis proceeded to link his fortune to that of African-American sailmaker James Forten. In 1831 he married Harriet Davy Forten (1810–1875), James Forten's daughter (note 118).

Robert Purvis often spoke of his father's commitment to abolition (although a close examination of the business affairs of both William Purvis and Harriet Judah indicates both owned and traded slaves). He immersed himself in the antislavery cause and a host of related reforms. He was one of the founders of the Colored Free Produce Society of Pennsylvania. He helped finance Garrison's *Liberator*. He was on the board of the projected manual labor college (note 44). He was one of three men of color who signed the constitution of the American Anti-Slavery Society in 1833. The following year, after a struggle to secure a passport, he embarked on a trip to Britain to visit his father's family and settle some business affairs, and to advance the antislavery cause. He traveled extensively, met the leaders of the British antislavery movement, and was much sought after as a lecturer.

On his return to Philadelphia he joined the Young Men's Anti-Slavery Society. In 1837 he helped organize the Pennsylvania Anti-Slavery Society. (He was its president from 1845 to 1850.) He played a major role in writing the *Appeal of Forty Thousand* in 1838 in an effort to persuade white voters to reject the revised state constitution that would disfranchise African Americans. He was a stalwart of the American Moral Reform Society (note 45). He gave addresses, rallied support for the abolitionist cause and quickly established himself as one of the most influential members of Philadelphia's "higher classes of colored society." His reform work was made possible by the fact that he was independently wealthy. Like his sometime business partner, Joseph Cassey (note 110), he was accorded the title "gentleman" in the Philadelphia directories. Purvis inherited not only his father's money but also his sound business sense. He accumulated real estate in Pennsylvania and New Jersey, and invested in bank and railroad stock. Unlike his brother, Joseph, who died in debt, Robert Purvis was a shrewd man of business who knew how to read the often volatile market.

Although both were freeborn, Robert and Harriet Purvis threw themselves into the task of aiding fugitive slaves. In 1836 Robert Purvis was almost single-handedly responsible for the rescue of the Dorsey brothers, four runaway slaves from Maryland. He built secret hiding-places in his home in Philadelphia and in the farmhouse he owned in Byberry, just outside the city. He was a tireless officer of the Vigilance Committee and kept meticulous records of those he helped, until his family persuaded him to destroy his papers after the passage of the Fugitive Slave Act. It was word of Purvis's Vigilance Committee activities that provoked a white mob to attack his home in 1842 and precipitated the family's move to Byberry. During the riot the pacifist Purvis had to defend his home with a shotgun.

Purvis took a prominent part in organizing the state convention of 1848 to agitate for the restoration of the franchise, and he was chosen to head the organization that emerged from the convention, the Citizens' Union of the Commonwealth of Pennsylvania. During the 1850s, in common with other African-American abolitionists, he became increasingly militant, advocating force to rescue slaves. He also felt the full weight of racism when he was taxed to support schools his children could not attend. It was the wish to give their children more opportunities than they could find in the United States that prompted Robert and Harriet Purvis to consider emigrating to England, although they eventually opted to stay.

During the Civil War, Purvis helped enlist black troops. (One of his sons, Charles, became an army surgeon.) After the war Robert and Harriet Purvis worked for the passage of the Fourteenth and Fifteenth Amendments through the American Equal Rights Association and the Pennsylvania State Equal Rights League. Although a Republican, Purvis took an increasingly pragmatic view of party politics. When it became obvious that Philadelphia's Democratic mayor was doing more for African Americans than his Republican challenger, Purvis urged black voters to support him—and was roundly condemned by many black leaders. After that experience he left political infighting to his brother-in-law William Forten, a powerful figure in the state's Republican machine, and gave his time and energy to reform. He combined his commitment to equal rights for African-American men with a call for the enfranchisement of women. He and his wife had many friends in the women's rights movement, notable among them Elizabeth Cady Stanton and Susan B. Anthony, and Purvis attended a number of women's rights conventions.

Harriet Forten Purvis died in 1875, and Robert Purvis married again. His second wife was Tacie Townsend, a white Quaker abolitionist more than twenty years his junior. Robert Purvis died in 1898 at his home in Philadelphia. He was survived by his wife and four of his eight children. Robert Purvis, *A Tribute to the Memory of Thomas Shipley, The Philanthropist, Delivered at St. Thomas's Church, November 23d, 1836* (Philadelphia: Merrihew and Gunn, 1836); *Remarks on the Life and Character of James Forten, Delivered at Bethel Church, March 30, 1842* (Philadelphia: Merrihew and Thompson, 1842). *Speeches and Correspondence* (Philadelphia, n.d.). *Sermon Preached at the Funeral of Robert Purvis by Rev. Frederick A. Hinckley, of Philadelphia, PA, on Friday, April 15, 1898, at Spring Garden Unitarian Church* (Washington, D.C.: Judd and Detweiller, 1898). *First Annual Report of the American Anti-Slavery Society* (1834), 36, 38. *Second Annual Report* (1835), 27. *Third Annual Report* (1836), 23, 25, 27. *Fourth Annual Report* (1837), 21. *Fifth Annual Report* (1838), 5, 12. *Sixth Annual Report* (1839), 34, 38. *Seventh Annual Report* (1840), 20, 31. *Proceedings of the Pennsylvania Anti-Slavery Convention . . . 1837*, 5. *Appeal of Forty Thousand*, 2. *Third Annual Convention of the Free People of Colour*, 3. *Minutes of the Fifth Annual Convention for the Improvement of the Free People of Colour*, 20. *Minutes of the State Convention . . . 1848*, 2, 3, 4, 5–6, 8–12, 13–22. *Proceedings of the Colored National Convention . . . 1853*, 5. *Proceedings of the Colored National Convention . . . 1855*, 7. ASR, 1835, Appendix. *CA*, August 19, 1837; September 2, 1837; March 22, 1838; September 15, 1838; September 7, 1839; March 28, 1840; July 25, 1840; November 7, 1840; November 14, 1840; December 5, 1840; December 12, 1840; December 26, 1840; February 20, 1841; February 27, 1841; March 27, 1841;

April 3, 1841. *FDP,* April 1, 1852; April 8, 1852; April 15, 1852; April 29, 1852; May 6, 1852; May 20, 1852; June 10, 1852; August 6, 1852. *GUE,* May 1831. *HR,* November 1833. *Lib,* March 12, 1831; April 13, 1833; October 19, 1833; July 2, 1836; September 24, 1836; October 22, 1836; August 9, 1839; July 14, 1843. *NASS,* July 9, 1840; September 10, 1840; October 1, 1840; May 6, 1841; September 30, 1841; August 11, 1842; January 12, 1843; June 22, 1843; August 21, 1845; September 11, 1845; January 29, 1846. *NECAUL,* October 15, 1836. *NEW,* May 6, 1852. *NR,* September 1838; January 1839; February 1839; March 1839; September 1839; October 1839; November 1839. *NS,* August 25, 1848; September 1, 1848; October 6, 1848; October 20, 1848; January 5, 1849; February 9, 1849; June 15, 1849; June 22, 1849; July 6, 1849; November 2, 1849; April 3, 1851. *NYT,* April 16, 1898. *PF,* August 10, 1837; January 17, 1839; June 20, 1839; August 29, 1839; October 10, 1839; April 2, 1840; December 24, 1840; November 17, 1841; February 10, 1847; September 28, 1848. *PL,* August 5, 1890. *Poulson,* September 16, 1831. *ProvF,* November 11, 1854; September 8, 1855; April 18, 1857; May 30, 1857; August 15, 1857. Clarkson School, Tuition Account Book, 1819–22; Young Men's Anti-Slavery Society, in PAS MSS, HSP. Glasgow Female Anti-Slavery Society to Philadelphia Female Anti-Slavery Society, September 3, 1834; PFASS Records, HSP. George Thompson to Purvis, November 10, 1834, BPL. Thomas Fowell Buxton to William Lloyd Garrison, September 30, 1834; BPL. Ripley et al., *Black Abolitionist Papers,* vol. 3, 81–82. Joseph Sturge, *A Visit to the United States in 1841* (London: Hamilton, Adams and Co., 1842; reprint, New York: Augustus M. Kelley, 1969), 46–47. Wilbur H. Siebert, *The Underground Railroad from Slavery to Freedom* (New York: Macmillan, 1898; reprint, New York: Arno Press, 1968), 356–61. Still, *The Underground Railroad,* 711. Samuel J. May, *Recollections of Our Antislavery Conflict* (Boston: Fields, Osgood, 1869; reprint, New York: Arno Press, 1968), 288. Vigilance Committee Records, HSP. U.S. census (1840), Philadelphia, Cedar Ward, 251; (1850), Byberry Township, Philadelphia County, 124; (1860), Philadelphia, Ward 23, 975; (1870), Ward 23, dist. 76, 250. Wills of William Purvis Sr., William Purvis Jr., and Robert Purvis, PCA.

114. Amy Matilda Williams was born in New York City in 1809, the daughter of Episcopal clergyman Peter Williams Jr. and his wife, Sarah. She married Philadelphia businessman Joseph Cassey (note 110), a widower twenty years her senior, in 1826. Her husband's wealth—the family always employed at least one servant—freed Amy Cassey from many of the burdens of running a home and tending to eight children. (Only six of the eight survived infancy.) She devoted much of her time to antislavery work. For many years she was an active member of the interracial Philadelphia Female Anti-Slavery Society. Joseph Cassey died in 1848, and two years later his widow married Charles Lenox Remond, a prominent African-American antislavery lecturer from Salem, Massachusetts. In her new home she continued to be active in the twin causes of abolition and civil rights. In 1853, for example, when she was ejected from a Boston theater, she successfully brought suit against the management. She died in Salem on August 15, 1856. "Original and Selected Poetry of Amy Matilda Cassey," LC. *Lib,* August 22, 1856. *NASS,* October 19, 1848; October 24, 1850. *NS,* February 18, 1848; October 13, 1848; March 9, 1849; June 29, 1849; July 6, 1849; September 28, 1849; November 9, 1849. *Poulson,* September 28, 1826. Ripley et al., *Black Abolitionist Papers,* vol. 4, 183. Brenda Stevenson, ed., *The Journals of Charlotte Forten Grimké* (New York: Oxford University Press, 1987). Gloria Oden, "The Journal of Charlotte

L. Forten: The Salem-Philadelphia Years (1851–1862) Reexamined," *EIHC* 119 (April 1983), 119–36. U.S. census (1850), Philadelphia, New Market Ward, 400.

115. Sarah Mapps Douglass (1806–1882) was the daughter of Robert Douglass Sr. (note 109) and Grace Bustill (note 117). She and her four brothers were educated at a school established by her mother and by wealthy neighbor James Forten. In 1827 she took over the school when the teacher retired, and made it into one of the finest academies for black girls anywhere in the nation. The curriculum included much more than the "traditional" female subjects of reading, writing, ciphering, and sewing. An enthusiastic amateur scientist, Douglass shared her growing interest in chemistry, biology, and geology with her students. In 1853 she gave up her school and accepted an appointment at the Quaker-sponsored Institute for Colored Youth. She taught there until crippling rheumatism forced her to retire in 1877.

Her promotion of black literary societies and lyceums was a logical extension of her work as a teacher. In addition to her membership in the Gilbert Lyceum, she was president of the Female Literary Association in the 1830s, and in 1859 friends recognized her contributions in the area of intellectual improvement by naming a new organization the Sarah M. Douglass Literary Circle in her honor. Over the years poems and essays by Douglass appeared in the antislavery press under the pen-names "Zillah" and "Ella."

Douglass played an important role in the abolitionist movement. She attended all three of the female antislavery conventions in the 1830s, and for more than forty years she was a leading member of the Philadelphia Female Anti-Slavery Society. She and her mother had many friends in antislavery circles, among them Lucretia Mott, Abby Kelley Foster, William Lloyd Garrison, and Sarah and Angelina Grimké. An especially close bond developed between the Douglasses and the Grimkés. Grace and Sarah Douglass attended the wedding of Angelina Grimké to Theodore Weld in 1838. Sarah Douglass supplied the sisters with eloquent testimony of her and her mother's treatment at the hands of white Quakers for their "Prejudice Among Friends." The Grimkés sought information and advice from Sarah Douglass as they pressed ahead with their campaign for abolition and women's rights, and she responded by turning to them—and particularly Sarah—for counsel. In fact, it was Sarah Grimké's encouragement that prompted the hesitant Sarah Douglass to accept, at age forty-nine, a proposal of marriage from Reverend William Douglass (note 18), a widowed minister with twelve children. The couple were married on July 23, 1855.

Reverend Douglass died six years later. Sarah Douglass was ambivalent about what had apparently not been a happy marriage. She spoke of her misery "in that School of bitter discipline, the old Parsonage of St. Thomas," and yet she acknowledged William Douglass's intellectual abilities, his "sound judgment," and the positive aspects of their partnership. "He had his weak points . . . yet where he was *weak* I was *strong*." She had been a diligent and caring stepmother to his children, shepherding his two eldest daughters through courtship and marriage, finding respectable trades for the others, and nursing his eldest son through the final stages of consumption. She did not remarry.

Reverend Douglass had evidently not tried to curb one aspect of his wife's work that many husbands would have considered not merely unsuitable but positively scandalous. Some years before her marriage Sarah Douglass decided to embark on a career as a lecturer on female and pediatric health. To prepare herself she took courses at the Female Medical College of Pennsylvania (1852–53) and at Pennsylvania Medical University (1855–58). Her first lectures were given at her home, but interest spread and she soon received invitations to speak to larger audiences in Philadelphia and New York. She illustrated her lectures, which were always praised for being "chaste and decorous," with an anatomically correct "French mannequin."

After the death of her husband Sarah Douglass kept house for her two surviving brothers, Robert (note 20) and James, taught school, and continued to devote herself to a wide range of community endeavors. During the Civil War she was an officer of the American Freedmen's Aid Commission, and after the war she helped establish the Stephen Smith Home for Aged and Infirm Colored Persons. The achievement of which she was proudest was the education of two generations of black teachers. Graduates of her private school and the Institute for Colored Youth held teaching appointments at schools all over America. Sarah Mapps Douglass died on September 9, 1882. Bustill-Mossell Family Papers, UPA. *CA,* December 2, 1837; January 20, 1838. *CR,* March 30, 1861; April 6, 1861; May 11, 1861; February 22, 1862. *Eman,* December 21, 1833. *Lib,* July 21, 1832; October 6, 1837; June 21, 1839. *NASS,* May 4, 1843. *NECAUL,* December 3, 1836. *PF,* May 14, 1840; March 17, 1841; March 14, 1844. *NS,* March 9, 1849. *ProvF,* June 9, 1855; August 22, 1855. Ripley et al., *Black Abolitionist Papers,* vol. 3, 117–18. *Proceedings of the Anti-Slavery Convention of American Women Held by Adjournment in the City of New York from the 9th to the 12th of May, 1837* (New York: William S. Dorr, 1837), 4, 6, 15. *Proceedings of the Anti-Slavery Convention of American Women, Held in Philadelphia, May 15th, 16th, 17th and 18th, 1838* (Philadelphia: Merrihew and Gunn, 1838), 3, 4, 12. *Proceedings of the Third Anti-Slavery Convention of American Women, Held in Philadelphia, May 1st, 2d and 3d, 1839* (Philadelphia: Merrihew and Gunn, 1839), 6. William Lloyd Garrison to Douglass, March 5, 1832, BPL. Sarah and Angelina Grimké to Douglass, February 22, 1837; Sarah Grimké to Douglass, October 22, 1837, *Weld-Grimké Letters,* 362–65, 467–71. Douglass to Abby Kelley, March 19, 1839, AAS. Sarah Grimké to Elizabeth Pease, August 25, 1839; William Lloyd Garrison to Douglass, March 18, 1842; BPL. Angelina Grimké Weld to Douglass, March 21, 1839; Sarah Grimké to Douglass, September 8, 1839; Angelina Grimké Weld to Douglass, September 13, 1839; Angelina Grimké Weld to Douglass, October 4, 1839; Sarah Grimké to Douglass, October 10, 1839; Sarah and Grace Douglass to Charles Stuart Weld, September 28, 1840; Theodore D. Weld to Douglass, July 16, 1848; Sarah Grimké to Douglass, November 21, 1844, BAP Micro. Wills of Robert Douglass Sr. and Sarah M. Douglass, PCA. U.S. census (1850), Philadelphia, High Street Ward, 176; (1860), Ward 5, 563; (1870), 4th Ward, 14th dist., 314. Dorothy Sterling, ed. *We Are Your Sisters: Black Women in the Nineteenth Century* (New York: W. W. Norton, 1984), 126–33. Catherine H. Birney, *The Grimké Sisters: Sarah and Angelina Grimké: The First American Women Advocates for Abolition and Women's Rights* (Boston: Lee and Sheppard, 1885; reprint, St. Clair Shores, Mich.: Scholarly Press, 1970), 121–24, 171, 191, 248–50, 253, 266, 276–77, 294–95. Lindhorst, "Politics in a Box," 263–79.

116. Hester or Hetty Burr (1795–1862) was freeborn, a native of Pennsylvania, and the wife of community leader John P. Burr (note 11). A member of the Philadelphia Female Anti-Slavery Society for many years, she was also involved in the Women's Anti-Slavery Conventions of 1838 and 1839. Among her friends were white abolitionists Sarah and Angelina Grimké and Abby Kelley. Hetty Burr was active in the Episcopal Church, and was a stalwart of the Colored Female Free Produce Society of Pennsylvania. The Burrs kept their heads above water financially, but they

were never wealthy. In 1838 the PAS census listed Hetty Burr as doing her "own work." A decade later she was running an intelligence office or employment bureau. In 1860 she was a dressmaker, as were her two unmarried daughters, Elizabeth and Louisa. Register of Confirmations. Sarah Grimké to Sarah M. Douglass, October 22, 1837, in Barnes and Dumond, eds., *Weld-Grimké Letters*, 470. Sarah M. Douglass to Abby Kelley, March 19, 1839, BAP micro. *Anti-Slavery Convention of American Women . . . 1838*, 4. *Third Anti-Slavery Convention of American Women*, 6. *GUE*, June 1831, 12. *NR*, March 1839. *NS*, March 9, 1849; August 17, 1849; November 9, 1849; February 1, 1850. *PA*, June 21, 1862. *ProvF,* December 1, 1855. PAS census (1838); Friends' census (1847). U.S. census (1850) Philadelphia County, Moyamensing, 243; (1860), Philadelphia, Ward 7, 259.

117. Grace Bustill Douglass (1782–1842) was born in Philadelphia, the daughter of Cyrus Bustill (1732–1806), a former slave who had purchased his freedom and prospered as a baker and brewer, and Elizabeth Morey (1746–1827), a woman of English and Native American descent. After retiring from business, Cyrus Bustill opened a school for black children, and it was there that Grace received her education. She was also trained as a milliner.

In 1803 Grace Bustill married affluent West Indian barber Robert Douglass (note 109). The Douglasses had a comfortable income, and Grace Douglass recalled that in her new home at 54 Arch Street she entertained in style, with the best wine and cake. It was not poverty that eventually induced her to economize but the wish to put money aside to assist poorer members of her community.

The Douglasses had six children, and their education posed a serious problem. The public schools for African Americans were woefully inadequate, and private academies generally would not accept them. Their eldest child, Elizabeth, briefly attended a private school, where she excelled at her studies, but the teacher was forced to dismiss her when the white pupils complained to their parents. Elizabeth died young, and the Douglasses determined to spare their other children the humiliation she had endured. Eventually Grace and a family friend, sailmaker James Forten, opened their own school.

Having been raised a Quaker, Grace Douglass took her children to Friends' Meeting. Repelled by the coldness of white Quakers, all her sons left to join their father at the First African Presbyterian Church. Although she attended Meeting faithfully, and adopted Quaker dress and speech, Grace Douglass was advised not to apply for membership in the Society of Friends because her application would certainly be rejected. Saddened by the treatment meted out to her by most white Quakers, Grace Douglass recognized that there were a few individuals who shared her commitment to abolition and racial equality. She and her daughter developed close friendships with Lucretia Mott and the Grimké sisters, Sarah, and Angelina. In 1838 mother and daughter attended the wedding of Angelina Grimké to Theodore Weld.

Over the years Grace Douglass worked tirelessly in the antislavery cause. In 1833 she and Sarah became founding members of the Philadelphia Female Anti-Slavery Society. In 1837 she served as one of the vice-presidents of the first women's antislavery convention and took an active role in the third and final convention in 1839. When she died on March 9, 1842, her co-workers in the Philadelphia Female Anti-Slavery Society praised her as having been "one of (their) . . . most self-denying members." Bustill-Mossell Family Papers, UPA. Grace Douglass to Rev. John Gloucester, February 28, 1819, in Catto, *A Semi-Centenary Discourse*, 36–37. *Lib,*

June 21, 1839; October 24, 1839; March 18, 1842; April 15, 1842. *NR, September* 1839; November 1839. *NASS,* March 24, 1842. *PF,* March 17, 1841. *True American Commercial Advertiser,* November 22, 1803. Sarah M. Douglass to William Bassett, December 1837; William Lloyd Garrison to Sarah M. Douglass, March 18, 1842, BPL. *Proceedings of the Anti-Slavery Convention of American Women . . . 1837,* 3, 7, 15. *Proceedings of the Anti-Slavery Convention of American Women . . . 1838,* 12. *Proceedings of the Third Anti-Slavery Convention of American Women,* 6. Sarah and Grace Douglass to Charles Stuart Weld, September 28, 1840, BAP micro. Records of the Philadelphia Female Anti-Slavery Society, HSP. U.S. census (1800), Philadelphia County, 384. Lindhorst, "Politics in a Box," 272.

118. Harriet Davy Forten Purvis was the daughter of wealthy freeborn entrepreneur James Forten and his second wife, Charlotte Vandine. She was born in Philadelphia in 1810 and named for one of the daughters of Robert Bridges, the white sailmaker who had given Forten his start in business.

Like her brothers and sisters, Harriet Forten enjoyed the benefits of a private education at the school her father had established with family friend Grace Douglass (note 117). Forten also arranged for his daughters to be tutored at home in music and languages. Visitors to the Forten home at 92 Lombard Street often commented on the refinement of James Forten's daughters and one, the abolitionist poet John Greenleaf Whittier, was moved to express his admiration in verse in Harriet's album.

On September 13, 1831, in an elegant ceremony at the Forten home presided over by the Episcopal bishop of the diocese, Harriet Forten married the wealthy young South Carolina emigré Robert Purvis. Purvis (note 13) was lighter-skinned than his wife, and the marriage gave rise to much gossip. James Forten, so it was alleged, had made "some sacrifice of his fortune" to buy "a whiter species" of husband for his daughter. In fact, if there was any "sacrifice of fortune" it was on Robert Purvis's part, and the "whiter species" Forten had secured for Harriet was an ardent abolitionist who made no secret of his ancestry.

Robert Purvis traveled extensively as an antislavery lecturer. Caring for their growing family kept Harriet closer to home, but did not prevent her from participating in the struggle for abolition. Like her mother and sisters, she played an active role in the Philadelphia Female Anti-Slavery Society. She also participated in the antislavery struggle at the national level. Despite the fact that she was expecting her second child, she traveled to New York with two of her sisters in 1837 to be present at the first Women's Anti-Slavery Convention. A delegate to the second convention at Philadelphia's newly built Pennsylvania Hall in 1838, she inadvertently helped cause a riot. Her husband accompanied her and was seen helping her from their carriage. Hostile onlookers concluded that they were an interracial couple and that the hall was a haven for "amalgamationists." Undaunted by the mob scenes that accompanied the destruction of Pennsylvania Hall, Harriet Purvis was present the following year when the third and final women's anti-slavery convention was held in Philadelphia. She was also a member of the Pennsylvania Anti-Slavery Society and attended meetings of the American Anti-Slavery Society with her husband.

In many respects, raising a family deepened Harriet Purvis's commitment to abolition and the eradication of racial prejudice as she reflected on the nature of the society into which her children had been born. In seeking a good education for them she encountered many of the same problems that had faced her own parents decades before. Her husband's wealth could not shield them from the impact of prejudice. In

1853, angry that his children were excluded from the better public schools and relegated to a vastly inferior black school in the neighborhood, Robert Purvis refused to pay his school tax.

Her early education had instilled in Harriet Purvis a great love of literature. She read whatever came her way—antislavery works, religious literature, contemporary novels, and works of literary criticism. Like other members of the family, she had a clear speaking voice and a talent for reading aloud. She could also sustain her part in an argument. For instance, discussing the authorship of Shakespeare's plays with her niece, Charlotte Forten, she insisted on siding with the Baconians—although Charlotte believed she only did so to be perverse. Her love of music, art, and literature led her to seek out others who shared those tastes. In 1841, as Willson notes, she and her husband were among the founders of the Gilbert Lyceum.

The Purvises enjoyed a lifestyle far more comfortable and secure than that of the vast majority of Philadelphians, irrespective of race. Robert Purvis was a shrewd businessman who invested his father's legacy wisely. The Purvises spent their early married life in Philadelphia, but in 1843 they purchased an estate in Byberry, a few miles outside the city. Harriet Purvis had been a gracious hostess at her home in Philadelphia. Now, established at Byberry, she had far greater scope. Abolitionists from all over the United States and Europe were sure of a warm welcome at the Purvis home. There were often other guests at Byberry whose presence the Purvises were careful not to reveal. For many years Harriet and Robert Purvis sheltered fugitive slaves. Their home even had a hidden room where runways could hide until Robert could arrange their passage to Canada.

Unlike so many of their white co-workers, Harriet and Robert Purvis did not believe the abolitionist struggle had come to an end with the passage of the Thirteenth Amendment. In September 1866, as a member of the Female Anti-Slavery Society, Harriet Purvis attended a lecture on the state of affairs in the South. She did not hesitate to point out that there were battles to be won in the North as well. Keenly aware of the barriers that still had to be removed, she and her husband gave generously of their time and their money to the American Equal Rights Association and the Pennsylvania State Equal Rights League.

A series of personal tragedies beset Harriet and Robert Purvis. They lost two of their sons to consumption and a third to meningitis. A daughter survived Harriet by barely two years. Harriet Forten Purvis died of tuberculosis on June 11, 1875, and was buried at the Friends' Fair Hill Burial Ground in Germantown. *ASA*, June 1859. *CA*, April 3, 1841. *Lib*, December 16, 1853. *NASS*, April 25, 1844; December 20, 1849. *NS*, February 9, 1849. *PF*, April 7, 1841. *Poulson*, September 3, 1831. Register of Confirmations, 148. *St. Peter's P.E. Church, Philadelphia, PA.—Marriages, Burials, Confirmations, Communicants, 1828–1884*, 1, HSP. Abraham Ritter, *Philadelphia and Her Merchants, As Constituted Fifty and Seventy Years Ago* (Philadelphia: The Author, 1860), 46–47. *Anti-Slavery Convention of American Women . . . 1838*, 12. *Anti-Slavery Convention of American Women . . . 1839*, 6. *History of Pennsylvania Hall, Which Was Destroyed by a Mob on the 17th of May, 1838* (Philadelphia: Merrihew and Gunn, 1838). Stevenson, ed., *Journals of Charlotte Forten Grimké*. Philadelphia Death Registers, 1875. Records of Friends' Fair Hill Burial Ground, HSP.

119. Amelia Bogle (1810–1867) was the daughter of well-to-do caterer Robert Bogle and his first wife, Grace Banton. Her father died in 1837, and his will directed that his substantial real estate holdings be divided among his surviving children. With

a home of her own on Pine Street, Amelia Bogle was able to support herself in modest comfort as a dressmaker. Then, in 1841, she opened a private school for African-American children on Twelfth Street below Spruce. The school was still in successful operation in 1856. Although she was freeborn, Amelia Bogle knew her father had been born into slavery. Perhaps it was that knowledge that prompted her to become involved in the antislavery movement. In 1839 she was a corresponding member of the Women's Anti-Slavery Convention. She was also the secretary of the Dorcas Society, which distributed clothing to the sick and the poor in the African-American community, and a member of the Union Benevolent Daughters of Elijah and the Female Rush Assistant Society. Manumission Papers, PAS MSS, HSP. *Proceedings of the Third Anti-Slavery Convention of American Women*, 6. *Statistical Inquiry* (1849). *Statistics of the Colored People* (1856). *NASS*, May 4, 1843. *PA*, January 25, 1868. *Poulson*, February 16, 1831. "Notes on Beneficial Societies, 1828–1838," in PAS MSS, HSP. Charters of Incorporation, Book 7, 221, 243, PSA. St. Thomas's Parish Registers. *Records of Christ Church, Philadelphia: Marriages, 1800–1900*, HSP. Philadelphia Board of Health Records. Board of Health, Cemetery Returns, St. Thomas's Church, 1816, PCA. Will of Robert Bogle, PCA. Friends' census (1847). U.S. census, (1820), Philadelphia, South Ward, 157; (1830), Cedar Ward, 15; (1840) Northern Liberties, Ward 2, 23. Philadelphia directories, 1841, 1843–48.

120. See above, note 73.

121. This is Willson's rather garbled version of Philippians 2:13: "You must work out your own salvation in fear and trembling; for it is God who works in you, inspiring both the will and the deed, for his own chosen purpose."

Bibliography

Manuscript Collections

American Antiquarian Society, Worcester, Massachusetts
    Abby Kelley Foster Papers
Boston Public Library, Department of Rare Books and Manuscripts
    Antislavery Manuscripts
Bucks County Courthouse, Doylestown, Pennsylvania
    Deeds
    Mortgages
Canadian National Archives, Ottawa
    Census of 1871
Crown Hill Cemetery, Indianapolis
    Burial Records
Cuyahoga County Archives, Cleveland, Ohio
    Cuyahoga County Wills (1895, 1901)
Howard University, Moorland Spingarn Research Center
    Francis J. Grimké Papers
Historical Society of Pennsylvania
    Burlington County, New Jersey, Deeds (microfilm)
    Christ Church, Philadelphia: Marriages, 1800–1900
    Friends' Fair Hill Burial Ground, Records
    Leon Gardiner Collection
    Pennsylvania Abolition Society Manuscripts
    Philadelphia Crew Lists, 1809, 1814 (WPA, typescript)
    Philadelphia Female Anti-Slavery Society Records
    Records of the Philadelphia Vigilance Committee
    Register of Confirmations by Bishop White, 1787 to 1836 Inclusive
    St. Peter's P.E. Church, Philadelphia—Marriages, Burials, Confirmations, Communicants, 1828–84
    Society of Friends Census (1847)
    Young Men's Anti-Slavery Society of Philadelphia, Records
Library Company of Philadelphia
    "Original and Selected Poetry of Amy Matilda Cassey"
    Stevens-Cogdell, Saunders-Venning Papers
Library of Congress
    American Colonization Society Records, Incoming Correspondence
National Archives
    Second Census of the United States (1800)
    Third Census of the United States (1810)
    Fourth Census of the United States (1820)
    Fifth Census of the United States (1830)
    Sixth Census of the United States (1840)
    Seventh Census of the United States (1850)
    Eighth Census of the United States (1860)
    Ninth Census of the United States (1870)

Tenth Census of the United States (1880)
Twelfth Census of the United States (1900)
Thirteenth Census of the United States (1910)
Seamen's Protection Certificate Applications, Port of Philadelphia, 1807–33. Record Group 36
Pennsylvania State Archives, Harrisburg
    Charters of Incorporation, 1812–75
Philadelphia City Archives
    Cemetery Returns, 1803–60
    Philadelphia County Deeds
    Probate Records
Richmond County Courthouse, Augusta, Georgia
    Accounts, Books D (1823–28), E (1827–32), F (1833–40), G (1840–41)
    Deeds, Books F and G
    Will Book A
St. Thomas's African Episcopal Church, Philadelphia
    Parish Registers
University of Pennsylvania Archives, Bustill-Mossell Family Papers
Western Reserve Historical Society, Cleveland, Ohio
    Cleveland Necrology
    Marriage Records, Cuyahoga County, 1810–1949

NEWSPAPERS

African Repository (Washington, D.C.)
Anglo-African Magazine (New York)
Anti-Slavery Advocate (London)
Anti-Slavery Bugle (Salem, Ohio; New Lisbon, Ohio)
Anti-Slavery Record (New York)
Christian Recorder (Philadelphia)
Cleveland Gazette (Cleveland, Ohio)
Cleveland Plain Dealer (Cleveland, Ohio)
Colored American (New York)
Emancipator (Boston; New York, New York)
Frederick Douglass' Paper (Rochester, New York)
Freedom's Journal (New York)
Genius of Universal Emancipation (Mount Pleasant, Ohio; Greenville, Tennessee; Baltimore; Washington, D.C.; Hennepin, Illinois)
Hazard's Register (Philadelphia)
Juvenile Magazine (Philadelphia)
Liberator (Boston)
Morning Journal (Kingston, Jamaica)
National Anti-Slavery Standard (New York)
National Enquirer and Constitutional Advocate of Universal Liberty (Philadelphia)
National Era (Washington, D.C.)
National Reformer (Philadelphia)
New York Times (New York)
North Star (Rochester, New York)
Pacific Appeal (San Francisco)

Pennsylvania Freeman (Philadelphia)
Philadelphia Tribune (Philadelphia)
Poulson's American Daily Advertiser (Philadelphia)
Provincial Freeman (Windsor, Ontario; Toronto, Ontario; Chatham, Ontario)
Public Ledger (Philadelphia)
Raleigh Register (Raleigh, North Carolina)
Rights of All (New York)
True American Commercial Advertiser (Philadelphia)
Voice of the Fugitive (Sandwich, Ontario: Windsor, Ontario)
Washington Bee (Washington, D.C.)
Weekly Advocate (New York)
Weekly Anglo-African (New York)

CITY DIRECTORIES

Cleveland, Ohio, 1856–1901
Philadelphia, 1785–1860

ADDITIONAL PRINTED SOURCES

Abajian, James de T., comp. *Blacks in Selected Newspapers, Censuses and Other Sources: An Index to Names and Subjects.* 3 vols. Boston: G. K. Hall, 1977.
———. *Supplement.* 2 vols. Boston: G. K. Hall, 1985.
Abdy, Edward S. *Journal of a Residence and Tour in the United States of North America, from April, 1833 to October, 1834.* 3 vols. London: John Murray, 1835; reprint, New York: Negro Universities Press, 1969.
American Anti-Slavery Society. *First Annual Report of the American Anti-Slavery Society.* New York: Dorr and Butterfield, 1834.
———. *Second Annual Report of the American Anti-Slavery Society.* New York, 1835.
———. *Third Annual Report of the American Anti-Slavery Society.* New York, 1836.
———. *Fourth Annual Report.* New York, 1837.
———. *Fifth Annual Report.* New York, 1838.
———. *Sixth Annual Report.* New York, 1839.
———. *Seventh Annual Report.* New York, 1840.
Augustine Society of Pennsylvania. *Constitution of the Augustine Society of Pennsylvania.* N.p., n.d.
Bacon, Benjamin C. *Statistics of the Colored People of Philadelphia.* Philadelphia: Pennsylvania Abolition Society, 1856.
Barnes, Gilbert H., and Dwight L. Dumond., eds. *Letters of Theodore Dwight Weld, Angelina Grimké Weld, and Sarah Grimké, 1822–1844.* 2 vols. New York: D. Appleton-Century, 1934.
Betts, Edward Chambers, ed. *Early History of Huntsville, Alabama, 1804 to 1870.* Montgomery, Ala.: The Brown Printing Co., 1916.
Biddle, Nicholas. *An Ode to Bogle.* Philadelphia: Privately printed for Ferdinand J. Dreer, 1865.

Birney, Catherine H. *The Grimké Sisters, Sarah and Angelina Grimké: The First American Women Advocates of Abolition and Women's Rights.* Boston: Lee and Sheppard, 1885; reprint, St. Clair Shores, Mich.: Scholarly Press, 1970.

Black Abolitionist Papers. Microfilm, 17 reels. New York: Microfilming Corporation of America, 1981–83.

Brown, William Wells. *The Black Man: His Antecedents, His Genius, and His Achievements.* 2nd ed. New York: Thomas Hamilton, 1863; reprint, New York: Johnson Reprint, 1968.

Catto, William W. *A Semi-Centenary Discourse Delivered in the First African Presbyterian Church, Philadelphia, on the Fourth Sabbath of May, 1857.* Philadelphia: Joseph M. Wilson, 1857.

Chambers, William. *American Slavery and Colour.* London: W. & R. Chambers; New York: Dix and Edwards, 1857.

College for Colored Youth: An Account of the New-Haven City Meeting and Resolutions, With Recommendations of the College, and Strictures Upon the Doings of New-Haven. New York: By the Committee, 1831.

Combe, George. *Notes on the United States of North America, during a Phrenological Visit in 1838-9-40.* Philadelphia: Carey & Hart, 1841.

Constitution of the American Society of Free Persons of Colour, For Improving Their Condition in the United States; For Purchasing Lands; And For the Establishment of a Settlement in Canada, Also The Proceedings of the Convention, With Their Address To The Free Persons of Colour in The United States. Philadelphia: J. W. Allen, 1831.

Delany, Martin R. *The Condition, Elevation, Emigration, and Destiny of the Colored People of the United States.* Philadelphia: The Author, 1852; reprint, New York: Arno Press, 1968.

Douglass, William. *Annals of the First African Church in the United States of America, Now Styled the African Episcopal Church of St. Thomas.* Philadelphia: King and Baird, 1862.

———. *A Discourse Commemorative of the Rt. Rev. William White, Delivered in St. Thomas's Church, Philadelphia, August 18, 1836.* Philadelphia: William Stavely, 1836.

———. *Sermons Preached in the African Protestant Episcopal Church of St. Thomas's, Philadelphia.* Philadelphia: King and Baird, 1854.

Eaklor, Vicki L., comp. *American Anti-Slavery Songs: A Collection and Analysis.* Westport, Conn.: Greenwood, 1988.

Forten, James, Robert Purvis, and William Whipper. *To the Honourable the Senate and House of Representatives of the Commonwealth of Pennsylvania.* Philadelphia, 1832.

Gandrud, Pauline Jones. *Alabama Records.* N.p., n.d.

Gardner, Charles W. *Speech of the Rev. Charles W. Gardner (A Presbyterian Clergyman of Philadelphia) at the Fourth Anniversary of the American Anti-Slavery Society, May 9th, 1837.* Philadelphia: Merrihew and Gunn, 1837.

Georgia Society of Colonial Dames of America. *Some Early Epitaphs in Georgia.* Durham, N.C.: The Seeman Printers for the Society, 1924.

Gibbs, Mifflin Wistar. *Shadow and Light: An Autobiography.* Washington, D.C., 1902; reprint, New York: Arno Press, 1968.

Gloucester, Jeremiah. *An Oration, Delivered on January 1, 1823, In Bethel Church: On the Abolition of the Slave Trade.* Philadelphia: John Young, 1823.

Gloucester, John, Jr. *A Sermon, Delivered in the First African Presbyterian Church*

in Philadelphia, on the 1st of January, 1830, Before the Different Coloured Societies of Philadelphia. Philadelphia, 1830.
Griffin, Edward Dorr. *A Plea for Africa. A Sermon Preached October 26, 1817, to the First Presbyterian Church in the City of New York, Before the Synod of New York and New Jersey, at the Request of the Board of Directors of the African School Established by the Synod.* New York: Gould, 1817.
Gurney, John Joseph. *A Visit to North America, Described in Familiar Letters to Amelia Opie.* Norwich, England: Joseph Fletcher, 1841.
Hallowell, Anna Davis, ed. *James and Lucretia Mott, Life and Letters.* Boston: Houghton Mifflin, 1884.
Hamilton, William. *Address to the Fourth Annual Convention of Free People of Colour in the United States, Delivered at the Opening of Their Session in the City of New-York, June 2, 1834.* New York: S. W. Benedict & Co., 1834.
―――. *An Address to the New York African Society, for Mutual Relief, Delivered in the Universalist Church, January 2, 1809.* New York, 1809.
―――. *An Oration Delivered in the African Zion Church, on the Fourth of July, 1827, in Commemoration of the Abolition of Domestic Slavery in this State.* New York: Gray and Bunce, 1827.
―――. *An Oration, on the Abolition of the Slave Trade, Delivered in the Episcopal Asbury African Church, in Elizabeth St., New-York, January 2, 1815.* New York: C. W. Bunce for the New York African Society, 1815.
Haytien Emigration Society of Philadelphia. *Information for the Free People of Colour, Who Are Inclined to Emigrate to Hayti.* Philadelphia: J. H. Cunningham, 1825.
History of Pennsylvania Hall, Which Was Destroyed by a Mob on the 17th of May, 1838. Philadelphia: Merrihew and Gunn, 1838; reprint, New York: Negro Universities Press, 1969.
Johnson, Michael P., and James L. Roark, eds. *No Chariot Let Down: Charleston's Free People of Color on the Eve of the Civil War.* Chapel Hill: University of North Carolina Press, 1984.
May, Samuel J. *Recollections of Our Antislavery Conflict.* Boston: Fields, Osgood, 1869; reprint, New York: Arno Press, 1968.
Memorial to the Honourable the Senate and House of Representatives of the Commonwealth of Pennsylvania, in General Assembly Met, the Memorial of the Subscribers, Free People of Colour, Residing in the City of Philadelphia. Philadelphia: n.p., 1833.
Merrill, Walter M., ed. *The Letters of William Lloyd Garrison.* Cambridge, Mass.: Belknap Press of Harvard University Press, 1971.
Miller, William. *A Sermon on the Abolition of the Slave Trade: Delivered in the African Church, New-York on the First of January, 1810. By the Rev. William Miller. Minister of the African Methodist Episcopal Church.* New York: John C. Totten, 1810.
Minutes and Proceedings of the First Annual Convention of the People of Colour, Held by Adjournments in the City of Philadelphia, From the Sixth to the Eleventh of June, Inclusive, 1831. Philadelphia: By Order of the Committee of Arrangements, 1831.
Minutes and Proceedings of the Second Annual Convention, for the Improvement of the Free People of Color in these United States, Held by Adjournments in the City of Philadelphia, from the 4th to the 13th of June Inclusive, 1832. Philadelphia: By Order of the Convention, 1832.

Minutes and Proceedings of the Third Annual Convention, for the Improvement of the Free People of Colour in these United States, Held by Adjournments in the City of Philadelphia, from the 3d to the 13th of June Inclusive, 1833. New York: By Order of the Convention, 1833.

Minutes of Proceedings at the Council of the Philadelphia Association for the Moral and Mental Improvement of the People of Color, June 5th-9th, 1837. Philadelphia: Merrihew and Gunn, 1837.

Minutes of the Fifth Annual Convention for the Improvement of the Free People of Color in the United States, Held by Adjournments, in the Wesley Church, Philadelphia, from the First to the Fifth of June, Inclusive, 1835. Philadelphia: William P. Gibbons, 1835.

Minutes of the Fourth Annual Convention, for the Improvement of the Free People of Colour, in the United States, Held by Adjournments in the Asbury Church, New York, from the 2d to the 13th of June Inclusive, 1834. New York: By Order of the Convention, 1834.

Minutes of the State Convention of the Colored Citizens of Pennsylvania, Convened at Harrisburg, December 13th and 13th, 1848. In Philip S. Foner and George E. Walker, eds., *Proceedings of the Black State Conventions, 1840–1865.* 2 vols. Philadelphia: Temple University Press, 1979–81.

Moak, Jefferson M., comp. *Philadelphia Guardians of the Poor: Bonds for the Support of Illegitimate Children and Other Indigent Persons, 1811–1859.* The Chestnut Hill Almanac, Genealogical Series, 1996.

Moses, Wilson Jeremiah, ed. *Liberian Dreams: Back-to-Africa Narratives from the 1850s.* University Park: The Pennsylvania State University Press, 1998.

Nordmann, Chris. "Georgia Registration of Free People of Color, 1819." *National Genealogical Society Quarterly* 77 (December 1989), 295–301.

Parrott, Russell. *An Oration on the Abolition of the Slave Trade, Delivered on the First of January, 1812, At the African Church of St. Thomas, Philadelphia.* Philadelphia: James Maxwell for the Different Societies, 1812.

———. *An Address, On the Abolition of the Slave Trade, Delivered Before the Different African Benevolent Societies, on the 1st of January, 1816.* Philadelphia: T. S. Manning, 1816.

Payne, Daniel Alexander. *Recollections of Seventy Years.* Nashville: AME Sunday School Union, 1888; reprint, New York: Arno Press, 1968.

Pennsylvania Abolition Society. *The Present State and Condition of the Free People of Color in the City of Philadelphia, and Adjoining Districts.* Philadelphia: Merrihew and Gunn, 1838.

———. *Register of the Trades of the Colored People in the City of Philadelphia and Districts.* Philadelphia: Merrihew and Gunn, 1838.

Porter, Dorothy, ed. *Early Negro Writing, 1760–1837.* Boston: Beacon Press, 1971.

Proceedings of the Anti-Slavery Convention, Assembled at Philadelphia, December 4, 5 and 6, 1833. New York: Dorr and Butterfield, 1833.

Proceedings of the Anti-Slavery Convention of American Women Held by Adjournment in the City of New York from the 9th to the 12th of May, 1837. New York: William S. Dorr, 1837.

Proceedings of the Anti-Slavery Convention of American Women, Held in Philadelphia, May 15th, 16th, 17th and 18th, 1838. Philadelphia: Merrihew and Gunn, 1838.

Proceedings of the Colored National Convention, Held in Rochester, July 6th, 7th and 8th, 1853. Rochester: At the Office of Frederick Douglass' Paper, 1853.

Proceedings of the Colored National Convention, Held in Franklin Hall, Sixth Street Below Arch, Philadelphia, October 16th, 17th and 18th, 1855. Salem, N.J.: By Order of the Convention, 1856.

Proceedings of the National Convention of Colored Men, Held in the City of Syracuse, New York, October 4, 5, 6, and 7, 1864: With the Bill of Wrongs and Rights, and the Address to the American People. Boston: J. S. Rock and George L. Ruffin, 1864.

Proceedings of the National Convention of Colored People, and Their Friends, Held in Troy, New York, on the 6th, 7th, 8th and 9th of October, 1847. Troy: J. C. Kneeland, 1847.

Proceedings of the Pennsylvania Convention, Assembled to Organize a State Anti-Slavery Society, at Harrisburg, on the 31st of January and 1st, 2d and 3d of February, 1837. Philadelphia: Merrihew and Gunn, 1837.

Proceedings of the State Convention of the Colored Freemen of Pennsylvania, Held in Pittsburgh, on the 23d, 24th and 25th of August, 1841, for the Purpose of Considering Their Condition, and the Means of Its Improvement. Pittsburgh, 1841.

Proceedings of the Third Anti-Slavery Convention of American Women, Held in Philadelphia, May 1st, 2d and 3d, 1839. Philadelphia: Merrihew and Gunn, 1838.

Protestant Episcopal Church. *Proceedings of the 51st Convention of the P.E. Church in the State of Pennsylvania*. Philadelphia: By Order of the Convention, 1835.

———. *Proceedings of the 52nd Convention of the P.E. Church in the State of Pennsylvania*. Philadelphia: By Order of the Convention, 1836.

Purvis, Robert. *Appeal of Forty Thousand Citizens, Threatened with Disfranchisement, To the People of Pennsylvania*. Philadelphia: Merrihew and Gunn, 1838.

———. *Remarks on the Life and Character of James Forten, Delivered at Bethel Church, March 30, 1842*. Philadelphia: Merrihew and Thompson, 1842.

———. *Speeches and Correspondence*. Philadelphia, n.d.

———. *A Tribute to the Memory of Thomas Shipley, The Philanthropist, Delivered at St. Thomas's Church, Nov. 23d, 1836*. Philadelphia: Merrihew and Gunn, 1836.

Resolutions and Remonstrances of the People of Colour Against Colonization on the Coast of Africa. Philadelphia, 1817.

Ripley, C. Peter, et al., eds. *Black Abolitionist Papers*. 5 vols. Chapel Hill: University of North Carolina Press, 1985–92.

Rush Education Society. *Purpose of the Rush Education Society of Philadelphia*. N.p., n.d.

Sipkins, Henry. *An Oration on the Abolition of the Slave Trade, in the City of New-York, January 2, 1809. By Henry Sipkins, A Descendant of Africa*. New York: John C. Totten, 1809.

Small, R. H. *Philadelphia; or, Glances at Lawyers, Physicians, First-Circle, Wistar Parties, &c. &c*. Philadelphia: R. H. Small, 1826.

A Statistical Inquiry into the Condition of the People of Colour in the City and Districts of Philadelphia. Philadelphia: Kite and Walton, 1849.

Sterling, Dorothy, ed. *Speak Out in Thunder Tones: Letters and Other Writings by Black Northerners, 1787–1865*. Garden City, N.Y.: Doubleday, 1973.

———, ed. *We Are Your Sisters: Black Women in the Nineteenth Century*. New York: W. W. Norton, 1984.

Stevenson, Brenda, ed. *Journals of Charlotte Forten Grimké*. New York: Oxford University Press, 1987.

Steward, Austin. *Twenty-Two Years a Slave and Forty Years a Freeman: Embracing a Correspondence of Several Years, While President of Wilberforce Colony, London, Canada West.* Rochester, N.Y.: William Alling, 1857.

Stott, Richard B., ed. *William Otter, History of My Own Times.* Ithaca: Cornell University Press, 1995.

Sturge, Joseph. *A Visit to the United States in 1841.* London: Hamilton, Adams & Co., 1842; reprint, New York: Augustus M. Kelley, 1969.

Tolles, Frederick B., ed. *Slavery and the "Woman Question": Lucretia Mott's Diary of Her Visit to Great Britain to Attend the World's Anti-Slavery Convention of 1840.* Haverford, Pennsylvania: Friends' Historical Association, 1952.

Webb, Frank J. *The Garies and Their Friends.* London: G. Routledge & Co., 1857; reprint, New York: Arno Press, 1969.

Whipper, William. *An Address Delivered in Wesley Church on the Evening of June 12, Before the Colored Reading Society of Philadelphia.* Philadelphia: John B. Roberts, n.d.

———. *Eulogy on William Wilberforce, Esq., Delivered at the Request of the People of Colour of the City of Philadelphia, in the Second African Presbyterian Church on the Sixth Day of December, 1833.* Philadelphia: W. P. Gibbons, 1833.

Williams, Peter, Jr. *An Oration on the Abolition of the Slave Trade.* New York: Samuel Wood, 1808.

Wooley, James E., and Vivian Wooley, eds. *Edgefield County, S.C. Wills, 1787–1836.* Greenville, S.C.: Southern Historical Press, 1991.

Yacovone, Donald, ed. *A Voice of Thunder: The Civil War Letters of George E. Stephens.* Urbana and Chicago: University of Illinois Press, 1997.

Secondary Works

Ames, Kenneth L. *Death in the Dining Room and Other Tales of Victorian Culture.* Philadelphia: Temple University Press, 1992.

Berlin, Ira. *Slaves Without Masters: The Free Negro in the Antebellum South.* New York: Vintage Books, 1976.

Blackett, R. J. M. " 'Freedom or the Martyr's Grave': Black Pittsburgh's Aid to the Fugitive Slave." In Joe William Trotter Jr. and Eric Ledell Smith, eds., *African Americans in Pennsylvania: Shifting Historical Perspectives.* University Park: The Pennsylvania State University Press, 1997.

———. *Beating Against the Barriers: Biographical Essays in Nineteenth-Century Afro-American History.* Baton Rouge and London: Louisiana State University Press, 1986.

Blight, David W. "In Search of Learning, Liberty, and Self Definition: James McCune Smith and the Ordeal of the Antebellum Black Intellectual." *Afro-Americans in New York Life and History* 9 (July 1985), 7–25.

Bolster, W. Jeffrey. *Black Jacks: African American Seamen in the Age of Sail.* Cambridge, Mass.: Harvard University Press, 1997.

Boylan, Anne M. "Benevolence and Antislavery Activity Among African American Women in New York and Boston, 1820–1840." In Jean Fagan Yellin and John C. Van Horne, eds., *The Abolitionist Sisterhood: Women's Political Culture in Antebellum America.* Ithaca: Cornell University Press, 1994.

Bushman, Richard L. *The Refinement of America: Persons, Houses, Cities.* New York: Vintage Books, 1992.
Curry, Leonard P. *The Free Black in Urban America, 1800-1850: The Shadow of the Dream.* Chicago: University of Chicago Press, 1981.
Davis, Russell H. *Black Americans in Cleveland.* Washington, D.C.: The Associated Publishers, 1972.
Gatewood, Willard B. *Aristocrats of Color: The Black Elite, 1880-1920.* Bloomington and Indianapolis: University of Indiana Press, 1990.
———. "Josephine Beall Willson Bruce." In Darlene Clark Hine, Elsa Barkley Brown, and Rosalyn Terborg-Penn, eds., *Black Women in America: An Historical Encyclopedia.* Bloomington and Indianapolis: University of Indiana Press, 1993.
Geffen, Elizabeth M. "Industrial Development and Social Crisis, 1841-1854." In Russell F. Weigley et al., eds., *Philadelphia: A 300-Year History.* New York: W. W. Norton, 1982.
Gilje, Paul A., and Howard B. Rock. " 'Sweep O! Sweep O!': African-American Chimney-Sweeps and Citizenship in the New Nation." *William and Mary Quarterly* 51 (July 1994), 507-38.
Graham, Leroy. *Baltimore: The Nineteenth-Century Black Capital.* Washington, D.C.: University Press of America, 1982.
Griffith, Cyril E. *The African Dream: Martin R. Delany and the Emergence of Pan-African Thought.* University Park: The Pennsylvania State University Press, 1975.
Gronowicz, Anthony. *Race and Class Politics in New York City Before the Civil War.* Boston: Northeastern University Press, 1998.
Hershberg, Theodore. "Free Blacks in Antebellum Philadelphia: A Study of Ex-Slaves, Freeborn, and Socio-Economic Decline." In Trotter and Smith, eds., *African Americans in Pennsylvania.*
Hinks, Peter P. *To Awaken My Afflicted Brethren: David Walker and the Problem of Antebellum Slave Resistance.* University Park: The Pennsylvania State University Press, 1997.
Horton, James Oliver. "Freedom's Yoke: Gender Conventions Among Free Blacks." In James O. Horton, ed., *Free People of Color: Inside the African American Community.* Washington, D.C.: Smithsonian Institution Press, 1993.
———, and Lois E. Horton. *Black Bostonians: Family Life and Community Struggle in the Antebellum North.* New York: Holmes and Meier, 1978.
Johnson, Michael P., and James L. Roark. *Black Masters: A Free Family of Color in the Old South.* New York: W. W. Norton, 1984.
Johnson, Whittington B. "Free Blacks in Antebellum Augusta, Georgia: A Demographic and Economic Profile." *Richmond County History* 14 (1982), 10-21.
Jones, Charles C., Jr. *Memorial History of Augusta, Georgia.* Syracuse, N.Y.: D. Mason & Co., 1890.
Jones, Louis C. "A Leader Ahead of His Times." *American Heritage* 14 (June 1963), 58-59, 63.
Kaplan, Michael. "New York City Tavern Violence and the Creation of a Working-Class Male Identity." *Journal of the Early Republic* 15 (Winter 1995), 591-617.
Kashatus, William C., III. "The Inner Light and Popular Enlightenment: Philadelphia Quakers and Charity Schooling, 1790-1820." *Pennsylvania Magazine of History and Biography* 118 (January-April, 1994), 87-116.
Kasson, John F. *Rudeness and Civility: Manners in Nineteenth-Century Urban America.* New York: Hill and Wang, 1990.

Kusmer, Kenneth L. *A Ghetto Takes Shape: Black Cleveland, 1870–1930.* Urbana and Chicago: University of Illinois Press, 1976.
Lapsansky, Emma J. " 'Discipline to the Mind': Philadelphia's Banneker Institute, 1854–1872." *Pennsylvania Magazine of History and Biography* 117 (January 1993), 83–102.
———. "Friends, Wives, and Strivings: Networks and Community Values Among Nineteenth-Century Philadelphia Afroamerican Elites." *Pennsylvania Magazine of History and Biography* 108 (January 1984), 3–24.
———. *Neighborhoods in Transition: William Penn's Dream and Urban Reality.* New York: Garland, 1994.
———. " 'Since They Got Those Separate Churches': Afro-Americans and Racism in Jacksonian Philadelphia." *American Quarterly* 32 (Spring 1980), 54–78.
Larkin, Jack. *The Reshaping of Everyday Life, 1790–1840.* New York: Harper and Row, 1988.
Laurie, Bruce. *Working People of Philadelphia, 1800–1850.* Philadelphia: Temple University Press, 1980.
Lindhorst, Marie. "Politics in a Box: Sarah Mapps Douglass and the Female Literary Association, 1831–1833." *Pennsylvania History* 65 (Summer 1998), 263–79.
Litwack, Leon. *North of Slavery: The Negro in the Free States, 1790–1860.* Chicago: University of Chicago Press, 1961.
Lott, Eric. *Love and Theft: Blackface Minstrelsy and the American Working Class.* New York: Oxford University Press, 1993.
McBride, David. "Black Protest Against Racial Politics: Gardner, Hinton, and Their Memorial of 1838." *Pennsylvania History* 46 (April 1979), 149–62.
McCormick, Richard P. "William Whipper: Moral Reformer." *Pennsylvania History* 43 (January 1976), 23–46.
Mabee, Carleton. *Black Education in New York State from Colonial to Modern Times.* Syracuse: Syracuse University Press, 1979.
Minton, Henry W. *The Early History of the Negro in Business in Philadelphia, Read Before the American Negro Historical Society, March, 1913.* Nashville, Tenn.: AMESS Union, 1913.
Nash, Gary B. *Forging Freedom: The Formation of Philadelphia's Black Community, 1720–1840.* Cambridge, Mass.: Harvard University Press, 1988.
———. "Slaves and Slaveowners in Colonial Philadelphia." In Gary B. Nash, ed., *Race, Class and Politics: Essays on American Colonial and Revolutionary Society.* Urbana and Chicago: University of Illinois Press, 1986.
Oden, Gloria. "The Journal of Charlotte L. Forten: The Salem-Philadelphia Years (1851–1861) Reexamined." *Essex Institute Historical Collections* 119 (April 1983), 119–36.
Pease, Jane H., and William H. Pease. *They Who Would Be Free: Blacks' Search for Freedom, 1830–1861.* New York: Atheneum, 1974.
Phillips, Christopher. *Freedom's Port: The African American Community of Baltimore, 1790–1860.* Urbana and Chicago: University of Illinois Press, 1997.
Pool, Daniel. *What Jane Austen Ate and Charles Dickens Knew: From Fox-Hunting to Whist, The Facts of Daily Life in Nineteenth-Century England.* New York: Simon and Schuster, 1993.
Quarles, Benjamin. *Black Abolitionists.* New York: Oxford University Press, 1969.
Rhodes, Jane. *Mary Ann Shadd Cary: The Black Press and Protest in the Nineteenth Century.* Bloomington: University of Indiana Press, 1998.
Ritter, Abraham. *Philadelphia and Her Merchants, As Constituted Fifty and Seventy Years Ago.* Philadelphia: The Author, 1860.

Roediger, David R. *The Wages of Whiteness: Race and the Making of the American Working Class*. 2nd ed. New York and London: Verso, 1999.
Runcie, John. " 'Hunting the Nigs' in Philadelphia: The Race Riot of August 1834." *Pennsylvania History* 39 (April 1972), 187-218.
Salvatore, Nick. *We All Got History: The Memory Books of Amos Webber*. New York: Random House, 1996.
Schweninger, Loren. *Black Property Owners in the South, 1790-1915*. Urbana and Chicago: University of Illinois, 1990.
———. "John Carruthers Stanly and the Anomaly of Black Slaveholding." *North Carolina Historical Review* 67 (April 1990), 158-92.
Sermon Preached at the Funeral of Robert Purvis by Rev. Frederic A. Hinckley, of Philadelphia, Pa., on Friday, April 15, 1898, at Spring Garden Unitarian Church. Washington, D.C., 1898.
Siebert, Wilbur H. *The Underground Railroad from Slavery to Freedom*. New York and London: Macmillan, 1898; reprint, New York: Arno, 1968.
Silcox, Harry C. "Delay and Neglect: Negro Education in Antebellum Philadelphia, 1800-1860." *Pennsylvania Magazine of History and Biography* 97 (October 1973), 444-64.
Simmons, William J. *Men of Mark: Eminent, Progressive, and Rising*. Cleveland: George M. Rewell & Co., 1887.
Smith, Edward D. *Climbing Jacob's Ladder: The Rise of Black Churches in Eastern American Cities, 1740-1877*. Washington, D.C.: Smithsonian Institution Press, 1988.
Southern, Eileen. *The Music of Black Americans: A History*. 2nd ed. New York: W. W. Norton, 1983.
Stewart, James Brewer. "The Emergence of Racial Modernity and the Rise of the White North, 1790-1840." *Journal of the Early Republic* 18 (Summer 1998), 181-236.
Still, William. *The Underground Railroad*. Philadelphia: People's Publishing Co., 1879; reprint, New York: Arno, 1968.
Sweat, Edward F. "The Free Negro in Ante-bellum Georgia." Ph.D. dissertation, Indiana University, 1957.
Swift, David E. *Black Prophets of Justice: Activist Clergy Before the Civil War*. Baton Rouge: Louisiana State University Press, 1989.
Walls, William J. *The African Methodist Episcopal Zion Church*. Charlotte, N.C.: AME Zion Publishing House, 1974.
Warner, Sam Bass, Jr., *The Private City: Philadelphia in Three Periods of Its Growth*. Philadelphia: University of Pennsylvania Press, 1968.
White, Shane. " 'It Was a Proud Day': African Americans, Festivals, and Parades in the North, 1741-1834." *Journal of American History* 81 (June 1994), 13-50.
———. *Somewhat More Independent: The End of Slavery in New York City, 1770-1810*. Athens: University of Georgia Press, 1991.
Wikramanayake, Marina. *A World in Shadow: The Free Black in Antebellum South Carolina*. Columbia: University of South Carolina Press, 1973.
Winch, Julie. *Philadelphia's Black Elite: Activism, Accommodation, and the Struggle for Autonomy, 1787-1848*. Philadelphia: Temple University Press, 1988.
———. " 'You Have Talents—Only Cultivate Them': Philadelphia's Black Female Literary Societies and the Abolitionist Crusade." In Yellin and Van Horne, eds., *The Antislavery Sisterhood*.
Yacovone, Donald. "The Transformation of the Black Temperance Movement, 1827-1854: An Interpretation." *Journal of the Early Republic* 8 (Fall 1988), 281-97.

Index

Unless otherwise indicated, all the churches and organizations referred to here are in Philadelphia.

Abyssinian Baptist Church, New York, 142 n. 56
Adam (slave), 54 n. 71
African Asbury Church, New York, 141 n. 54
African Dorcas Society, New York, 141 n. 54
African Friendly Society of St. Thomas, 122 n. 7
African Masonic Lodge, New York, 141 n. 54
African Methodist Episcopal (AME) denomination, 57, 139 n. 51, 141 n. 54, 147 n. 60, 148 n. 63
African Methodist Episcopal Wesley Church, 121 n. 6
African Methodist Episcopal Zion (AMEZ) denomination, 141 n. 54
African Porters' Benevolent Society, 15 n. 16, 157 n. 89
African Society for Mutual Relief, New York, 143 n. 57
Agricultural and Mechanical Association of Pennsylvania and New Jersey, 164 n. 111
A.H.B. (writer), 36
Alabama, 7
Allen, Richard, 103n., 134 n. 47
The American (newspaper), 135 n. 49
American and Foreign Anti-Slavery Society, 148 n. 62
American Anti-Slavery Society, 146 n. 59, 148 n. 62, 154 n. 78, 163 n. 110, 165 n. 113, 171 n. 118
American Colonization Society, 63, 132 n. 43, 137 n. 50, 142–44 nn. 56–58, 147 n. 62, 152 n. 73, 153 n. 76, 156 n. 88
American Equal Rights Association, 166 n. 113, 172 n. 118
American Freedmen's Aid Commission, 169 n. 115
American Moral Reform Society, 84, 123 nn. 10–11, 133 n. 45, 135 n. 49, 137 n. 50, 144 n. 58, 147 n. 62, 150–51 nn. 71–72, 154 n. 78, 156 nn. 86–87, 157 n. 90, 158 n. 93, 163–64 nn. 110–11, 165 n. 113
American Notes (Dickens), 121 n. 1

American Society of Free Persons of Color, for Improving their Condition, 103n.
Amherst Academy, 165 n. 113
Amistad, 136 n. 49
Anthony, Susan B., 166 n. 113
Appeal of Forty Thousand (pamphlet), 27, 151 n. 72, 154 n. 78, 156 n. 88, 165 n. 113
Appo family, 10
apprenticeships, difficulty in securing, 18, 59–60
Association for Moral and Mental Improvement. *See* Philadelphia Association for Moral and Mental Improvement
Augusta, Georgia, 7, 11, 51, 54
Augusta, Bank of, 53
Augustine, Peter, 21
Avery, Charles, 139 n. 51
Avery College, 139 n. 51

Bacchus (slave), 54 n. 71
Ballygallon, Londonderry, 51
Baltimore, 7, 28, 56, 125 n. 18, 140 nn. 52–53, 147 n. 62
Banneker Institute, 164 n. 111
Banton, Grace. *See* Bogle, Grace
Banton, William D., 114, 156 n. 85
Baptists, 84, 121 n. 6
Barbados, 10, 153 n. 75
barbers, 20, 59, 122 n. 8, 127 n. 19, 139 n. 51, 150 nn. 71–72, 158 n. 92, 160 nn. 100 and 102, 163 n. 111, 170 n. 117
Bastien, David, 10 n. 13
benevolent societies, 26, 84, 85, 122 n. 7
Benezet Philanthropic Association, 147 n. 60, 162–63 nn. 109–10
Bennett, Richard, 10 n. 13
Bethel Education Society, 124 n. 13
Bias, James J. G., 21, 23, 127 n. 19
Bias, Eliza, 127 n. 19
Binah (slave), 54 n. 71
Bird, James, 114, 156 n. 88
Black, Ebenezer, 150 n. 71
bleeders, 20–23, 127 n. 19, 163 n. 111

Index

boardinghouses, 12, 130 n. 37, 147 n. 60
Bob (slave), 54 n. 71
Bogle, Amelia, 117, 122 nn. 8 and 9, 172 n. 119
Bogle, Grace (Banton), 172 n. 119
Bogle, Robert, 21, 172 n. 119
Bolivar, William Carl, 160 n. 103
bootblacks, 156 n. 85
Boston, 10, 11, 56–57, 60, 133 n. 46, 167 n. 114
Bowers, Henrietta (wife of John), 153 n. 78
Bowers, Henrietta. *See* Duterte, Henrietta
Bowers, John, 10, 15, 18, 21, 105, 133 n. 46, 153 n. 78
Bowers, John C., 18, 113, 117, 153 n. 78, 161 n. 105
Bowers, Mary, 154 n. 78
Bowers, Thomas, 18
Bowser, David Bustill, 124 n. 16
Brick Wesley Church, 156 n. 85
Brister, Charles, 18, 114, 157 n. 89
Britain, 11, 144 n. 58, 165 n. 113
Brown, John, 10 n. 13
Brown, Morris, Jr., 150 n. 71
Brown, Morris, Sr., 150 n. 71
Brownhill, Daniel B., 150 n. 71
Bruce, Blanche K., 68, 70–71
Bruce, Josephine. *See* Willson, Josephine Beall
Bruce, Roscoe Conkling, 71
Burr, Aaron, 123 n. 11
Burr, David, 123 n. 11, 158 n. 92
Burr, Edward, 158 n. 92
Burr, Elizabeth, 170 n. 116
Burr, Hetty, 18, 117, 123 n. 11, 158 n. 92, 169 n. 116
Burr, J. Matilda, 18
Burr, John Emery, 115, 123 n. 11, 158 n. 92
Burr, John P., 18, 84, 115, 123 n. 11, 158 n. 92, 169 n. 116
Burr, Louisa, 170 n. 116
Burr, Martin, 158 n. 92
Burton, Belfast, 105, 127 n. 19, 134 n. 47
Bustill, Cyrus, 162 n. 109, 170 n. 117
Bustill, Grace. *See* Douglass, Grace
Butler, Elizabeth, 122 n. 8
Butler, Thomas, 20, 122 n. 7, 127 n. 19, 150 n. 71
Byberry, Pennsylvania, 165 n. 113, 172 n. 118

cabinetmakers, 20, 23
"calling," 98–99, 130 n. 34

Canada, emigration to, 132 n. 43, 135 n. 49, 138 n. 50, 140 n. 51, 146–47 nn. 59–60
carpenters, 20, 159 n. 96
Cassey, Alfred, 124 n. 16
Cassey, Amy M. (Williams), 10, 117, 163 n. 10, 167 n. 114
Cassey, Joseph, 10, 20, 23, 24, 117, 151 n. 72, 162 n. 110, 165 n. 113, 167 n. 114
Cassey, Peter, 20
caterers, 21, 172 n. 119
Catholics, 31, 83, 121 n. 6, 139 n. 51
Central College, New York, 132 n. 44
Charleston, South Carolina, 55–56, 164 n. 113
Charlotte (slave), 54 n. 71
Chicago, 56
China, black Philadelphians in, 15–16, 133 n. 46
cholera, 64, 150 n. 72
Christiana Riot (1851), 123 n. 11
churches, African-American, in Philadelphia, 23, 30–31, 40, 84, 121 n. 6. *See also under names of individual churches*
Cincinnati, 56
Citizen Sons of Philadelphia, 156 nn. 85 and 88
Citizens' Union of the Commonwealth of Pennsylvania, 146 n. 59, 166 n. 113
Clarkson, Thomas, 145 n. 58
The Clarksonian (newspaper), 144 n. 58
Clarkson School, 31, 57–58, 159 n. 97, 160 n. 100, 164 n. 113
Clay, Edward W., 36
Cleveland, 11, 49, 56, 67–68, 71–72
clothing dealers, 18, 21, 133 n. 46, 156 n. 87
coachmen, 15, 122 n. 7
Coachmen's Benevolent Society, 15 n. 17
Coker, Abner, 105, 140 n. 52
Coker, Daniel, 125 n. 18, 140 n. 52
Coker, Sarah, 140 n. 52
Collins, Mary. *See* Bowers, Mary
Colly, Daniel, 150 n. 71, 155 n. 83
colonization, African, 57, 135 n. 49, 146 n. 59, 147 n. 62
Colored American (newspaper), 49, 146 n. 59, 150 n. 72, 153 n. 75, 154 n. 78, 159 n. 99, 160 n. 103, 164 n. 111
Colored Female Free Produce Society of Pennsylvania, 169 n. 116
Colored Free Produce Society of Pennsylvania, 134 n. 48, 151 n. 72, 165 n. 113

Colored Reading Room Society, 137 n. 50
Columbia, Pennsylvania, 138 n. 50
Connecticut, 158 n. 93
Consolidation Act (1854), 5, 6
conventions, black national, 57, 123 n. 10, 133 n. 45, 134 n. 48, 135 n. 49, 137–39 nn. 50–51, 143–44 nn. 57–58, 146 n. 59, 147 nn. 60 and 62, 151–52 nn. 72–73, 156 nn. 86 and 88
  (1830), 103n., 133–34 nn. 46–47, 135 n. 49, 147–48 nn. 61–63
  (1831), 103–5, 132 n. 44, 134 n. 47, 149 n. 67
  (1832), 132 n. 44, 133 n. 46, 140 n. 53, 141 n. 55, 149 n. 67, 155 n. 81
  (1833), 132 n. 44, 140 n. 53, 142 n. 56, 153 n. 76
  (1834), 137 n. 50, 141 n. 55, 152 n. 73
  (1835), 126 n. 19, 142 n. 56, 152 n. 73
  (1836), 133 n. 45
  (1847), 159 n. 99
  (1853), 64, 139 n. 51
  (1855), 136 n. 49, 152 n. 73, 154 n. 78
  (1864), 152 n. 73
conventions, Pennsylvania state,
  (1841), 139 n. 51, 146 n. 59, 159 n. 99
  (1848), 138 n. 50, 146 n. 59, 166 n. 113
Cornish, James, 105, 113, 134 n. 48
Cornish, Mary, 134 n. 48
Cornish, Samuel E., 134 n. 48, 137 n. 50, 160 n. 103
Corr, Joseph M., 125 n. 17
Cowley, Robert, 105, 140 n. 53
Cowperthwaite, Joseph, 57
Crandall, Prudence, 133 n. 46
Crouch, Thomas Smith, 115, 160 n. 102
Crown Hill Cemetery, Indianapolis, 71

daguerreotypists, 128 n. 20
debating, 33, 85, 89, 113, 114–15, 116
Delany, Martin R., 128 n. 20, 139 n. 51
Delaware, 9, 103, 134 nn. 47–48, 145 n. 59, 152 n. 73, 155 n. 84, 156 n. 86
Demosthenian Institute, 33, 115–16, 147 n. 62, 157 n. 91
Demosthenian Shield (newspaper), 116n., 159 n. 96, 160 n. 103
dentists, 20, 127 n. 19
Depee. *See* Dupee, John
A Diary in America (Marryat), 121 n. 1

Dickens, Charles, 121 n. 1
dining, in antebellum America, 100, 130 n. 36
divisions, within the "higher classes," 91–96
Domestic Manners of the Americans (Trollope), 121 n. 1
domestics, 12
Donaldson, Arthur, 157 n. 89
Dorcas Society, 122 n. 8, 173 n. 119
Dorsey, Thomas J., 21
Douglass, Charles (son of Robert and Grace), 162 n. 109
Douglass, Elizabeth (daughter of Robert and Grace), 162 n. 109, 170 n. 117
Douglass, Elizabeth (Grice) (1st wife of Rev. William), 126 n. 18
Douglass, Frederick (abolitionist), 126 n. 18, 148 n. 62
Douglass, Grace (Bustill), 117, 127 n. 20, 162 n. 109, 168 n. 115, 170–71 nn. 117–18
Douglass, James (son of Robert and Grace), 20, 162 n. 109, 169 n. 115
Douglass, Robert, Jr. (son of Robert and Grace), 113, 117, 127 n. 20, 162 n. 109, 169 n. 115
Douglass, Robert, Sr., 10, 20, 23, 117, 127 n. 20, 160 n. 103, 162 n. 109, 168 n. 115
Douglass, Sarah M. (daughter of Robert and Grace), 12, 117, 124 n. 16, 126 n. 18, 160 n. 107, 162 n. 109, 168 n. 115
Douglass, Rev. William, 23, 24, 40, 89, 125 n. 18, 168 n. 115, 170 n. 117
Douglass, William P. (son of Robert and Grace), 124 n. 16, 162 n. 109
draymen, 15
dressmakers, 18, 170 n. 116, 173 n. 119. *See also* seamstresses
Duncan, William, 105, 147 n. 61
Dupee, John, 113, 153 n. 76
Dupuy family, 10
Durnford, Andrew, 55
Dustan, Ina. *See* Willson, Ina Dustan
Duterte, Francis, 154 n. 78
Duterte, Henrietta (Bowers), 154 n. 78
Duterte family, 10

Edgefield County, South Carolina, 51
Edgeworth, Maria, 161 n. 106
Edgeworth Literary Association, 117, 161 n. 106
Edmondston, Mary, 64 n. 96

Index

education, African-American, 31–33, 87–88, 89, 111–12, 124 n. 13
"Ella," 168 n. 115
Ellison, William, 55
Elsey (slave), 54 n. 71
Emancipator (newspaper), 133 n. 46, 139 n. 51, 146 n. 59, 150 n. 72
employment patterns, African-American, 11–13, 15–21, 23, 28 n. 36
Episcopalians, 84, 121 n. 6, 169 n. 116

Female Benevolent Society of St. Thomas, 122 n. 7
Female Literary Association of Philadelphia, 161 n. 104, 168 n. 115
Female Medical College of Pennsylvania, 168 n. 115
Female Minervian Literary Society, 116–17, 151 n. 81, 161 n. 105
Female Rush Assistant Society, 173 n. 119
Female Simeon Society, 155 n. 84
Female Vigilance Committee, 159 n. 97
feuding, Willson criticizes, 43, 46, 91–93, 101, 108–11
First African Baptist Church, 121 n. 6
First African Presbyterian Church, 121 n. 6, 147 n. 62, 162 n. 109, 170 n. 117
First Colored Wesley Methodist Church, 141 n. 54, 155 n. 84
"Flying Horses" riot (1834), 29
Foote, Anna L. *See* Willson, Anna Foote
Forten, Charlotte Vandine, 171 n. 118
Forten, Harriet. *See* Purvis, Harriet
Forten, James, 7, 11, 15 n. 15, 18, 23, 24, 26 n. 33, 121 n. 4, 127 n. 20, 130 n. 35, 132 n. 44, 137 n. 50, 149 n. 67, 160 n. 103, 163 n. 110, 165 n. 113, 168 n. 115, 170–71 nn. 117–18
Forten, James, Jr., 124 n. 16, 150 n. 71
Forten, Robert Bridges, 24, 121 n. 4
Forten, Sarah Louisa, 130 n. 35
Forten, William D., 166 n. 113
Foster, Abby Kelley, 168–69 nn. 115–16
franchise, 3, 26–28, 102–3, 131 n. 42, 142 n. 55, 145–46 nn. 58–59, 149 n. 68, 152 n. 73, 153 n. 75, 154 n. 78, 158 n. 94, 166 n. 113
Franklin Institute, 121 n. 4
Free African Society, 122 n. 7
Freedman's Savings Bank, 138 n. 50

free labor, 137 n. 50, 164 n. 111
Friendly Daughters of Nehemiah, 155 n. 84
Friendly West Indian Society, 10 n. 13
Friends, Society of, 12, 57, 168 n. 115, 170 n. 117
The Fugitive Blacksmith (Pennington), 145 n. 58
Fugitive Slave Law, 136 n. 49, 158 n. 94, 165 n. 113
fugitive slaves, 122 n. 8, 138–39 nn. 50–51, 146 n. 59, 148 n. 62, 152 n. 73, 159 n. 97, 164 n. 111, 165 n. 113, 172 n. 118

Ganges, as last name, 10
Gardiner, Elizabeth. *See* Howell, Elizabeth
Gardiner, Peter, 105, 127 n. 19, 130 n. 37, 146 n. 60
Gardiner, Serena, 130 n. 37, 147 n. 60
Gardner, Charles W., 105, 147 n. 62, 151 n. 72
The Garies and Their Friends (Webb), 25 n. 30
Garrison, William Lloyd, 36, 59–60, 104n., 132 n. 44, 142 n. 56, 149 n. 67, 163 n. 110, 168 n. 115
"Gentleman's Dressing Room," 20, 59, 150 n. 72
Georgia, laws regarding free people of color, 9, 55
Gibbons, Anne B. (Poole), 159 n. 96
Gibbons, George Washington, 20, 115, 159 n. 96
Gibbons, James, 18, 19, 20, 130 n. 37, 159 n. 96
Gilbert, Howard W., 162 n. 107
Gilbert Lyceum, 33, 117–18, 161 n. 107
Glasgow, Elizabeth, 65
Glasgow, Peter, 65
Gloucester, James, 125 n. 17
Gloucester, Jeremiah, 125 n. 17
Gloucester, John, Jr., 46, 125 n. 17
Gloucester, John, Sr., 125 n. 17
Gloucester, Stephen H., 125 n. 17
Goines, George Washington, 157 n. 91
Gordon, Alice (daughter of David), 158 n. 93
Gordon, David, 115, 158 n. 93
Gordon, David, Jr. (son of David), 158 n. 93
Gordon, Eliza (daughter of David), 158 n. 93
Gordon, Ella (daughter of David), 158 n. 93
Gordon, Mary (wife of David), 158 n. 93
Gordon, Mary (daughter of David), 158 n. 93

Index

Gordon, Mary (2d wife of Robert C.), 153 n. 75
Gordon, Robert (father of Robert C.), 153 n. 75
Gordon, Robert III (son of Robert C.), 153 n. 75
Gordon, Robert C., 113, 153 n. 75
Gordon, Sarah (1st wife of Robert C.), 153 n. 75
Gordon, Sarah Ann (mother of Robert C.), 153 n. 75
Gordon, Walter (son of Robert C.), 153 n. 75
Gordon, Walter (son of David), 158 n. 93
Gordon, William S., 150 n. 71
Gradual Abolition Act (Pennsylvania, 1780), 7, 25
Grice, Hezekiah, 126 n. 18
Grimké, Angelina, 130 n. 35, 168–70 nn. 115–17
Grimké, Sarah, 126 n. 18, 168–70 nn. 115–17

hairdressers, 123 n. 11, 152 n. 73, 154 n. 81, 159 nn. 97 and 99, 162 nn. 109–10. *See also* barbers
Haiti, 123 n. 11, 134 n. 47, 147 n. 60
Hamilton, Alexander, 143 n. 57
Hamilton, William, 105, 143 n. 57
Hamilton Institute, New York, 143 n. 57
Harang, Mr., 71 n. 117
Harnett, Elizabeth. *See* Willson, Elizabeth Harnett
Harris, Andrew, 125 n. 17
Harry (slave), 54 n. 71
Hart, Elizabeth, 155 n. 84
Hart, Henry Edward, 58
Hart, John L., 41, 114, 155 n. 84
Haytien Emigration Society, 162 n. 110
Henderson, John, 66
Henrico County, Virginia, 147 n. 61
"higher classes of colored society"
 definition of, 40–41, 83, 86–88
 existence of, 82–83
 praised, 36
 ridiculed, 36
 role of, 47–48
 violence against, 40
Hinton, Eliza Ann (Howell), 147 n. 60, 150 n. 72
Hinton, Frederick Augustus, 9, 10, 20, 58–60, 63, 64, 113, 137 n. 50, 147 n. 60, 148 n. 62, 150 n. 72
Howell, Eliza Ann. *See* Hinton, Eliza Ann
Howell, Elizabeth (Gardiner), 147 n. 60
Howell, Richard, 147 n. 60, 150 n. 72
Hubert, Ann, 156 n. 86
Hubert, Littleton, 23, 114, 156 n. 86
Hughes, Benjamin, 115, 160 n. 101
Humane Mechanics' Association, 134 n. 48, 157 n. 90, 164 n. 111
Huntsville, Alabama, 11, 55
Hutchinson, Alexander F., 20, 115, 158 n. 94, 160 n. 100

Indianapolis, 11, 71
Institute for Colored Youth, 168 n. 115

Jackson, Elizabeth, 145 n. 59
Jacksonville, Florida, 145 n. 58
Jacob (slave), 54 n. 71
Jamaica, 128 n. 20, 145 n. 58
Jematrice, John, 10 n. 13
Jennings, Elizabeth, 143 n. 56
Jennings, Thomas L., 105, 142 n. 56
Jennings, William M., 115, 158 n. 95
Jocelyn, Simeon S., 104n., 132 n. 44
Johnson, Mrs. E., 130 n. 37
Judah, Harriet, 141 n. 54, 164 n. 113
Juvenile Singing School, 152 n. 73

Keating, Aaron (son of Edward and Rose), 51, 52
Keating, Betsy. *See* Willson, Elizabeth
Keating, Betsy ("Little Betsy"), 53
Keating, Caroline. *See* Willson, Caroline
Keating, Charles (son of Edward and Rose), 51, 52
Keating, Edward, 51, 52
Keating, Eliza. *See* Willson, Elizabeth or Eliza
Keating, Emily. *See* Willson, Emily
Keating, Jenny (wife of William), 52
Keating, John. *See* Willson, John
Keating, Joseph. *See* Willson, Joseph
Keating, Martha (daughter of Jenny and William), 52
Keating, Mary (daughter of Edward and Rose), 51, 52
Keating, Moses (son of Edward and Rose), 51
Keating, Polly (daughter of Jenny and William), 52
Keating, Richard, Jr. (nephew of Edward), 51

Keating, Richard, Sr. (brother of Edward), 51
Keating, William or Billy (son of Edward and Rose), 51, 52, 53
Kensington, Philadelphia County, 5
King, John P., 54–55, 57–58
Knapp, Isaac, 60
Kossuth, Louis, 136 n. 49
Kuzel, Frank, 72

laborers, 12–13, 15
Lancaster, Pennsylvania, 154 n. 78
laundresses, 11–12
Lebanon Cemetery, 164 n. 111
Liberator (newspaper), 59, 123 n. 11, 133 n. 46, 135–39 nn. 49–51, 146 n. 59, 150 n. 72, 154 n. 79, 155 n. 84, 158 n. 92, 162–64 nn. 109–11, 165 n. 113
Liberia, 11, 26, 60, 63, 135 n. 49, 151 n. 72
"Life in Philadelphia" cartoons, 36
literary societies, African-American, 33, 85, 89, 111–19, 155 n. 82. *See also under names of individual societies*
Little Britain Township, Lancaster County, Pa., 136 n. 50
London, England, 127 n. 20
longshoremen, 15
Louisiana, 55
Lundy, Benjamin, 162 n. 107
Lutherans, 121 n. 6

Male Harrison Benevolent Society, 155 n. 84
manual labor college, 104, 132 n. 43, 155 n. 82, 162 nn. 109–10, 165 n. 113
maritime trades, African Americans in, 18
Marryat, Frederick (author), 121 n. 1
Martineau, Harriet (author), 121 n. 1
Maryland, 9, 103, 139 n. 51, 140 n. 54, 144 n. 58, 148 n. 63
Mathews, Henrietta, 155 n. 81, 161 n. 105
Mathews, James C., 113, 154 n. 81, 161 n. 105
Mayflower School, Cleveland, 68
McClendon, Joseph Greenfield, 58
McCrummill, James, 20
Mead, Lewis, Jr., 115, 159 n. 97
Mead, Lewis, Sr., 159 n. 97
Mead, Mary, 159 n. 97
Mechanics' Association of Philadelphia. *See* Humane Mechanics' Association
Mechanics' Enterprise Hall, 123 n. 11, 156 n. 88, 157 n. 90

medical practitioners, African-American, 21, 23, 89–90, 126 n. 19, 147 n. 60
meetings, Willson on, 106–11
Methodists, 83, 121 n. 6
midwives, 23, 127 n. 19
Miller, Clayton, 150 n. 71
Miller, Henry B., 161 n. 105
Miller, William, 105, 140 n. 54
milliners, 12, 170 n. 117
Minerva Literary Association. *See* Female Minervian Literary Society
ministers, 23, 84, 89, 124 n. 17
Minton family, 21
money-lending, 20, 162 n. 110
Montier family, 10
Morel, Alice, 136 n. 49
Morel, Caroline, 135 n. 49
Morel, Junius C., 9, 11, 16, 105, 135–37 nn. 49–50, 150 n. 71
Morel, Sarah, 136 n. 49
Morey, Elizabeth, 170 n. 117
"Mother" Bethel AME Church, 121 n. 6, 134 n. 47
Mott, Lucretia, 161 n. 105, 168 n. 115, 170 n. 117
Moyamensing, Philadelphia County, 5, 6, 24–25, 65

Nash, Charles, 23, 127 n. 19
National Association for the Advancement of Colored People (NAACP), 73
National Association of Colored Women, 73
National Council of the Colored People, 136 n. 49, 140 n. 51
National Reformer (periodical), 123 n. 11, 137 n. 50, 146 n. 59
Needham, Elizabeth, 152 n. 73
Needham, James, Jr., 113, 118, 152 n. 73
Needham, James, Sr., 152 n. 73
Needham, Martha, 152 n. 73
New Haven, Connecticut, 132 n. 44, 155 n. 82
New Jersey, 9–10, 123 n. 11, 147 n. 62, 162 n. 110
New Orleans, 7, 55–56
New York (state), 103
New York City, 7, 10, 11, 12, 28, 49, 57, 133 n. 45, 140–42 nn. 54–56, 144 n. 58, 158 n. 94, 159 n. 96, 160 n. 103, 167 n. 114
New York African Bible Society, 141 n. 54

Index

New York African Society for Mutual Relief, 142 n. 55
New York Legal Rights Association, 143 n. 56
North Carolina, 9, 135 n. 49, 150 n. 72, 158 n. 94
"northerners" versus "southerners," 95
Northern Liberties, Philadelphia County, 5, 28

Oakland, California, 160 n. 99
Oberlin College, 68
O'Connell, Daniel, 11
Onderdonk, Bishop Henry, 126 n. 18
Oneida Institute, 132 n. 44, 163 n. 110
Otter, William, 28

Parkenson, Eben, 115, 159 n. 98
parlor, significance of, 98, 129 n. 32
Parnell, Harriet. *See* Shadd, Harriet
Parrott, Russell, 125 n. 17
passport, problems securing, 128 n. 20, 165 n. 113
Payne, Daniel Alexander, 121 n. 4, 122 n. 9, 125 n. 17
Peck, David J., 127 n. 19, 140 n. 51
Peck, John C., 105, 139 n. 51
Pembroke, James. *See* Pennington, James W. C.
"Pencil Pusher." *See* Bolivar, William Carl
Pennington, James W. C., 105, 143 n. 58
Pennsylvania Abolition Society, 12, 24, 31, 60, 122 n. 9, 148 n. 62
Pennsylvania Anti-Slavery Society, 123 n. 11, 133 n. 46, 139 n. 51, 148 n. 62, 151–52 nn. 72–73, 154 n. 78, 158 nn. 92 and 94, 165 n. 113, 171 n. 118
Pennsylvania Augustine Society, 124 n. 13, 162–63 nn. 109–10
Pennsylvania Constitutions
  (1790), 26–27, 131 n. 42
  (1838), 27
Pennsylvania Freeman (newspaper), 48
Pennsylvania Grand Lodge of Prince Hall Masons, 152 n. 73
Pennsylvania Hall, 30, 171 n. 118
Pennsylvania Medical University, 168 n. 115
Pennsylvania State Equal Rights League, 138 n. 50, 152 n. 73, 154 n. 78, 166 n. 113, 172 n. 118
Petersburg, Virginia, 56

Philadelphia Anti-Slavery Society, 151 n. 72
Philadelphia Association for Moral and Mental Improvement, 122 n. 8, 124 n. 13, 133 n. 46, 134 n. 48, 147 n. 62, 150–52 nn. 71–73, 153 n. 75, 154 n. 78, 158 n. 94, 164 n. 111
Philadelphia Female Anti-Slavery Society, 60, 167–71 nn. 114–18
Philadelphia Library Company of Colored Persons, 113, 134 n. 48, 137 n. 50, 149 n. 71, 162 n. 109
Philadelphia Young Men's Anti-Slavery Society, 60, 134–36 nn. 48–49, 152 n. 73, 153 n. 75, 154 n. 78, 165 n. 113
Philanthropic Society, Pittsburgh, 139 n. 51
Philomathean Society, New York, 143 n. 57
Phoenixonian Society, New York, 142–43 nn. 56–57
phrenologists, 22–23, 127 n. 19
Pittsburgh, 56, 139 n. 51
Pittsburgh Mystery (newspaper), 139 n. 51, 154 n. 78, 159 n. 99
Political Association, 135 n. 49
Polly (slave), 52, 53 n. 68
Poole, Anne B. *See* Gibbons, Anne B.
population statistics, Philadelphia, 5–6
porters, 15, 122 n. 7, 155 n. 84
prejudice, Willson on, 32–33, 47–49, 87–88, 99–100, 101, 119
"Prejudice Reproved" (poem by Lydia Sigourney), 129 n. 21
Presbyterians, 83, 121 n. 6
proceedings, editing of, 110, 147 n. 67
Prosser, James, 21
Provincial Freeman (newspaper), 146 n. 59
Public Ledger (newspaper), 48–49
Purdy, John, 23, 127 n. 19
Purnell, Ann, 159 n. 99
Purnell, Zedekiah Johnson, 115, 159 n. 99
Purvis, Charles Burleigh, 166 n. 113
Purvis, Harriet (Forten), 117, 165 n. 113, 171 n. 118
Purvis, Joseph, 141 n. 54, 164 n. 113
Purvis, Robert, 11, 23, 27 n. 35, 30, 40, 117, 137 n. 50, 141 n. 54, 150–51 nn. 71–72, 163 n. 110, 164 n. 113, 171 n. 118
Purvis, Tacie (Townsend), 166 n. 113
Purvis, William, Jr., 141 n. 54, 164 n. 113
Purvis, William, Sr., 141 n. 54, 164 n. 113

Quakers. *See* Friends, Society of
Quamine (slave), 54 n. 71

race riots, 6–7, 28–30, 49
rag-pickers, 21
Raleigh, North Carolina, 9, 10, 58
Raleigh, Ontario, 146 n. 59
Ray, Charles B., 49, 160 n. 103
Reform Convention, 3 n. 4, 27, 148 n. 62, 149 n. 68, 151 n. 72
Remond, Charles Lenox, 167 n. 114
"Remus," 157 n. 91
Retrospect of Western Travel (Martineau), 121 n. 1
Rhode Island, 146 n. 60
Richmond, Virginia, 56
Rights of All (newspaper), 135–37 nn. 49–50, 147 n. 60, 150 n. 72
Roberts, John B., 155 n. 83
Rose (slave), 51
Rush, Dr. Benjamin, 155 n. 83
Rush Benevolent Society, 155 n. 84
Rush Education Society, 124 n. 13, 133 n. 46
Rush Librarian Debating Society, 114, 155 n. 83

Sabbath schools, 32, 84
sailmakers, 7, 18
sailors, 10, 11, 15–16, 18, 133 n. 46, 135 n. 49, 159 n. 99
St. Kitts, 10, 162 n. 109
St. Paul's Protestant Episcopal Church, Cleveland, 68
St. Paul's Protestant Episcopal Church, Indianapolis, 71
St. Thomas's African Episcopal Church, 41, 58, 114, 121 n. 6, 125 nn. 17–18, 133–34 nn. 46–47, 150 nn. 70–71, 152 n. 73, 153 n. 75, 154 n. 78, 155 nn. 81 and 84, 157 n. 90, 161 n. 105, 162–63 nn. 109–10
Salem, Massachusetts, 167 n. 114
Salter, Paris, 18, 157 n. 90
Salter's Hall, 115, 157 n. 90
Sammons, Ann. *See* Purnell, Ann
San Bernardino County, California, 160 n. 102
Sarah M. Douglass Literary Circle, 168 n. 115
Saunders, Prince, 163 n. 110
Schad, Hans, 145 n. 59
schooling, of African-American children, 31, 84, 122 n. 9
scientists, 121 n. 4

seamstresses, 12, 164 n. 111. *See also* dressmakers
Second African Presbyterian Church, 121 n. 6, 125 n. 17, 164 n. 111
"secrets papers," 100, 131 n. 38
segregation, residential, 2, 4
Shadd, Abraham D., 105, 145 n. 59
Shadd, Amelia, 130 n. 37
Shadd, Harriet, 146 n. 59
Shadd, Mary Ann, 146 n. 59
Shaw, Bertram Willson, 72
Shippen Street, Southwark, 65–67
shoemakers, 18, 23, 153 n. 75
Sigourney, Lydia (poet), 129 n. 20
Sipkins, Henry, 105, 141 n. 55
slaves, former, in "higher classes," 8–9, 127 n. 19, 130 n. 37, 134 n. 47, 135 n. 49, 155 n. 84, 173 n. 119
Smith, Harriet L. L. *See* Whipper, Harriet
Smith, James McCune, 126 n. 19
Smith, Stephen, 138 n. 50, 163 n. 110
Social Circle, Cleveland, 68
Society in America (Martineau), 121 n. 1
Sons of St. Thomas, 134 n. 48, 150 n. 72, 152 n. 73, 153 n. 75, 155 n. 81, 163 n. 110
South Carolina, 9, 51, 55, 141 n. 54, 150 n. 71, 158 n. 93
South Street corridor, Philadelphia, 6, 7, 29, 49, 66–67
Southwark, Philadelphia County, 5
Spring Garden, Philadelphia County, 5, 6, 58, 66
Squash (slave), 54 n. 71
Stanly, Benjamin, 115, 158 n. 94, 160 nn. 100 and 103
Stanly, Congressman Edward, 158 n. 94
Stanly, John Carruthers, 158 n. 94
Stanton, Elizabeth Cady, 166 n. 113
Stephen Smith Home for Aged and Infirm Colored Persons, 169 n. 115
"street culture," 33
street-vendors, 12
Sully, Thomas (artist), 128 n. 20
sweeps, 15
Sykora, Mr., 68
Sylva, Harrison R., 21, 114, 156 n. 87
Sylvan, Garretson, 155 n. 83

tailors, 18, 142 n. 56, 153 n. 78
Talcott Street Congregational Church, Hartford, Connecticut, 144 n. 58

Index

Tappan, Arthur, 104n., 132 n. 44
teachers, 12, 84, 122 n. 9, 168 n. 115, 173 n. 119
temperance, 30, 85, 100–101, 131 n. 39, 137 n. 50, 154 n. 78, 155 n. 84, 164 n. 111
Text Book of the Origin and History of the Colored People (Pennington), 144 n. 58
Thompson, John P., 135 n. 49
Thoughts on African Colonization (Garrison), 142 n. 56
Todd, Samuel, 105, 148 n. 63
Tom (slave), 54 n. 71
Tompkins, Richard T., 67
Townsend, Tacie. *See* Purvis, Tacie
Trinidad, 63, 151 n. 72
Trollope, Frances (writer), 121 n. 1
Trulier, Charles, 113, 154 n. 79
Turner, Nat, 9
Tuskegee Institute, 73

Union AME Church, 121 n. 6
Union Baptist Church, 121 n. 6
Union Benevolent Daughters of Elijah, 173 n. 119
Union Hall, 155 n. 83
Union Methodist Church, 121 n. 6
Union Sons of Industry, 155 n. 84
Unitarians, 84
United Daughters of Wilberforce, 155 n. 84
United Sons of Wilberforce, 155 n. 84
Universalists, 83, 121 n. 5

Vandine, Charlotte. *See* Forten, Charlotte Vandine
Varick, James, 140 n. 54
Veitch, Andrew D., 55
Vesey, Denmark, 9, 56
Vigilance Committee, 148 n. 62, 150 n. 71, 152 n. 73, 165 n. 113
violence, racial, 3, 28–30, 40, 130 n. 35, 166 n. 113
Virginia, 9, 103, 139 n. 51, 159 n. 97, 160 n. 102
visiting, in the "higher classes," 100

Walker, David, 57
War of 1812, 26
Washington, D.C., 56
Washington, Booker T., 73
Watson, John Fanning, on the "higher classes," 36

wealth distribution, among black Philadelphians, 23–25, 85
Webb, Frank J., 25 n. 30
Webber, Amos, 9
Weekly Advocate (newspaper), 154 n. 78
Weld, Theodore Dwight, 168 n. 115, 170 n. 117
Wesley Methodist Church, 121 n. 6
West Chester, Pennsylvania, 146 n. 59
West Indies, 10
Whipper, Harriet (Smith), 137 n. 50
Whipper, William, 26 n. 33, 103n., 105, 113, 136 n. 50, 151 n. 72
White, Elizabeth (Miller), 164 n. 111
White, Isaac J., 157 n. 91
White, Jacob C., 20, 23, 117, 127 n. 19, 163 n. 111
White, Bishop William, 114, 153 n. 75, 155 n. 82
whitewashers, 15
Whittier, John Greenleaf (poet), 171 n. 118
Wilberforce, William, 137 n. 50
Wilberforce Benevolent Society, 155 n. 84
Wilberforce Society, New York, 142 n. 56
Williams, Amy Matilda. *See* Cassey, Amy M.
Williams, Peter, Jr., 167 n. 114
Williams, Peter, Sr., 140 n. 54
Williams, Sarah, 167 n. 114
Willson, Albert (Joseph's nephew), 67 n. 104
Willson, Anna Foote (2d wife of Leonidas), 71–72
Willson, Caroline (Joseph's sister), 53, 58
Willson, Elizabeth (alias Betsy Keating, Joseph's mother), 51, 53, 54, 55, 57, 58, 64–65
Willson, Elizabeth or Eliza (Joseph's sister), 53, 60, 63, 151 n. 72
Willson, Elizabeth Harnett (Joseph's wife), 62, 68–71
Willson, Emily (Joseph's sister), 10, 53, 55 n. 73, 60 n. 90
Willson, Emily (Joseph's daughter), 65, 68, 70–71, 73 n. 124
Willson, Hannah (Joseph's sister-in-law), 67 n. 104
Willson, Henry. *See* Hart, Henry Edward
Willson, Ina Dustan (1st wife of Leonidas), 68, 71
Willson, John, Jr. (Joseph's father), 51, 53–54
Willson, John, Sr. (Joseph's great-uncle), 52–53

Willson, John (Joseph's brother), 53, 66–67
Willson, Joseph (author of *Sketches*), 50–72
Willson, Josephine Beall (Joseph's daughter), 65, 68, 70–71, 73
Willson, Laverne (Joseph's granddaughter), 71, 72
Willson, Leona (Joseph's granddaughter), 71, 72
Willson, Leonidas (Joseph's son), 64, 68, 71
Willson, Mary (Joseph's daughter), 67, 68, 71
Willson, Victoria (Joseph's daughter), 67, 68, 71
Wilson, Samuel, 127 n. 19
women, Willson on role of, 43, 89, 93–96, 124 n. 15
women's anti-slavery conventions (1837–39), 10, 168–73 nn. 115–19

Women's Christian Temperance Union, 73
Wood, Mary Virginia, 129 n. 21
Wylie Street AME Church, Pittsburgh, 139 n. 51

Yale Divinity School, 144 n. 58
yellow fever epidemic (1793), 26
Young Men's Philadelphia Library Association, 134 n. 48, 152 n. 73
Young Men's Union Literary Association, 157 n. 91

"Zillah," 168 n. 115
Zion Methodist Church, New York, 140 n. 54
Zoar Methodist Episcopal Church, 121 n. 6

F
158.9
.N4
W54